FILMING DEATH

FILMING DEATH
End-of-Life Documentary Cinema

Outi Hakola

EDINBURGH
University Press

Edinburgh University Press is one of the leading university presses in the UK. We publish academic books and journals in our selected subject areas across the humanities and social sciences, combining cutting-edge scholarship with high editorial and production values to produce academic works of lasting importance. For more information visit our website: edinburghuniversitypress.com

We are committed to making research available to a wide audience and are pleased to be publishing a Gold Open Access ebook edition of this title.

© Outi Hakola, 2024 under a Creative Commons Attribution-NonCommercial licence

Grateful acknowledgement is made to the sources listed in the List of Illustrations for permission to reproduce material previously published elsewhere. Every effort has been made to trace the copyright holders, but if any have been inadvertently overlooked, the publisher will be pleased to make the necessary arrangements at the first opportunity.

Edinburgh University Press Ltd
13 Infirmary Street
Edinburgh EH1 1LT

Typeset in 10/12.5pt Sabon by
Cheshire Typesetting Ltd, Cuddington, Cheshire
and printed and bound in Great Britain

A CIP record for this book is available from the British Library

ISBN 9781399523264 (hardback)
ISBN 9781399523288 (webready PDF)
ISBN 9781399523295 (epub)

The right of Outi Hakola to be identified as the author of this work has been asserted in accordance with the Copyright, Designs and Patents Act 1988, and the Copyright and Related Rights Regulations 2003 (SI No. 2498).

CONTENTS

List of Figures	vii
1. Introduction	1

SECTION I: INSTITUTIONAL VOICES

2. Medical Documentaries: Demedicalisation of Death	29
3. Hospice Documentaries: Responsibility to Care	52
4. Spiritual Documentaries: Making Death Meaningful	71
5. Advocacy Documentaries: Investigating the Legalisation of Assisted Dying	91

SECTION II: THE VOICES OF DYING PEOPLE

6. Performative Documentaries: Life-Affirming Stories about Mortality	113
7. Legacy Documentaries: Reaching beyond Death	134
8. Physical Documentaries: Experiencing the Process of Dying	153
9. Dialogical Documentaries: Understanding Personal End-of-Life Choices	174

SECTION III: PERSONAL VOICES

10. First-Person Documentaries: Filmmakers' Personal Journeys 195

11. Collaborative Documentaries: Intimate Testimonials of
    End of Life 214

12. Conclusion 235

Index 244

FIGURES

2.1	The shot focuses on the breathing machine in the documentary *Facing Death* (Navasky and O'Connor 2010)	43
3.1	Staff members complimenting Carlo on his pictures in *Here & Now* (Banci 2018)	56
4.1	A wintery landscape and Alfons in *Die Weisse Arche* (Beeler 2016)	85
5.1	Split-screen image of interviewed authorities in *Fatal Flaws* (Dunn 2018)	100
6.1	Noël faces a skeleton in *Before We Go* (León 2014)	114
6.2	Johana's last performance, a journey towards the unknown in *Bouton* (Balzli 2011)	122
6.3	Opening of *Seven Songs for a Long Life* where Tosh sings during an arts and crafts session (Hardie 2015)	124
7.1	Jack on his deathbed, fragile, comforted by his family in *Prison Terminal* (Barens 2013)	139
8.1	Close-up of Meris at the birthday party in *The Perfect Circle* (Tosi 2014)	162
8.2	Death scene of Alan in *ISLAND* (Eastwood 2017)	168
9.1	Nathan in his bathroom, looking at himself in the mirror, tears in his eyes (Nollet 2014a)	186
10.1	Animated opening of *Living while Dying* (Zheutlin 2017)	200
10.2	Colourful arrangement of a shaman and his disciples in *Living while Dying* (Zheutlin 2017)	202

10.3	The filmmaker sitting by Mari's deathbed, reflecting her emotions through diary writing (Luostarinen 2003)	204
11.1	Sam Niver taking the first steps towards his suicide in *Live and Let Go: An American Death* (Spain 2002)	224
11.2	Leverne on her deathbed in *All in Her Stride* (Cochrane 2014)	226
11.3	Laura's peaceful death scene in *Laura's Choice* (Henkel and Lara 2020)	228
11.4	Death of Eli Timoner in *Last Flight Home* (Timoner 2022)	230

1. INTRODUCTION

In a scene from Amy Hardie's documentary film *Seven Songs for a Long Life* (2015), hospice patient Dorene is having physiotherapy. The scene opens with Dorene pleading that nurse Mandy won't laugh at her. Mandy promises to do 'it' with her. The comment does not refer to physical activities, but to the song 'Wouldn't It Be Loverly' from the musical *My Fair Lady*, which Dorene starts to sing and perform. Amid the series of exercises Dorene sings, Mandy nods along, and both smile and laugh at the line where the song's protagonist wishes for someone to take care of her. The 'Loverly' singing scene is one of many in this documentary where hospice patients choose and perform their favourite 'last' songs as empowering expressions of still being alive, even when dying. *Seven Songs for a Long Life* was also one of the end-of-life films I was asked to review for the Finnish documentary film festival DocPoint a few years ago. At the time, I described Hardie's film as follows:

> This documentary was inspired by her time as a filmmaker in residence at Strathcarron Hospice, where singing has become one of the ways to celebrate life, create shared memories and to articulate feelings in the face of death. The scenes where people sing to the camera, be it solo or along with others, are very moving. The songs speak of wistfulness, of letting go and of love; the themes that the imminent death stirs in people's minds. At the same time, they give the documentary its fresh and warm tone, highlighting its zest for life. (Hakola 2018)

In other words, I was impressed by the positive mood and how it eases the viewer into the intimate lives of dying people. After the festival and its screenings were over, I kept returning to the films I had reviewed, and particularly to the closing words of my blog post: 'Hence, the most important observation of documentaries about death is not learning to accept our own mortality, but rather learning to understand that we are alive' (Hakola 2018). I started to wonder whether we ever document dying people to discuss mortality as such? Or are we using these documentaries to push our own mortality further away?

I joined a long line of those who have pondered the relationship between mortality and cinema. For example, some have debated (moving) images' symbolic relationship with temporality and mortality (Bazin 1960; Bakhtin 1984; Barthes 2010; Mulvey 2006; Sontag 2001). Others have discussed how sociocultural aspects of death are communicated through cinema (Aaron 2014) or what technological potential film has to represent death and dying (Malkowski 2017). Regarding the study of film narratives, death certainly has thematic, structural and plot uses as it often functions as a starting point, turning point, or closure for the stories as has been discussed by Catharine Russell in *Narrative Mortality* (1995) and by Boaz Hagin in *Death in Classical Hollywood Cinema* (2010). Yet, in a critique of Hagin's storyline-oriented approach, Robert Armstrong (2011, 126) writes that 'we get little sense of what death entails as experience'. Also, most of the above discussions are based on fictional representations, which prompts me to ask: Would contemporary documentary cinema be better equipped to shine a light on what dying is as an experience, given that it has moved towards subjective, personal and embodied practices?

Death is a key transformative event and experience in life, which several documentary filmmakers have wanted to discuss and represent in their work. Particularly, it seems that this topic has become increasingly popular in the western countries in the twenty-first century with new films popping up every few months. For this study, I watched about ninety and analysed forty-five end-of-life documentaries from the past twenty years in Europe, Australia and New Zealand, as well as Canada and the United States. I interviewed eighteen of these filmmakers to gain insight into their goals and backgrounds in these projects, and when not possible, I have used the directors' interviews with the media and other supporting material, such as commentary tracks, directors' statements and blog posts.

When I asked them what inspired them to film dying people, the filmmakers recognised their own fear of death as a key motivation. They either admitted having a personal desire to understand their emotional relationship with death or they recognised fear of death as a sociocultural issue that limited people's understanding of death and communication with dying people.

INTRODUCTION

Tom Murray, director of *Love in Our Own Time* (Murray and Hetherton 2011), explains:

> We filmmakers, we all have to be driven by something very personal – in this film, perhaps it was a need to deal with an immortality complex. You know, that I couldn't possibly consider my own death, and if I did, I did so with profound fear and terror. I suppose we fear that of which we least know. So, I was very fearful of death as a concept, and of my own death as a fact. So, I'm going to be really blunt, it [filming the documentary] was kind of exposure therapy, with the aim of getting closer to death, trying to deal with my own fear of death. (Murray 2020)

Paul Davidson, director of *Helen's Story* (Davidson and Gibb 2016), takes the argument to a societal level:

> Dying, we all are gonna face it. You don't need to be that afraid of it. It doesn't have to be a terrible process, and that a hospice is not just a place to die, that a hospice can help you live until you die. [...] I think that part of me is proud of that message. People understand after watching this [documentary] a lot more. (Davidson and Gibb 2020)

These notions of fear of death suggest that while death as a personal experience awaits us all, documentary filmmakers can help us to try to understand our emotional relationship with the topic.

Inspired by these interviews, I interpret end-of-life documentaries as maps to alleviate commonly experienced death anxiety. Death anxiety, or the response to our awareness of mortality, is a widely recognised phenomenon in psychology (Lehto and Stein 2009; Cai et al. 2017; Neimeyer, Wittkowski, and Moser 2004). Psychological studies understand death anxiety as a non-conscious and emotionally negative response to (repressed) death and dying. Yet, death anxiety also involves cognitive and sociocultural processes: the subjective knowledge and sociocultural practices and representations influence the anxiety that we experience. Thus, death anxiety varies in different stages of life (Lehto and Stein 2009, 25–30). The field which studies our death-related attitudes has developed various standardised questionnaires and scales to empirically measure and understand attributes of death attitudes, yet many of these standardised models frame the topic in negative terms, such as fear (Neimeyer, Moser, and Wittkowski 2003; Cai et al. 2017). At the same time, studies have shown that positive affective and cognitive attitudes, such as death awareness, support life satisfaction and lessen death-related fears (Neimeyer, Wittkowski, and Moser 2004). Death anxiety can become more than a life-limiting condition: it can also motivate people to overcome death in

3

different ways, such as using symbolical options of artmaking (Lehto and Stein 2009, 25–30). Psychological research suggests that art, including documentary cinema, can offer a way to respond to death anxiety and it can even help to manage this anxiety in a positive and productive manner.

For example, psychologists Ryan Niemiec and Stefan Schulenberg (2011) have analysed death narratives in fiction films. They recognise two main narratives – death acceptance and death denial – which they value according to their capability to reduce death anxiety. Their argument is that positive stories where dying people embrace and acknowledge their deaths are culturally desirable because such stories call forth personal strength in a difficult emotional situation. In comparison, death denial stories exemplify unwanted death, because they give space to despair and suffering (Niemiec and Schulenberg 2011). They suggest therefore that positive outlooks, such as musical scenes from *Seven Songs for a Long Life*, could be influential in managing and alleviating death anxiety.

However, from the perspective of documentary cinema, the request to narrate only the stories that represent desirable behavioural habits (and exclude other experiences) seems absurd. After all, documentary films have a specific relationship with 'real', as the viewer expects documentaries to have a close connection to the actualities of the world. One of the most durable definitions of documentary cinema comes from John Grierson, an early documentary filmmaker and social activist. His approach has been captured in the formulation that documentary is 'the creative treatment of actuality' (Hardy 1966, 13). This formulation combines the two aspects of documentary filmmaking, the cinematic art and actualities. In his essay 'First Principles of Documentary' (1932–34), Grierson discusses the relationship between these aspects and argues that documentary filmmaking describes the world and its natural material in a way that creatively rearranges and interprets it (Grierson 1966, 145–56). Since Grierson, the connection between the real and the art has remained at the core of documentary theories (Borum Chattoo and Jenkins 2019, 1109). For example, Bill Nichols (2017, 105) argues that we should separate 'documents', which refers to such indexical nonfiction audiovisual material as surveillance footage or informational videos, from 'documentaries', which have personal perspective and voice. Recognising the link between represented realities and cinematic expressions is vital to understanding how end of life and fear of death are discussed in documentary films. While cinematic expressions could allow only positive stories, the desire to represent actualities demands space for various experiences and voices.

The death acceptance approach also summons criticism. For example, Michele Aaron (2014, 103–26) complains that in mainstream media, the images of everyday deaths too often turn into exceptional tales about self-improvement and beauty of the experience. Another film that I reviewed for the DocPoint festival was the Italian documentary *The Perfect Circle* (2015) by Claudia Tosi. This film embraces the vitality of its two main characters in a hospice home, but the story focuses on their difficulty accepting the situation. I described the film thus:

> What makes this documentary interesting is that unlike in many depictions of end-of-life care, the dying aren't presented as courageous and emotionally mature people, in charge of their emotions and ready to let go of life. Ivano in particular is defiant and stubborn to the point of frustration in his will to hold on for dear life, raging at impending death. (Hakola 2018)

In this narrative choice, Claudia Tosi rewrote the heroic acceptance story to make room for complex emotions that people encounter at the end of their lives.

After the festival, I started to wonder whether we would need more of these varied perspectives on the topic. I became inspired by Angela Armstrong-Coster's ethnographic study on a television documentary project about a woman with breast cancer. The study revealed mixed emotions about the documentary's positive handling of the topic, particularly its image of heroic battle and the empowering experience of dying. On purpose, the filmmaker emphasised the cancer patient's active and empowered life after the diagnosis and left out images of suffering. The filmmaker's reasoning was familiar, wanting to give the audience a comforting image of dying (Armstrong-Coster 2001). While the documentary project followed the preferred cultural model of death acceptance, I was struck by that section of the study in which Armstrong-Coster had shown the film to people diagnosed with cancer. For them, the documentary raised 'personal feelings of shame and failure at not being able to live up to these media images that presented people with cancer appearing to be in radiant good health' (Armstrong-Coster 2001, 297). While the chosen representation can be comforting for some, for others it may appear unreasonable and inauthentic. These notions encourage me to ask what kind of knowledge documentaries create on end of life. Do they provide complex images of mortality, or do they create normative pressure about acceptable ways to die?

I have a strong preference for complex and varied images, which partly comes from my understanding of documentary cinema's relationship with 'reality' or 'real'. At its best, documentary cinema thrives on differences in experiences and contributes to the construction of the reality (Hongisto 2015). Thus, while reality is something that exists in the world, such as death, we can understand and experience death differently. This view follows social constructivism theories which discuss how our approach to reality is socially situated and constructed through our previous experiences as well as through interaction with others. For example, in the above-mentioned cancer story, the heroic acceptance of illness did not resonate with those who had cancer themselves but appeared acceptable to those with no personal experience. Consequently, if documentaries have a specific, yet interpretative, relationship with realities, the simple division between death acceptance and death denial might simplify the experiences and stories of end of life. This book is an exploration of how end of life has been represented in documentary films, what variety of experiences are filmed and how these different understandings of the topic also provide different takes on how to manage our complicated relationship with dying.

Contextual Background: Social Issue Documentaries and End of Life

In this book, my focus is on western documentaries dealing with topics such as terminal illness, hospice and palliative care, and assisted dying. Because I focus on end-of-life (care) choices and experiences, I exclude violent and sudden deaths, such as accidents, suicides, murders and war deaths. The drama related to sudden and violent deaths has made them popular for cinematic content, not least because it makes death exceptional and something that happens to others (Schultz and Huet 2001; Gibson 2007). Vivian Sobchack (1984) argues that in the media, violent and often somewhat exaggerated death has replaced the role of everyday death because exaggerated events are easier to narrate. The end of life due to illness or ageing, in turn, is something that most of us encounter in our own lives and in the lives of our loved ones. Thus, while many theories about representations of death in cinema are grounded in violent and sudden deaths, the everyday deaths can help us to deepen our understanding of the relationship between death and cinema.

End-of-life documentaries are by no means an existing genre or category in documentary cinema, nor do I claim that we should define such a genre. These films have various production backgrounds, aims, distribution channels, funding models, and narrative and aesthetic solutions. However, they all explore how to cope with end of life, death and dying. Rather than a genre, I see these films as 'social issue documentaries'; they centre on the issue of death and dying and aim to influence how the viewer understands this. Grierson (1966), whose career was built on social issue documentaries, sees documentaries as a way to make social problems comprehensible and understandable. One of the ways in which filmmakers can make their topics meaningful is to dramatise the issue. More recently, social issue documentaries have been defined as films that aim to create conversation on a certain topic, hope to intervene in our understanding of the world and to contribute to social change. Social issue films also take an active and a determined role in civil society

INTRODUCTION

(Nichols 2017, 26; Borum Chattoo 2020, 5). These definitions stress two components: an issue and the desire to impact.

In their research on documentary filmmakers, Caty Borum Chattoo and William Harder (2018) discovered that most documentary makers saw themselves as artists with a flavour of issue advocacy and motivated by wanting to impact on social issues. My own interviews with end-of-life filmmakers agreed with this desire to make a difference. The filmmakers recognised that death and dying are a problematic issue that causes unnecessary anxiety, avoidance of the topic and decreases individuals' preparedness to comfort dying people. For example, Mike Hill, director of the Australian end-of-life documentaries *Life Before Death* (2012) and *Little Stars* (2015) describes his aims thus:

> Normalising death would be a key thing. And that dying, also, is a perfectly normal process that we will all go through. That is a quite important message for people in more developed countries, in more developed systems, where they rely on interventions at the end of life. It has sort of become not normal in places like I live. There are also more specific goals. Like in *Little Stars* it was about creating empathy for families who are going through with this. So they would feel less isolated and more supported. And again, it is about normalising it. (Hill 2020)

By giving visibility to death and dying, the filmmakers want to increase understanding of a social issue and enhance compassion towards dying people and their families.

However, focusing on an issue and wanting to make an impact is a rather vague definition – after all, most documentaries fit these criteria. Nichols (2017, 186) deepens the description by arguing that social issue documentaries bring the social issue to the fore instead of leaving it as something to be interpreted. Borum Chattoo (2020, 22), in turn, engages a contextualising approach by arguing that social issue documentaries work in the field of civic practice. End-of-life documentaries are influenced by the death awareness movement and campaigns to legalise assisted dying, which highlights these films' social issue approach.

Social issue documentaries have a long history. They were popular already in the 1930s, campaigning for social reforms. Yet, in the early decades of cinema, they were often seen as part of governmental and educational programming. The early documentaries tended to be didactic reportages or featured expository storylines that commonly rendered the subjects as victims (Winston 2008, 20; Borum Chattoo 2020, 35). For example, in Finland, early documentaries desired to educate or enlighten the citizens about social problems, such as poverty or alcohol use, in a way that often reduced the agency of those who ended up being part of the stories (Aaltonen 2022).

The 1960s civil rights movements and political activism around the globe changed documentary traditions. The sociocultural climate that idealised social responsibility and demanded social justice encouraged a new generation of documentary filmmakers to discuss the stories from the insider perspective. Consequently, social issue documentaries transformed from governmental stories to community-focused stories with a social activist perspective. Along with the renewal of social issue documentaries, innovative direct cinema methods transformed documentary filming. The showcasing of lived experiences and complexities of daily lives replaced educational approaches. Lighter and more movable film cameras and smaller crews contributed to the opportunities to capture human life and its intimate moments. The new funding channels, such as the public broadcasting services' requirement to produce non-fiction content, and alternative distribution channels, such as the possibility of showing documentaries at educational institutions and non-profit organisations, provided resources and audiences for social issue documentaries (Borum Chattoo 2020, 30–47). Even today, institutions and organisations offer important distribution channels for end-of-life documentary filmmakers. In addition to cinemas, film festivals and television broadcasting, the interviewed filmmakers had shown their films in local churches and community spaces, hospice institutions, educational institutions and (medical) conferences.

Social issue documentaries, in other words, established themselves as part of social and political movements. One of these civic engagements was the death awareness movement. Its origins have been traced to the late 1950s, when scholars from various fields started to demand that death and dying should receive interdisciplinary and public attention (Doka 2003; Incorvaia 2022). For example, demands for death awareness were raised by such works as the English anthropologist Geoffrey Gorer's essay 'The Pornography of Death' (1955), American psychologist Herman Feifel's study *The Meaning of Death* (1959), American journalist Jessica Mitford's investigative work *The American Way of Death* (1963) and Swiss-American psychiatrist Elisabeth Kübler-Ross's ethnographic research *On Death and Dying* (1969). Later, death was deemed as marginalised in western societies in French historian Philippe Ariès's key work *Western Attitudes toward Death: From the Middle Ages to the Present* (1974) and in German sociologist Norbert Elias's book *The Loneliness of the Dying* (1982).

With educational goals, the death awareness movement campaigns to include death-related education in higher education, medical education and other educational areas. The movement also supports therapy for the dying and the bereaved through counsellors, therapy groups and programmes, and influences public opinion particularly through such media products as documentary films (Doka 2003). On a practical level, the death awareness movement has paraded modern hospice practices and occasionally even voiced demands for legislation on assisted dying (Incorvaia 2022). The movement is a loosely defined network of academics, advocate organisations and institutions, and people working in the end-of-life field. The movement has mostly American origins, yet certain philosophical and ethical aspects related to the desire to improve death-related communication – including an interest in thanatology and death education – can be recognised in all western countries (Bregman 2017; Orkibi, Biancalani, and Bucu 2021). While not well organised, the movement centres on general ideals and goals, such as bringing attention and openness to dying, death and bereavement, and advocates for the rights and dignity of the dying.

Today, the death awareness movement is often discussed in the context of the death positivity movement, which shifts the focus from sociocultural aspects of dying to emotionally positive attitudes towards death and dying, perhaps with an aim of reducing death anxiety. The demand for positivity emphasises death as a natural and personal event (Incorvaia 2022). The death positivity movement inspires emotionally supportive practices, such as discussion events at death cafés (Richards et al. 2020) and death over dinner (Lambert South and Elton 2017) as well as practices of end-of-life (or death) doulas, who provide non-medical company for the dying and their families (Rawlings et al. 2020). These practices give further life to the themes familiar from the death awareness movement, including the desire to erase taboos around death, the search for meaningful end-of-life communication, rejection of medicalised death and advocating for death education. Death positivity also embraces self-reflection, self-improvement and emotional growth over sociocultural changes (Incorvaia 2022). Lucy Bregman (2017) argues that personal stories have given credibility and emotional depth to the movement, and in turn, the movement has provided the language and concepts for people to frame their experiences.

Documentary films have this desired ability to tell personal stories as a part of social issue argumentation. However, it took time for the issue of end of life to become a focus for documentary filmmakers. In 1974, Amos Vogel (2006) argued that while lightweight cameras had inspired documentarians to engage with various topics, the natural death remained an untouched taboo subject. Quite soon after this, Michael Roemer produced *Dying* (1976), a documentary with three terminally ill individuals telling their stories. A West-German–Swedish documentary *Lightning Over Water* (Ray and Wenders 1984) focused on the last days of film director Nicholas Ray. Frederick Wiseman even produced an ambitious, almost six-hour-long documentary *Near Death* (1989) that draws from medical staff's care for patients with life-threatening conditions.

In the 1990s, end-of-life documentaries gained increasing visibility, not least due to the AIDS epidemic. Many documentary filmmakers were moved by their own experiences or those in their family and turned to the camera to witness these deaths. For example, *Silverlake Life* (Friedman and Joslin 1993),

The Andre Show (Peterson 1998) and *Death: A Love Story* (LeBrun 1999) narrate intimate and personal stories of and by AIDS patients, whereas *Common Threads: Stories from the Quilt* (Epstein and Friedman 1989) connects personalised stories with sociopolitical aspects. Personal stories were also visible in other films, such as the Dutch euthanasia documentary *Death on Request* (Nederhorst 1994) or Kirby Dick's *Sick: The Life and Death of Bob Flanagan, Supermasochist* (1997). All of these narrate an inside view on dying, and as Jennifer Malkowski (2017, 88–104) argues, they provide views to 'unique natural deaths' because they refuse to generalise death as an experience while forcing death into a public space.

The twenty-first century has seen a proliferation of end-of-life documentaries, so much so that several projects are produced each year, and I was not able to include all potential documentaries into my study. Instead, the forty-five analysed documentaries aim to give an idea of the variety of films. Their popularity can be understood as an outcome of the death awareness movement. The movement's popularity has been explained by the ageing population of the western countries (Doka 2003), and existential anxieties that arise from modern fragility of life due to the nuclear age, global wars, social unrest, health pandemics and the climate crisis (Staudt 2009; Walter 2020; Incorvaia 2022; Doka 2003). Also, there is the ongoing process of secularisation, where the death awareness movement has started to assume the cultural tasks of religion in understanding death (Doka et al. 2011), and dissatisfaction with institutionalised, bureaucratic and medicalised end-of-life care (Incorvaia 2022; Walter 2020). Shifting media landscapes have similarly paved the way for end-of-life documentaries. The available and affordable digital filmmaking technology and various distribution channels, such as social media, have made non-fiction content increasingly accessible and useful for various producers, such as independent filmmakers, institutions and organisations, journalists and the public sphere (Karlin and Johnson 2011; Borum Chattoo and Jenkins 2019; Nash and Corner 2016; Aufderheide 2008; Coffman 2009). Documentary filmmaking has thus become a significant tool for many social issue campaigns and discussions.

David Lipson and Zachary Baqué (2019, 2–5) argue that Grierson's legacy to see social issue documentaries as didactic contrast to entertaining mainstream cinema is still evident in current discussions, for example in Bill Nichols's (1991) emphasis on discourses and rhetoric in knowledge building, and in Carl Plantinga's (1997) pragmatic approach to studying the social functions and tasks of the documentaries. However, Lipson and Baqué recognise that some others, like Michael Renov (1999) and Elizabeth Cowie (1999), have brought forward how documentaries can move beyond their truth claims, even to the sphere of spectacle. As such, Lipson and Baqué (2019) suggest that social issues can be narrated in various ways, not merely through rational argumentation and devoid of entertainment. For example, in the case of social issue documentaries, creative and emotional storytelling has become a persuasive way to move and impact the viewer (Borum Chattoo and Feldman 2017; Borum Chattoo and Jenkins 2019; Nash and Corner 2016; Smaill 2010). These notions resonate with changes in the documentary field. The seemingly objective and all-knowing narration has given way to openly subjective and personal approaches, where the filmmakers become part of their stories and bring their voices into a dialogue with the filmed subjects and the viewers (e.g. Renov 2004; Önen 2021). In other words, understanding of social issue documentaries has moved beyond focusing on representations and discourses to activities that the documentaries enable.

Inspired by these evolvements, I approach end-of-life documentaries through a metaphor of space. That is, documentary films create space where the social issue occurs in time and place and is framed by evolving activities and meaning-making. Patricia Zimmerman and Helen De Michiel suggest that documentaries could be understood through the concept of 'open space'. They take inspiration from open-space architecture that plans spaces where people can encounter others, to engage in dialogue and collaboration, and they apply the concept to collaborative and community-based filmmaking (Zimmermann and De Michiel 2018). I suggest that we recognise documentary films themselves as collaborative spaces that encourage intersubjectivity between the filmmaker, the subject and the viewer, who all contribute towards having a dialogue on chosen social issues. Intersubjectivity within this space highlights co-experiencing and co-living (see also Gallagher 2008), where the embodied connections to others can enable us to try to understand others' experiences, such as their sense of mortality. In end-of-life documentaries, the dying subjects offer their experiences for the viewer to connect with, and through engagement the viewer can contribute to making these experiences meaningful. In this way, the documentaries open spaces for experiencing, feeling, thinking and learning about mortality and death as a social issue.

THEORETICAL BACKGROUND: END-OF-LIFE EXPERIENCES AS ETHICAL SPACE

End-of-life documentary filmmakers aim to bear upon our relationship with death and dying, particularly by alleviating our fear of death. The desire to influence raises ethical questions and generates ethical potential. Debates of the ethical aspects of documentary films are at the core of documentary studies, even more so after the 'ethical turn', which has given these discussions a fresh perspective. Traditionally, discussions have targeted ethical ways of making the documentaries, such as respecting consent and privacy issues of the filmed subjects and the authenticity of representations. The ethical turn has shifted the attention towards the ethical potential of films' impact on the viewers (Choi and Frey 2014, 1; Sinnerbrink 2016, 5; Fleming 2017, 8–9). As I describe above through a metaphor of space, documentary cinema can evoke ethical experiences in the viewers, make them feel, embody and think about ethical dilemmas, the world and the perspectives of others in such a way as transforms their attitudes, values and beliefs. As such, documentary cinema can offer a space for transformation that is ethical by nature.

In the field of cinema, discussions on ethical cinema draw from narrative theory, philosophy and cultural studies. Narrative theories paint stories as integral to our thinking, remembering and understanding the world. In philosophy, phenomenological theories have paid special attention to the importance of experiences in our learning and evolving attitudes. The cultural studies approach has emphasised the relationship with the other, particularly by studying marginalised groups, othering processes and relationships of power. In the intersection of these approaches, cinematic ethics emerges. It suggests that films can offer insight into the experiences of others, and the witnessing of these experiences can open the viewer to new ways of knowing, feeling and thinking, or at least, to increased understanding of others' experiences.

Cinematic ethics and transformative potential coexist. While ethics can be understood as theories or standards about right and wrong, it is also a continuous effort to re-evaluate and shape what can be considered reasonable ethical standards (Velasquez et al. 2010). Films offer material for the viewers to feel, embody and think about ethical, moral and existential issues. They offer an ethical space where viewers can experience the everyday of other people with an openness to experiences that can be both similar and different from their own. It is these encounters that have the potential to transform the viewer (Raviv 2021, 2–4). Gilles Deleuze (1986b), an influential figure in cinematic ethics, argues that cinema can affect us in ways that makes it possible to become something else, to transform through audiovisual imagery. Particularly, Deleuze's two *Cinema* books (Deleuze 1986a; 1986b) have generated plenty of discussion regarding ethics. For example, D. N. Rodowick (2010, 99) sees Deleuze's books as ethical exercises on how art provokes and transforms the viewer.

In the context of end-of-life documentaries in particular, I draw inspiration from David Fleming's use of the Deleuzian tradition. Fleming builds on Deleuze's distinction between 'mechanical' and 'machinic' forms of living. Here, mechanical refers to repetitive, fixed and undesirable closed cycles of being. Machinic, in comparison, embraces experimental and open ways of being which can empower a person. Empowering ways of being can increase a person's ability to live and act. Cinema, in turn, can explore our and others' being in the world and help us to think differently. In other words, Fleming sees cinema as a machinic force that can introduce alternative ways of thinking and acting (Fleming 2017, 4, 14–15, 34). Here, Fleming emphasises that the film's ethical potential is tied in its potential to make us live better and fuller. As discussed above, the filmmakers' desire to use end-of-life documentaries to alleviate our death anxiety in a manner that would make us value life and encourage us to live fully, ties into this idea of ethical transformation through cinematic expression. As is argued by Ilona Hongisto (2015, 135–7), also based on Deleuze, the documentary film can show the potential of what could be and what we could become. Here lies the true revolutionary and social change that documentaries can induce.

The ethical turn in film studies overlaps with the affective shift, which has added affective, embodied and haptic aesthetics to the discussion (Fleming 2017, 10). For example, Lisa Downing and Libby Saxton (2010, 2) argue that cinema can make ethics tangible, and Jinhee Choi and Mattias Frey (2014, 2) note that cinematic ethics emphasises 'singularity over universality, affectivity over rationality, and ethics of the particular over ethics of moral imperatives'. These aspects of cinematic ethics build on the understanding that cinema holds a specific ethical potential by virtue of its non-linguistic, embodied and affective approach to existence and behaviour (Sinnerbrink 2016; Grønstad 2016; Choi and Frey 2014). Edward Lamberti, for example, writes that cinema is an expressive study on human behaviour, which cannot be reduced to cognitive aspects often expected by linguistic expressions. In addition, non-linguistic expressions should not be reduced to mere aesthetic questions, but should also include affective experiences, which, similar to cognitive traits of films, carry ethical potential in them (Lamberti 2019, 1–26). In other words, cinematic ethics moves its interest beyond cognitive interpretations of filmic representations of ethical issues. It moves towards understanding how cinema engages the viewer by embodying themes, visualising ethical issues, creating potential for affective experiences and by helping the viewer to emotionally commit to feeling and thinking about ethical and social issues. In end-of-life documentaries, the films rarely openly claim to offer ways to alleviate death anxiety. They rather inspire the viewers to be open to changing their emotional relationship with death through witnessing the other, through creating intimate and empathetic relationships with the other, and through embodying experiences related to death and dying. By studying how documentaries inspire the viewers to feel and think, we can better understand the draw of personal and intimate stories about death and dying.

This approach highlights films as material entities, as described in Deleuze's work on cinema. The ways in which films make use of image, movement and time give films a material body that flows and transforms, and in turn, invites the viewer to transform (Deleuze 1986a; 1986b). In this study, these notions translate into a phenomenological approach (with occasional flavours from cognitive theory). Maurice Merleau-Ponty argues that cinema is based on perceptions that can challenge the cultural assumptions of mind–body dualism.

As such, films can provide access to emotions and senses in ways that aim to create new meanings and experiences of the world (Merleau-Ponty 2019; 2012). While Merleau-Ponty sees film as a potential to show how meanings emerge through embodied experiences, Vivian Sobchack takes the idea further. Sobchack writes about phenomenal body and 'film's body', where the viewing experience entails all the senses, including bodily experiences. But similarly, film sees, hears and is constantly moving. As such, film has its own material status (Sobchack 1992). Sobchack thus creates a strong, embodied connection between the viewer's experience and film as a flow of movements and transitions. The phenomenological approach allows us to understand how cinematic ethics is more than a question of representation, it is about experiences that challenge us to respond and potentially to change accordingly.

Because cinema is a narrative art form that tells us stories of the other in a way that evolves our thinking and feeling, the 'other' emerges as a key concept of cinematic ethics. In the context of filming real-life deaths, several scholars have raised ethical concerns that the viewer too often remains an outsider who distantly observes the 'death of the other' (e.g. Pryluck 2005; Sobchack 1992; Malkowski 2017; Grue 2022). Susan Sontag, for example, has questioned whether we can ever imagine or experience the suffering of the other through visual media. She argues that particularly photographs remain too distant and without enough context or emotional connection to make the death of the other meaningful or comprehensible for the viewer (Sontag 2004). These concerns echo the thoughts of Emmanuel Levinas about otherness, which have inspired contemporary ethical debates in film studies. According to Levinas (2011), explaining and understanding others through familiar categories leads westerners to violate the complexity of otherness. For Michael Renov (2004, 148), Levinas's argument raises criticism of documentary practices where the filmmaker's and the viewer's search for knowledge risks de-contextualising or objectifying the subjects' experiences. Thus, in the worst-case scenario, both the filmmakers and the viewers could push their own agenda over the filmed subjects.

How, then, could we avoid this kind of self-centred and distanced viewing position? Merleau-Ponty sees our relationships with otherness arise from situated, empirical and historical ways of perception. As we perceive others against their horizon, we can only understand the other in relation to ourselves. Yet, this relationship and connection can be guided through embodied emotions, which encourages the viewer to open up their thinking and understanding of the other (Merleau-Ponty 2012; 2019). Janet Stadler recognises compassion as the core of cinematic ethics and argues that when a film manages to engage cognitive as well as embodied and affective responses, it creates a link between the viewer and the other. It offers an intersubjective experience that ethical experience relies on (Stadler 2014, 38). While this ethical engagement does not always take place in mainstream cinema's spectacles of violent deaths, many end-of-life documentaries aim to build embodied and affective connections between the viewer and the dying people. As such, these films prove to be excellent material for exploring ethical space for discussions on mortality. Here, I turn to Deleuze's (1986b) understanding of the viewing experience as an engagement with the moving images. In affective participation, the imagery can help the viewer 'become' or be transformed. Deleuze's arguments have inspired various readings, but I prefer to read them as the viewer's potential to engage with the film in a way that fosters openness to others' experiences and to change. In other words, rather than forcing the subjects into a pre-existing understanding of the topic, the viewers' openness to experience can transform their thinking models and thus encourage ethical encounters with dying people.

In this process, the concept of witnessing becomes central. Emily West (2018, 1483) and Tal Morse (2018, 245), for example, contend that end-of-life documentaries can create an ethical space when they invite the viewer to 'bear witness' in situations where dying people have agreed to die on camera and to turn their personal vulnerable moments into shared intimacies with other people. Media witnessing, according to John Ellis, is 'witnessing from privileged position' because the viewer is given a holistic view from various perspectives while eyewitnesses often get only a partial view of the events. For Ellis, the privileged position is not merely about evaluation or judgement, but about emotional commitment as well (Ellis 2000, 124–32). Maria Kyriakidou looks at this viewer's position in more detail in her empirical reception study on how viewers react to media imagery on real-life suffering. She recognises four witnessing models: 'affective witnessing' refers to deep emotional connection that the viewer creates to the other through media; 'ecstatic witnessing' emphasises immediacy of the experience and urgency of the situation that is happening while we watch (life footage from disaster areas, for example); 'politicised witnessing' enables the viewer to evaluate the events through political and societal lenses in a rather distant manner; and 'detached witnessing' takes place when the viewer distances themselves from the suffering. Kyriakidou points out that different viewers may react differently to the same media images, yet for ethical experience affective witnessing appears as the preferred mode (Kyriakidou 2015, 220–9). These notions on witnessing further emphasise the importance of creating potential for the viewer's affective engagement when filming end-of-life documentaries.

Witnessing, then, is an active position, something that goes beyond watching or viewing. It builds on engaging with the film, on being open to others and on willingness to transform by becoming involved (see also Kyriakidou 2015, 217; Peters 2001, 708; Ashuri 2010, 172, 177; Morse 2018, 245). Enrica Colusso, for example, argues that documentaries provide spaces for encounter, which has the potential to transform the filmmaker and the filmed subject in a dialogic process, and which allows the viewer to take part in it through witnessing. These ethical encounters in themselves raise 'awareness of the responsibility towards the other' (Colusso 2017, 155). For example, in her analysis of migrant workers' films, Darshana Sreedhar Mini argues that when the films prioritise the experiences and rights of the other, they demand the viewer responds to the workers' vulnerability and suffering (Mini 2020, 145). The responsibility over the other is created through embodied engagement, which helps the viewer to understand the other better.

However, it has been questioned whether mere understanding or responsibility is enough of an act. This notion is at the core of Sontag's (2004, 34) criticism when she argues that we should not have the right to watch someone else's death unless we can do something to alleviate their suffering. Yet, as Ellis (2000, 122) reminds us, mediated witnessing differs from being an eyewitness because no immediate action is possible. However, I argue that a different type of action is possible. While we may not be able to alleviate that person's suffering, we can change societal practices towards inclusive and accessible end-of-life care. For example, as Morse (2018, 245) argues, the required action can be about thinking how suffering can be relieved, or about simply mourning the deaths of others. Along with the argumentation of cinematic ethics, the action can then relate to being willing to learn from these encounters and willing to learn to create an open relationship with another mortal being. As such, responsibility over the other can lead to our transformation, making the death of the other meaningful.

Maria Arman discusses a similar question in her empirical study of how witnessing takes place in the context of palliative care. In her study, witnessing includes addressing the patients' vulnerability and suffering as well as the staff's willingness to be present, emotional and open to existential questions. Consequently, Arman talks about 'daring to bear witness', because witnessing may change both parties in the process and requires the ability to become vulnerable when encountering mortality (Arman 2007, 86–91). Thus, affective witnessing is not an easy position, it requires the viewer to become vulnerable themselves. This makes witnessing an intersubjective engagement, not a one-way street where we watch and evaluate the death of the other. Instead, it invites us to care. This thinking leads us to Emma Wilson (2012, 3–20), who argues that audiovisual art can become a form of palliative care itself. The art creates space for caring connections and engagement between the viewers and the participants in the documentary projects, and this space allows and acknowledges all kinds of lived feelings ranging from fear and suffering to love and compassion. As such, witnessing and responsibility start to function as an ethical premise for the relationship between the viewer and the cinematic other (Davis 2019; Lamberti 2019). Based on these arguments, it seems that

INTRODUCTION

end-of-life documentaries, which allow us to witness the death and dying of others, can help us understand what these people and their families are going through. In end-of-life documentaries, the encounters with dying people can increase death awareness, increase our willingness to discuss the topic with others and encourage us to engage with dying people.

End-of-life documentaries have different strategies for providing ethical space. At the beginning of this Introduction, I gave an example of positive and life-affirming end-of-life documentaries that encouraged feelings of empowerment. An empowering approach can, indeed, foster in the viewer new ways of feeling, acting and living (Stadler 2014). However, negative emotions, too, can create ethical engagement with cinema: being uncomfortable and anxious, and sensing injustice or unfairness can stimulate strong responses that invite the viewer to ethically imagine what could be done to live better (Fleming 2017, 8). The viewers can challenge the chosen approach or perhaps even their own reactions to the documentary. Thus, an ethical space can be created through varied affective, embodied and cognitive responses. Instead of creating a unified picture of what dying is, end-of-life documentaries propose how it could be experienced. Particularly, they address death anxiety with various strategies and provide their own solutions to dealing with this fear, and in this process affects carry potential for social change. These films challenge the viewer to transform with the films, not to experience death itself, but to alleviate their death anxiety. The transformation process is built through witnessing the experiences of others from which the viewer can learn to better understand what dying people are going through, and perhaps gain insights for their own lives.

ORGANISATION OF THE BOOK: DOCUMENTARY VOICES

I approach the variety of end-of-life documentaries through the concept of voice. In documentary films, voice exceeds dialogue by referring to the space and time that a certain perspective has in the narration. Voice is a combination of several cinematic forms of expression, such as editing decisions, shot length, framing, music and represented spaces and people (Nichols 1983). Filmed subjects can have their own voice on-screen, as can the filmmaker, the narrator and various institutions and organisations represented in the story. Voice is an active choice whose perspective guides the viewer's experience and how the chosen issue is represented. While each film can include multiple, even contradicting voices, it is interesting to study which voices are offered as those of experts of end of life, and whose experience the viewer is expected to witness, engage and transform with.

Outside documentary films' context, voice refers to practices where the voiceless are given space to share their stories and perspectives. However,

17

some have questioned whether we should be more concerned that these voices are heard and valued. As an alternative, Tanja Dreher and Anshuman Mondal, among others, offer listening. They argue that this would turn the focus towards ethics of witnessing because unlike voice, listening includes the possibility of being unsettled and vulnerable, of changing one's mind and of transforming (Dreher and Mondal 2018, 4–6). Their argument is in line with my emphasis on affective witnessing, yet I use the voice as an organisational tool for my study. Understanding documentary film as an ethical space where the filmmaker and the viewer are asked to listen to the voices of the subjects places the responsibility on us, the viewers and readers, to respond to these voices.

While all documentaries discussed in *Filming Death* bring different voices to the fore, I have divided this book into three sections based on the main perspectives offered in the documentaries. These perspectives build on institutional voices, voices of the dying people and personal voices. Institutional voices showcase documentaries that emphasise the authorities' and professionals' viewpoints on end of life. The voices of the dying people refer to stories where the filmmakers give dying people the main voice. Personal voices include stories where the filmmakers narrate their experiences (often in collaboration with dying subjects) from their first-person perspective. This division calls to mind what William Stott has written about early documentaries from the 1930s. According to Stott, these documentaries were either about facts and information, about the lived experience (case studies) or about the filmmaker's personal experience (Stott 1986, 172). The division seems applicable in contemporary social issue documentaries. Borum Chattoo (2020, 8), for example, argues that social issue documentaries continue to locate social issues within a factual framework, but they also want to showcase real experiences and are shaped by the filmmaker's viewpoint. Similarly, in the documentary films discussed in this book, all these three aspects can be seen in all films, yet various films emphasise these elements differently.

These three categories also emerged in the content analysis of some of the films studied (thirty-five out of ninety viewed films). I studied how much space and time were given to dying people's voices in these films. The analysis revealed three categories, which turned out to follow the guidelines of institutional, dying and personal voices. The documentaries which allocated the least time to the voices of those about to die, were institutional films: about 29 per cent of the narration took place through dying people. The films highlighting dying people's voices dedicated about 71 per cent of the content to their perspectives. The filmmaker's perspective was situated in-between with about 40 per cent of the narration telling the story of dying people (Hakola 2021). This quantitative approach shows that none of the films is narrated through only one type of voice, but each film contains multiple perspectives and experiences for the

INTRODUCTION

viewer. What the varied emphasis of voices does is provide a starting point to further explore end-of-life documentaries.

First, the institutional approach follows Bill Nichols's view of traditional social issue documentaries. Nichols argues that social issue documentaries use an authoritative voice that is supplemented by experts and witnesses endorsing the message. Knowledge of the social issue is preferred over personal stories. Consequently, these documentaries have minimal psychological depth. Also, these films emphasise content and rhetorical arguments, which makes style a secondary notion. As such, Nichols argues, social issue documentaries aim to direct attention to the film's mission, and often they propose or seek a solution to the presented social issue (Nichols 2017, 192). Similarly, some end-of-life documentaries focus their attention on institutional, factual and generalisable knowledge of dying. In these films, the focus is on how we should care for dying people, and what kind of care options we should offer to dying people. These films inform the viewer about end-of-life care choices and explore their potential and limits. In the following chapters, I will first discuss medical care within medicalised death (Chapter 2) and will then turn to examine how hospice care is represented in the documentary films (Chapter 3). The third theme includes spiritual aspects that are related to end-of-life care (Chapter 4). Lastly, I will discuss the heated debate of assisted dying and the forms that it takes in the end-of-life documentaries (Chapter 5). These documentaries suggest that good end-of-life care can diminish our death anxiety, because it promises that we do not have to be afraid of the dying process itself. This promise is given by the professionals – medical doctors, hospice and palliative care workers, spiritual and religious leaders, and advocacy organisations – who share their knowledge with the viewer. While these documentaries include the personal stories of dying people, they are often used as engaging examples that support the educational message of the documentaries.

The second part of the book is dedicated to documentaries that prioritise the voices of dying people. In these documentaries, the filmmakers invite their filmed subjects to be equal partners in the conversation to create understanding of lived experiences. For Nichols (2017, 193), personal portraits provide a situated perspective on social issues, and this singularity of experience would lead the social issue to take a secondary role. While Nichols excludes portraits from 'traditional' social issue films, the current understanding sees that personal touch increases the effectiveness of the message. These films blur the line between public and private by focusing on how the issue feels from an individual's perspective. In personal portraits, Nichols argues, style becomes at least as important as the content, and their approaches can be subjective or poetic. Typically, these films do not aim to provide a solution or a conclusion. Their goal is to increase empathy and understanding of others' experiences (Nichols 2017, 193). As this description connects dying voices to theories of

19

ethical space and encounters, the second section of the book moves on to films where filmmakers provide space for dying people's voices. Instead of trying to educate viewers with a 'one-size-fits-all' model, these documentaries showcase various perspectives on what a dying process can look and feel like. Above all, in allowing space for the dying people, these kinds of documentaries aim to empower the dying subjects and make them visible in the public discussions on death. In these chapters, I discuss how dying people participate in performing their experiences for the viewer (Chapter 6), how they use documentaries to create personal legacies (Chapter 7), how some dying people dedicate their last moments for the viewer to witness physical fragilities related to dying and the moment of death (Chapter 8), and how people seeking assisted dying want to make the viewer understand why they have chosen to die (Chapter 9). Here, dying is an individual path towards death, which is more tolerable to tread when one's personal needs and desires are met.

The third perspective in *Filming Death* is the personal voice of those participating in the filmmaking processes. For Nichols, personal perspectives connect to first-person or autobiographical narratives, which are performative by nature. They focus on personal accounts of someone's experiences, self-reflection and individual development (Nichols 2017, 106–9). Furthermore, personal documentaries delve deep into private experience, and provide an intimate connection for the viewer where the filmmakers offer themselves and their experiences for the viewer to engage with. This category therefore also provides a strong connection to experiences, perhaps even more so than in those documentaries that focus on dying people's voices. In this section of the book, I turn to subjective voices, where the filmmakers reflect their own thoughts about death (Chapter 10) and where the dying subjects participate in making films of their dying and death (Chapter 11). These documentaries stress subjective knowledge and experience and ask the viewer to witness these experiences. The self-reflection of those participating in the filmmaking reveals how they learn to accommodate their own death anxiety and how they come to acknowledge the idea of death in their own lives. These personal transformation stories invite the viewer to transform along with them, and as such, learn to think about death and dying with less fear and anxiety.

While the organisation of the book borrows elements from Nichols's categorisations of documentary films, I recognise that these categorisations also have their limits. Documentaries are rarely produced to fit into a theoretical category. They are clearly more driven by an idea of a message and theme. I can appreciate the artificiality of forcing documentaries into neat categories, but at the same time I realise that discussing films which have common attributes allows us to recognise the variety of ways end of life can be discussed through the art of documentary film. In my study, unlike in Nichols's categorisation, social issue documentaries are not limited to their 'traditional'

INTRODUCTION

category. Contemporary social issue documentaries embrace the use of emotions, experiences and personal stories in their desire to create social change. In end-of-life documentaries, the desired social change is often related to our emotional relationship with death and dying, and as such, embodied and affective elements are important aspects of this quest for change in attitudes and values.

References

Aaltonen, Jouko. 2022. 'Valistaa, Taistella Vai Haastaa? Suomalaisen Ei-Fiktiivisen Elokuvan Retoriikkaa Ja Strategioita'. In *Repeämän Kuvat: Dokumentaarinen Elokuva Ja Hyvinvointivaltion Murtumia*, edited by Susanna Helke and Essi Viitanen, 16–61. Espoo: Aalto ARTS Books.

Aaron, Michele. 2014. *Death and the Moving Image: Ideology, Iconography and I*. Edinburgh: Edinburgh University Press.

Arman, Maria. 2007. 'Bearing Witness: An Existential Position in Caring'. *Contemporary Nurse* 27 (1): 84–93. https://doi.org/10.5172/conu.2007.27.1.84.

Armstrong, Richard. 2011. 'Review: Boaz Hagin (2010) Death in Classical Hollywood Cinema'. *Film-Philosophy* 15 (2): 126–8.

Armstrong-Coster, Angela. 2001. 'In Morte Media Jubilate [1]: An Empirical Study of Cancer-Related Documentary Film'. *Mortality* 6 (3): 287–305. https://doi.org/10.1080/13576270120082943.

Ashuri, Tamar. 2010. 'I Witness: Re-presenting Trauma in and by Cinema'. *The Communication Review* 13 (3): 171–92. https://doi.org/10.1080/10714421.2010.5 05145.

Aufderheide, Patricia. 2008. *Documentary Film: A Very Short Introduction*. Oxford: Oxford University Press.

Bakhtin, M. M. 1984. *Rabelais and His World*. First published 1965. Bloomington: Indiana University Press.

Barthes, Roland. 2010. *Camera Lucida: Reflections on Photography*. Translated by Richard Howard. First published 1980. New York: Hill and Wang.

Bazin, André. 1960. 'The Ontology of the Photographic Image'. Translated by Hugh Gray. *Film Quarterly* 13 (4): 4–9. https://doi.org/10.2307/1210183.

Borum Chattoo, Caty. 2020. *Story Movements: How Documentaries Empower People and Inspire Social Change*. New York: Oxford University Press. https://doi.org/10.1093/oso/9780190943417.001.0001.

Borum Chattoo, Caty, and Lauren Feldman. 2017. 'Storytelling for Social Change: Leveraging Documentary and Comedy for Public Engagement in Global Poverty'. *Journal of Communication* 67 (5): 678–701. https://doi.org/10.1111/jcom.12318. Last accessed 11 May 2022.

Borum Chattoo, Caty, and William Harder. 2018. 'The State of the Documentary Field: 2018 Study of Documentary Professionals'. Washington DC: Center for Media & Social Impact; American University School of Communication. https://dra.american.edu/islandora/object/socialmediapubs%3A87.

Borum Chattoo, Caty, and Will Jenkins. 2019. 'From Reel Life to Real Social Change: The Role of Contemporary Social-Issue Documentary in U.S. Public Policy'. *Media, Culture & Society* 41 (8): 1107–24. https://doi.org/10.1177/0163443718823145.

Bregman, Lucy. 2017. 'The Death Awareness Movement'. In *The Routledge Companion to Death and Dying*, edited by Christopher M. Moreman. London; New York: Routledge, Taylor & Francis Group.

Cai, Wei, Yung-lung Tang, Song Wu, and Hong Li. 2017. 'Scale of Death Anxiety (SDA): Development and Validation'. *Frontiers in Psychology* 8 (May): 858. https://doi.org/10.3389/fpsyg.2017.00858.

Choi, Jinhee, and Mattias Frey. 2014. 'Introduction'. In *Cine-Ethics: Ethical Dimensions of Film Theory, Practice, and Spectatorship*, edited by Jinhee Choi and Mattias Frey, 1–13. London; New York: Routledge.

Coffman, Elizabeth. 2009. 'Documentary and Collaboration: Placing the Camera in the Community'. *Journal of Film and Video* 61 (1): 62–78.

Colusso, Enrica. 2017. 'The Space between the Filmmaker and the Subject – the Ethical Encounter'. *Studies in Documentary Film* 11 (2): 141–56. https://doi.org/10.1080/17503280.2017.1342072.

Cowie, Elizabeth. 1999. 'The Spectacle of Actuality'. In *Collecting Visible Evidence*, edited by Jane Gaines and Michael Renov, 19–45. Minneapolis: University of Minnesota Press.

Davidson, Paul, and Barbara Gibb. 2016. *Helen's Story*. Documentary. Bytesize Productions.

———. 2020. Personal interview by Outi Hakola.

Davis, Colin. 2019. 'Levinas and Film'. In *The Oxford Handbook of Levinas*, online edition. Oxford Academic. https://doi.org/10.1093/oxfordhb/9780190455934.013.19.

Deleuze, Gilles. 1986a. *Cinema 1: The Movement-Image*. First published 1983. Minneapolis: University of Minnesota.

———. 1986b. *Cinema 2: The Time-Image*. Translated by Hugh Tomlinson and Robert Galeta. First published 1985. Minneapolis: University of Minnesota.

Dick, Kirby. 1997. *Sick: The Life and Death of Bob Flanagan, Supermasochist*. Documentary. Lionsgate Films.

Doka, Kenneth J. 2003. 'The Death Awareness Movement: Description, History, and Analysis'. In *Handbook of Death & Dying*, 50–6. Thousand Oaks: SAGE Publications. https://doi.org/10.4135/9781412914291.n6.

Doka, Kenneth J., E. Neil Heflin-Wells, Terry L. Martin, Lula M. Redmond, and Sherry R. Schachter. 2011. 'The Organization of Thanatology'. *OMEGA – Journal of Death and Dying* 63 (2): 113–24. https://doi.org/10.2190/OM.63.2.a.

Downing, Lisa, and Libby Saxton. 2010. *Film and Ethics: Foreclosed Encounters*. London; New York: Routledge.

Dreher, Tanja, and Anshuman A. Mondal. 2018. 'From Voice to Response: Ethical Responsiveness and the Politics of Difference'. In *Ethical Responsiveness and the Politics of Difference*, edited by Tanja Dreher and Anshuman A. Mondal, 1–20. Cham: Palgrave Macmillan.

Ellis, John. 2000. *Seeing Things: Television in the Age of Uncertainty*. London: I. B. Tauris & Co. Ltd. https://doi.org/10.5040/9780755604784.

Epstein, Rob, and Jeffrey Friedman. 1989. *Common Threads: Stories from the Quilt*. Documentary. Couterie, Home Box Office (HBO), Saul Zaentz Film Center.

Fleming, David H. 2017. *Unbecoming Cinema: Unsettling Encounters with Ethical Event Films*. Bristol: Intellect.

Friedman, Peter, and Tom Joslin. 1993. *Silverlake Life: The View from Here*. Documentary. Strange Attractions.

Gallagher, Shaun. 2008. 'Intersubjectivity in Perception'. *Continental Philosophy Review* 41 (2): 163–78. https://doi.org/10.1007/s11007-008-9075-8.

Gibson, Margaret. 2007. 'Death and Mourning in Technologically Mediated Culture'. *Health Sociology Review* 16 (5): 415–24. https://doi.org/10.5172/hesr.2007.16.5.415.

Grierson, John. 1966. *Grierson on Documentary*, edited by Forsyth Hardy. Berkeley; Los Angeles: University of California Press.

Grønstad, Asbjørn. 2016. *Film and the Ethical Imagination*. London: Palgrave Macmillan. https://doi.org/10.1057/978-1-137-58374-1_10.

Grue, Jan. 2022. 'The Death of Others. On the Narrative Rhetoric of Neoliberal Thanatopolitics'. *Disability Studies Quarterly* 42 (1). https://doi.org/10.18061/dsq.v42i1.7799.

Hagin, B. 2010. *Death in Classical Hollywood Cinema*. Basingstoke; New York: Palgrave Macmillan.

Hakola, Outi. 2018. 'Death in Documentary Film'. *The Perfect Circle Film* (blog). 28 June 2018. http://www.theperfectcirclefilm.com/wordpress/en/2018/06/28/outi-j-hakola-la-morte-nei-film-documentari/. Last accessed 16 August 2022.

———. 2021. 'Diversity in Representations and Voices of Terminally Ill People in End-of-Life Documentaries'. *Journal of Palliative Care* 37 (2): 08258597211013961. https://doi.org/10.1177/08258597211013961.

Hardy, Forsyth. 1966. 'Introduction'. In *Grierson on Documentary*, edited by Forsyth Hardy, 13–39. Berkeley; Los Angeles: University of California Press.

Hill, Mike. 2012. *Life Before Death*. Documentary. Moonshine Agency.

———. 2015. *Little Stars*. Documentary. Moonshine Agency.

———. 2020. Personal interview by Outi Hakola.

Hongisto, Ilona. 2015. *Soul of the Documentary*. Amsterdam: Amsterdam University Press. https://doi.org/10.5117/9789089647559.

Incorvaia, Aubrey DeVeny. 2022. 'Death Positivity in America: The Movement – Its History and Literature'. *OMEGA – Journal of Death and Dying*, April, 00302228221085176. https://doi.org/10.1177/00302228221085176.

Karlin, Beth, and John Johnson. 2011. 'Measuring Impact: The Importance of Evaluation for Documentary Film Campaigns'. *M/C Journal* 14 (6). https://doi.org/10.5204/mcj.444.

Kyriakidou, Maria. 2015. 'Media Witnessing: Exploring the Audience of Distant Suffering'. *Media, Culture & Society* 37 (2): 215–31. https://doi.org/10.1177/0163443714557981.

Lambert South, Andrea, and Jessica Elton. 2017. 'Contradictions and Promise for End-of-Life Communication among Family and Friends: Death over Dinner Conversations'. *Behavioral Sciences* 7 (2): 24. https://doi.org/10.3390/bs7020024.

Lamberti, Edward. 2019. *Performing Ethics through Film Style: Levinas with the Dardenne Brothers, Barbet Schroeder and Paul Schrader*. Edinburgh: Edinburgh University Press.

LeBrun, Michelle. 1999. *Death: A Love Story*. Documentary. Harken Productions.

Lehto, Rebecca Helen, and Karen Farchaus Stein. 2009. 'Death Anxiety: An Analysis of an Evolving Concept'. *Research and Theory for Nursing Practice* 23 (1): 23–41. https://doi.org/10.1891/1541-6577.23.1.23.

Levinas, Emmanuel. 2011. *Totality and Infinity: An Essay on Exteriority*. First published 1969. Pittsburgh, PA: Duquesne University Press.

Lipson, David, and Zachary Baqué. 2019. 'Rethinking the Convergence of Documentary and Entertainment'. *InMedia*, no. 7.2. (December): 1–12. https://doi.org/10.4000/inmedia.1601.

Malkowski, Jennifer. 2017. *Dying in Full Detail: Mortality and Digital Documentary*. Durham, NC; London: Duke University Press. https://doi.org/10.1215/9780822373414.

Merleau-Ponty, Maurice. 2012. *Phenomenology of Perception*. Translated by Donald A. Landes. First published 1945. Abingdon; New York: Routledge.

———. 2019. 'The Film and the New Psychology'. In *Philosophers on Film from Bergson to Badiou*, edited by Christopher Kul-Want, 97–112. First published 1945. Columbia University Press. https://doi.org/10.7312/kul-17602-006.

Mini, Darshana Sreedhar. 2020. 'Transnational Ethical Screens: Empathetic Networks in Malayalam Short Films from the Gulf'. *Film History* 32 (3): 141. https://doi.org/10.2979/filmhistory.32.3.06.

Morse, Tal. 2018. 'The Construction of Grievable Death: Toward an Analytical Framework for the Study of Mediatized Death'. *European Journal of Cultural Studies* 21 (2): 242–58. https://doi.org/10.1177/1367549416656858.

Mulvey, Laura. 2006. *Death 24x a Second: Stillness and the Moving Image*. Repr. London: Reaktion Books.

Murray, Tom. 2020. Interview on documentary film *Love in Our Own Time*. Interview by Outi Hakola.

Murray, Tom, and Madeleine Hetherton. 2011. *Love in Our Own Time*. Documentary. Tarpaulin Productions.

Nash, Kate, and John Corner. 2016. 'Strategic Impact Documentary: Contexts of Production and Social Intervention'. *European Journal of Communication* 31 (3): 227–42. https://doi.org/10.1177/0267323116635831.

Nederhorst, Maarten. 1994. *Death on Request*. Documentary. Icarus Films.

Neimeyer, Robert A., Richard P. Moser, and Joachim Wittkowski. 2003. 'Assessing Attitudes Toward Dying and Death: Psychometric Considerations'. *OMEGA – Journal of Death and Dying* 47 (1): 45–76. https://doi.org/10.2190/EP4R-TULM-W52G-L3EX.

Neimeyer, Robert A., Joachim Wittkowski, and Richard P. Moser. 2004. 'Psychological Research on Death Attitudes: An Overview and Evaluation'. *Death Studies* 28 (4): 309–40. https://doi.org/10.1080/07481180490432324.

Nichols, Bill. 1983. 'The Voice of Documentary'. *Film Quarterly* 36 (3): 17–30. https://doi.org/10.2307/3697347.

———. 1991. *Representing Reality: Issues and Concepts in Documentary*. Bloomington; Indianapolis: Indiana University Press.

———. 2017. *Introduction to Documentary, Third Edition*. Bloomington: Indiana University Press.

Niemiec, Ryan M., and Stefan E. Schulenberg. 2011. 'Understanding Death Attitudes: The Integration of Movies, Positive Psychology, and Meaning Management'. *Death Studies* 35 (5): 387–407. https://doi.org/10.1080/07481187.2010.544517.

Önen, Ufuk. 2021. 'The Voice as a Narrative Element in Documentary Films'. *Resonance* 2 (1): 6–18. https://doi.org/10.1525/res.2021.2.1.6.

Orkibi, Hod, Gianmarco Biancalani, and Bucu. 2021. 'Students' Confidence and Interest in Palliative and Bereavement Care: A European Study'. *Frontiers in Psychology* 12. https://doi.org/10.3389/fpsyg.2021.616526.

Peters, John Durham. 2001. 'Witnessing'. *Media, Culture & Society* 23 (6): 707–23. https://doi.org/10.1177/016344301023006002.

Peterson, Beverly. 1998. *The Andre Show*. Documentary. Fanlight Productions.

Plantinga, Carl R. 1997. *Rhetoric and Representation in Nonfiction Film*. Cambridge Studies in Film. Cambridge; New York: Cambridge University Press.

Pryluck, Calvin. 2005. 'Ultimately We Are All Outsiders: The Ethics of Documentary Filming'. In *New Challenges for Documentary*, edited by Alan Rosenthal and John Corner, second edition, 194–208. Manchester; New York: Manchester University Press.

Raviv, Orna. 2021. *Ethics of Cinematic Experience: Screens of Alterity*. New York: Routledge.

Rawlings, Deb, Caroline Litster, Lauren Miller-Lewis, Jennifer Tieman, and Kate Swetenham. 2020. 'The Voices of Death Doulas about Their Role in End-of-Life Care'. *Health & Social Care in the Community* 28 (1): 12–21. https://doi.org/10.1111/hsc.12833.

Ray, Nicholas, and Wim Wenders. 1984. *Lightning Over Water*. Documentary. Road Movies Filmproduktion, Viking Film, Wim Wenders Productions.

Renov, Michael. 1999. 'Documentary Horizons: An Afterword'. In *Collecting Visible Evidence*, edited by Jane Gaines and Michael Renov, 313–26. Minneapolis: University of Minnesota Press.

———. 2004. *The Subject of Documentary*. Minneapolis: University of Minnesota Press.

Richards, Naomi, Gitte H. Koksvik, Sheri Mila Gerson, and David Clark. 2020. 'The Global Spread of Death Café: A Cultural Intervention Relevant to Policy?' *Social Policy and Society* 19 (4): 553–72. https://doi.org/10.1017/S1474746420000081.

Rodowick, D. N. 2010. 'The World, Time'. In *Afterimages of Gilles Deleuze's Film Philosophy*, edited by D. N. Rodowick, 97–114. Minneapolis: University of Minnesota Press. https://doi.org/10.5749/j.ctttsbsc.

Russell, Catherine. 1995. *Narrative Mortality: Death, Closure, and New Wave Cinemas*. Minneapolis: University of Minnesota Press.

Schultz, Ned W., and Lisa M. Huet. 2001. 'Sensational! Violent! Popular! Death in American Movies'. *OMEGA – Journal of Death and Dying* 42 (2): 137–49. https://doi.org/10.2190/6GDX-4W40-5B94-MX0G.

Sinnerbrink, Robert. 2016. *Cinematic Ethics: Exploring Ethical Experience through Film*. London; New York: Routledge.

Smaill, Belinda. 2010. *The Documentary: Politics, Emotion, Culture*. Basingstoke; New York: Palgrave Macmillan.

Sobchack, Vivian. 1984. 'Inscribing Ethical Space: Ten Propositions on Death, Representation, and Documentary'. *Quarterly Review of Film Studies* 9 (4): 283–300. https://doi.org/10.1080/10509208409361220.

———. 1992. *The Address of the Eye: A Phenomenology of Film Experience*. Princeton, NJ: Princeton University Press.

Sontag, Susan. 2001. *On Photography*. First published 1977. New York: Picador.

———. 2004. *Regarding the Pain of Others*. First published 2003. New York, NY: Picador.

Stadler, Jane. 2014. 'Cinema's Compassionate Gaze: Empathy, Affect, and Aesthetics in The Diving Bell and the Butterfly'. In *Cine-Ethics*, edited by Jinhee Choi and Mattias Frey, 26–42. New York: Routledge.

Staudt, Christina. 2009. 'From Concealment to Recognition: The Discourse on Death, Dying, and Grief'. In *Speaking of Death: America's New Sense of Mortality*, edited by Michael K. Bartalos, 3–41. Westport, CT; London: Praeger.

Stott, William. 1986. *Documentary Expression and Thirties America*. Chicago, IL: University of Chicago Press.

Velasquez, Manuel, Claire Andre, Tom Shanks, and Micheal J. Meyer. 2010. 'What Is Ethics? (Revised from an article that originally appeared in *Issues in Ethics* IIE V1 N1, Fall 1987)'. *Markkula Center for Applied Ethics at Santa Clara University* (blog). 2010. https://www.scu.edu/ethics/ethics-resources/ethical-decision-making/what-is-ethics/. Last accessed 1 January 2023.

Vogel, Amos. 2006. *Film as a Subversive Art*. First published 1974. London; New York: Distributed Art Publishers/CT Editions.

Walter, Tony. 2020. *Death in the Modern World*. London: SAGE Publications, Inc.

West, Emily. 2018. 'Invitation to Witness: The Role of Subjects in Documentary Representations of the End of Life'. *International Journal of Communication* 12: 1481–500.

Wilson, Emma. 2012. *Love, Mortality and the Moving Image*. London: Palgrave Macmillan. https://doi.org/10.1057/9780230367708.

Winston, Brian. 2008. *Claiming the Real II: Documentary: Grierson and Beyond.* Second edition. London; New York: Palgrave Macmillan.

Wiseman, Frederick. 1989. *Near Death.* Documentary. Exit Films Inc.

Zimmermann, Patricia R., and Helen De Michiel. 2018. *Open Space New Media Documentary: A Toolkit for Theory and Practice.* New York: Routledge.

SECTION I
INSTITUTIONAL VOICES

2. MEDICAL DOCUMENTARIES

Demedicalisation of Death

The first scene of the television documentary *Being Mortal* (Jennings 2015) leads the viewer from the street outside a Boston hospital to its busy hallways, where doctors and nurses navigate the floors. The camera follows Atul Gawande scrubbing in for surgery, while the surgeon's voiceover sets the scene:

> I've been a surgeon for more than a decade now. In medicine, your first fear as a doctor is that you're supposed to be able to fix a problem, and our anxieties include wanting to seem competent, and to us, competent means I can fix this. [...] Among the most uncomfortable difficulties was grappling with those cases where we couldn't solve the problem. The two big unfixables are aging and dying. You know, they're not – you can't fix those. (Jennings 2015)

The opening displays the conflict explored in the documentary – is death a medical failure, a broken promise for the patients, or something that should be embraced as a natural part of life?

Similar discussions emerge from cinema's relationship with death. Since the early twentieth century, cinema, along with medical technology, has served as a sign of modern society and cinema has eagerly supported a technological vision of society. Early documentary films, for example, represented scientific technology with authority and sociopolitical importance (Tabernero 2018). Since early cinema, Kirsten Ostherr (2013) and José van Dijck (2005) argue, audiovisual media has imagined, conceptualised, and represented medical knowledge to the public in ways that have both informed and entertained the audiences, and promoted and popularised medical technology and expertise. In addition, medical professionals have utilised film technology to document medical procedures to standardise and verify the medical practices (Ostherr 2013, 4–7; van Dijck 2005, 9–14). In other words, cinema and, subsequently, television programming have participated in building up the medical authority in western societies. These representations often promise that medicine and physicians have almost omnipotent powers to cure and save patients (Ostherr 2013, 168–9; Painter, Kubala, and Parsloe 2020, 330–1; van Dijck 2005, 33–4; Henderson 2010, 201–3). Consequently, typical storylines cast death in the problematic role of being a failure in modern society.

Since the late twentieth century, however, audiovisual narratives of the medical field have diversified. Contemporary end-of-life documentaries exemplify the critical voices about the conception of the omnipotence of the medical field. Many end-of-life documentaries align themselves with the death awareness movement's goals to make death visible, approachable and a natural part of life, instead of a sign of failure of care. In this chapter, I analyse medical documentaries that focus on end-of-life care at hospitals, particularly in the intensive care units (ICU), which provide critical care, life support and constant surveillance for patients whose lives are at immediate risk. These films include *Edge of Life* (Theroux 2014a), where British-American documentarist Louis Theroux explores the American way of death at the Cedars-Sinai Medical Center in Los Angeles; *The First Wave* (Heineman 2021), which observes Long Island Jewish Medical Center amid the Covid-19 pandemic in New York City; *Extremis* (Krauss 2016), which was filmed at the intensive care unit at Highland Hospital in Oakland, California; *Facing Death* (Navasky and O'Connor 2010), which investigates end-of-life care at an emergency care unit at the Mount Sinai Hospital in New York City; *Being Mortal* (Jennings 2015), which follows the journey of a surgeon, Dr Atul Gawande from Brigham and Women's Hospital in Boston, Massachusetts; and a short documentary *Dying in Your Mother's Arms* (Beder 2020), which shadows Dr Nadia Tremonti's work at Children's Hospital of Michigan, Detroit. All these documentaries discuss medical, social and emotional aspects of end-of-life care choices, and at the same time rewrite cinematic traditions that celebrate medical technologies.

As public affairs documentaries, these films take an investigative reporting approach to the social issue of end-of-life care in television broadcasting (Aufderheide 2008, 77). Commissioned by the BBC, Theroux's *Edge of Life* is part of the LA Stories documentary series on the underbelly of Los Angeles. *The First Wave*, distributed by National Geographic, an American television network known for its non-fiction programming, won several Emmy awards. *Extremis* is a Netflix-distributed documentary, which earned its director Dan

Krauss, a graduate from Berkeley Graduate School of Journalism, an Academy Award nomination in 2017. *Facing Death* and *Being Mortal* are Frontline documentaries in the American Public Broadcasting Service (PBS) investigative journalism series that explores controversial topics to 'spur change and reform' (GBH 2018). And last, *Dying in Your Mother's Arms* is distributed by the New York Times op-docs series, where filmmakers platform opinionated non-fiction films. These 'investigative' production contexts frame end-of-life care as a controversial topic that needs a public change of attitudes to embrace mortality and accept death.

Public affairs documentaries blur the boundaries between journalism and creative filmmaking. In the early twenty-first century, journalistic values such as neutrality, fairness, balance and a desire to inform and educate the viewer were still at the core of journalistic documentaries (Kemmitt 2007; Nichols 2017, 105–6). By the 2010s, however, television documentaries increasingly became tools for journalists to dive deep into the stories, give voice and faces to those involved, to engage audiences and communities, to advocate arguments and to promote social change (Nash and Corner 2016; Charles 2013, 384–8). Matthew Charles (2013, 384) argues that the change from idealisation of objectivity to telling engaging and persuasive stories also transforms the ethical practices of the public affairs documentaries. Traditionally, the evaluation of documentaries' ethical practices has favoured an assessment of film's rhetorical and discursive practices, or in other words, how credibly and truthfully the social issues are represented for the viewer (Eitzen 2007; Plantinga 2013; Austin 2012; Brylla and Kramer 2018). The increasing use of emotive and engaging storytelling guides the notion from cognitive evaluation towards the affective aspects of arguments (Brylla and Kramer 2018). This brings us back to Charles's argument that contemporary public affairs documentaries want to create social change through attachment, and as such, attachment becomes the documentaries' most important ethical practice (Charles 2013, 384–8). In this chapter, I argue that medical documentaries about end-of-life care combine rhetorical and affective arguments in ways that allow the viewer to cognitively evaluate both sides of medicalisation and demedicalisation arguments. At the same time, these films' affective aspects encourage attachment with the goals of demedicalisation.

Mediated and Cultural Traditions of Medicalisation

In the early days of death education and death awareness movements, one of the most common arguments was that western cultures suffer from a denial of death that leads to alienation and marginalisation of not only death but also of dying individuals (Ariès 1975; Bauman 1992; Elias 2001). Death denial is spurred on by institutionalisation and medicalisation of death, where professionals, and particularly medical professionals, take care of the dying process, and death takes place in hospitals, nursing homes and hospices (Quinlan 2009). Medicalisation processes place death firmly under medical authority and also transform social, psychological and spiritual aspects of dying to a medical problem that can be managed with medical interventions (Hetzler and Dugdale 2018, 767; Conrad 2007, 4; Sadler et al. 2009). The death movements have rallied against these processes, which they see as inhumane and bureaucratic (Walter 2020, 101–2). The criticism targets 'overmedicalisation', which refers to aggressive medical interventions such as tube-feeding or ventilators to extend life. Overmedicalisation is seen to favour physicians' experience in shaping end-of-life experience, which isolates patients into hospitals where they are treated as medical objects instead of autonomous beings whose social and mental well-being matters (Field 1994; Hetzler and Dugdale 2018; Zimmermann and Rodin 2004; Lofland 1978, 61–72). Thus, overmedicalisation is seen to prevent a 'natural' dying process where death is accepted as a part of life.

Many end-of-life documentaries align themselves with death movements' goals to make death visible and approachable in the public sphere. This premise also drives their critical referencing of medicalisation. At the same time, the documentary films come from a long filmic and televisual tradition of endorsing the medical field's scientific, social and cultural authority. Since the 1950s, the popular medical dramas in western countries have represented devoted and heroic physicians with omnipotent powers and superior medical technology to cure their patients, which has served to normalise the medical gaze and has reassured audiences about functioning medical systems (Ostherr 2013, 168–9; Painter, Kubala, and Parsloe 2020, 330–1; van Dijck 2005, 33–4; Henderson 2010, 201–3). Non-fiction films and programming established medical topics in the 1970s. Early medical documentaries, such as Frederick Wiseman's *Hospital* (1970) and the documentary series *Operation: Lifeline* (NCC, 1978–79) gave viewers behind-the-scenes access to witness how real, and respectable, doctors treated real patients. Investigative journalism shows, such as *60 Minutes* (CBS, 1968–), linked medicine to the idea of progress, and American television introduced television doctors advocating medical education (Ostherr 2013, 171–9). In these early representations, the medical approach could solve whatever problems there were, including the patients' social problems.

Fictional programming, such as the British medical drama *Casualty* (BBC One, 1986–), Australian drama *G.P.* (Australian Broadcasting Corporation, 1989–96), and the American series *ER* (NBC, 1994–2009) started to add social realism and criticism of healthcare systems to medical programming in the late 1980s and early 1990s (Henderson 2010; Lupton 1995), while non-fictional programming began to focus on reality television. This turned the gaze from doctors and hospital life towards patients, and promoted healthy lifestyles through inspirational, yet moral narratives (Painter, Kubala, and Parsloe 2020, 330–1; Ostherr 2013, 201). In hospital documentaries, such as *Hopkins 24/7* (ABC, 2000) or *Boston Med* (ABC, 2010), the occasional death of a patient provided realism to stories that were more frequently uplifting (Ostherr 2013, 193–200). Representations of the medical field have grown more complex over the years, but the grand narratives where patients can be fixed and discharged thanks to high-tech interventions and the staff's admirable efforts have endured (Hetzler and Dugdale 2018, 767; van Dijck 2005, 26; Ostherr 2013, 201). The mediated images thus continue to support medicalisation, which creates expectations of the omnipotent nature of modern medicine.

End-of-life documentaries, at least partially, challenge this tradition. Theroux's documentary *Edge of Life* (2014a) asks if something has gone wrong with the medical system when enormous amounts of money and resources are spent on aggressive care at the end of life. The filmmaker visits an LA hospital where he follows the stories of three young adults, Donta, Javier and Langston, who all have poor recovery prospects. During the filming, both Donta and Javier die after several cycles of aggressive cancer treatments. In Javier's case, the physician suspects that the treatments may have shortened rather than lengthened his life. The viewer is asked to evaluate whether the aggressive treatments are overmedicalisation and worth the risks.

Medical documentaries and programming have been criticised for promising the viewer that salvation comes in the guise of medical expertise and technologies. When the media focus has been on curing illnesses, saving the patients and framing the end of life as a medical issue, many physicians have claimed that the omnipotent view of medicine has created unreasonable expectations that most patients can be fixed (Hetzler and Dugdale 2018). *Edge of Life* discloses similar concerns among the physicians, who admit to Theroux that their patients do not want to listen and understand when they say that there are no more treatments available. In the case of Donta, a group of doctors enter his room to tell him that there is nothing more to be done and the next step is comfort care. Donta struggles to accept the news, and while he agrees to move back home, he sees this as an avenue to search for alternative treatments. A relative of Donta supports this decision, and when Theroux tries to challenge the need to fight, the relative asks what Donta is supposed to do. 'I mean, just sit there, and just die? I would not do it and I would not encourage him to do it. But to lay there and do nothing, I don't think that is an answer' (Theroux 2014a). The relative continues to believe in the power of medical interventions and reads the doctors' refusal to try anything new as a sign of 'human error'.

In Javier's case, similarly, both the patient and his girlfriend maintain their belief in medical processes until Javier's death. In a discussion by Javier's bedside, Dr Linhares is the bearer of bad news: the cancer treatments, once again, have failed, and the cancer has strengthened its hold. The physician suggests that it is time to start thinking about a different approach but also lists potential medical options. Javier chooses to try another set of treatments: 'Really, they are offering me nothing or something, so I might just take something.' Theroux interjects by asking what would justify not going through new treatments and allowing Javier to go home, instead of staying at the hospital. The physician admits that there would be benefits to discontinuing treatments, yet Javier is not convinced. To him, discontinued treatments represent a death sentence.

In the same discussion, Javier reveals that he blames himself for letting people down. When Theroux challenges this view, Javier falls back on the metaphor of fighting the cancer and sees himself as a 'garbage outcome of the struggle'. The fighting metaphor is a common way to make sense of illness. The metaphor aligns itself with a medicalised view of seeing death as a failure, but in addition, it internalises a view that one would have agency over illness. This sense of agency, in some cases, can turn to a positive asset that gives a sense of maintaining control in a difficult situation, but in most cases, it engenders negative feelings when patients blame themselves for their 'weakness' in stopping the progression of illness (Semino et al. 2017; Semino, Demjén, and Demmen 2018). In Javier's mind, the fighting metaphor becomes baggage that spurs him to continue treatments despite growing frailty. In the end, he dies only two days after starting the new round of treatments.

Theroux tries to place some responsibility over the situation on the physician. After their discussion by Javier's bedside, Theroux questions Dr Linhares in the corridor. Why did she make Javier's situation appear more optimistic than it was? The physician replies that she does not have the heart to take away Javier's hope. The film's audiences appear stricken by this contradiction as well. In a Q & A event on Theroux's Facebook page, a viewer asks, 'Do you feel that the doctors and nurses weren't being frank enough to the patients about their condition?' Theroux replies:

> I think Dr Jones and Dr Gould (Langston's doctor and Donta's, respectively) were aware of the dangers of soft-soaping the prognosis and so they were a little more blunt in the way they gave the news. Dr Linhares took the opposite approach, trusting Javier to read between the lines. Maybe there's a way of imparting the information in a way that is both clear and also open to the possibility of hope. (Theroux 2014b)

Theroux's answer speaks to the conflicting emotional aspects of the documentary. While the cognitive argument shows that the physicians recognise the challenges related to the medicalisation of terminal illnesses, the film also shows the situations from the perspective of those who are ill. Medicalisation, for them, is about hope. Donta and Javier do not choose to die a medicalised death, but they keep on hoping, a solution that is emotionally understandable. When Donta begs for any positive news, tears running down his face, the viewer can understand why the doctors might be tempted to try one more treatment.

In *Edge of Life*, Langston's story turns the scales in favour of hope. Langston has a traumatic head injury and the medical professionals predict that he will not wake up from coma. His family is unwilling to give up, arguing time after time that Langston is not a type to give up, that he is a fighter. After thirty-seven days in intensive care, Langston wakes up, and after rehabilitation he returns to his life. The unexpected and sudden turn of events, as Natalie Harrison (2014, 568) writes about the documentary, 'shows both sides to end-of-life care: when the time comes to give up fighting, and also when the fight can turn into a miracle Hollywood ending'. In a way, *Edge of Life* exemplifies the dilemma between hope and the realities of end-of-life care. In this film, it is the patients that keep on hoping and fighting, whereas the doctors maintain a realistic approach to what the medical field can do to prevent – or delay – death and dying.

Edge of Life understands the patients' individual choices, but it questions the sustainability of the medical system to meet these demands. In an interview for the *Daily Mail*, Theroux argues that the optimism of his documentary is linked to the US context and the American way of funding healthcare, where if one has insurance, there is a temptation to try every option available, even if this makes American end-of-life care one of the most expensive amongst western countries (Styles 2014). The article's writer, Ruth Styles (2014), boils the cultural difference down to claiming that in *Edge of Life*, 'doctors, families and patients continue to treat patients long after they would have been dispatched to a hospice in the UK'. All the documentaries in this chapter focus on American end-of-life care, which is not coincidental nor a random choice. While the theme is referenced and discussed in other western documentaries, American medical documentaries give this issue a front-row seat. These documentaries highlight the dilemma of an expensive and potentially overmedicalised healthcare system and the patients' expectations that are fuelled by media representations of medical technology and heroic doctors fighting off death.

In comparison, Matthew Heineman's Covid-19 pandemic film, *The First Wave*, never suggests that acute patients should not be given every option for recovery. Yet, even this documentary comments on the organisation of American healthcare. The high proportion of racial minorities among hospitalised patients connects the pandemic to questions of structural racism in society. In the film, the minority patients struggle for breath simultaneously when the camera visits the streets to film Black Lives Matter protests over

George Floyd's death in police custody. The protest slogan 'I Can't Breathe' becomes symbolic on several levels.

The First Wave focuses on the difficult situation that New York City faced during the spring of 2020, when the city became the hardest-hit region in the country in the early phases of the pandemic. The filmmaker Matthew Heineman, who had previously filmed *Escape Fire: The Fight to Rescue American Healthcare* (Froemke and Heineman 2012), used his contacts to gain access to show what was happening at the hospitals and to put a human face to the pandemic. He started filming in the early stages of the pandemic, and due to having no planning time, the team ended up filming events as they unfolded. The story was edited together later on, including the discussion on structural racism (Luers 2021).

Compared to *Edge of Life* and other films discussed in this chapter, intensive care is portrayed in positive light in *The First Wave*. The patients need critical care for acute conditions instead of chronic diseases. Thus, the film avoids discussions on overmedicalisation or whether these patients should be supported with expensive care. The focus is on healthcare professionals, such as Dr Nathalie Dougé, yet the events evolve around patients, some of whom survive while others die. The threat of death and loss is tangible in many scenes, where a staff member calls family members to inform them that their loved one has died, where staff rush to a patient's side only to return quietly and solemnly, or when resuscitation turns into disbelief and inaction. The medical experts' emotional and embodied reactions become the core of the story, for example, when Dr Dougé breaks down in the corridor and cries over the situation and her patients. These emotional reactions were important to the director, who comments in an interview with *Filmmaker Magazine*:

> There was so much fear and sadness and deeply troubling moments throughout the shoot, but the overall feeling we kept was to appreciate the incredible fortitude and courage and love we witnessed every single day between the staff and the patients we were documenting. That feeling of inspiration pushed us day in and day out. (Luers 2021)

The comment shows how in this film, the medical experts do more than discuss options and provide medical care. In many ways, the medical staff replaces the role that the family members play in medical documentaries. They connect with their patients and care for them, turning the medicalised environment into humane space. In comparison, family members depend on remote connections and video calls.

While *The First Wave* acknowledges the physical and affective care by the medical staff, it does not paint a rosy image of the deaths in the medicalised environment. On one occasion, Dr Dougé complains about how she hates the isolation the patients are forced into. The ability to communicate, say good-byes, and be accompanied by loved ones would be the preferred way to die, but in the face of a pandemic all care options are explored (most often this requires sedation of the patient) just in case one of them would work. Pandemic deaths are pictured as lonely, isolated and medicalised. While they are not pictured as good deaths, the blame is directed towards the novel virus instead of overmedi-calisation. This becomes clear in a few cases where the patients survive. From the beginning of the documentary, the filmmakers follow the stories of Ahmed, a NYPD school safety officer, and Brussels, a nurse who contracted the virus. They both are hospitalised for a long time, and at times, their recoveries seem unlikely. When both finally pull through and can return home to their rejoicing families, the documentary ends with a sense of hope and appreciation of what good the medicalisation can do when it is properly deployed in acute situations to prevent premature death, as opposed to being used as an alternative to end-of-life care.

DESIRE FOR DEATH ACCEPTANCE

Extremis (Krauss 2016) debates medical, emotional, social and moral dif-ficulties related to end-of-life care choices. The film foregrounds physicians, Dr Jessica Zitter and Dr Monica Bhargava, who care for their patients at a hectic intensive care unit. In an interview for *The Moveable Fest*, director Dan Krauss explains:

> What really fascinated me is that, as an ICU physician, she [Dr Zitter] is, on a daily basis, confronted with questions that really transcend medicine and science. I hadn't thought about doctors having to take on the role of a counselor that has to help shepherd families and patients through the most fundamental questions of their core humanity. (Saito 2017)

In the documentary, the two physicians represent different sides of the medi-calisation argument. Dr Zitter speaks against overmedicalisation. Halfway through the documentary, she recalls a time they tried every trick to save a patient before a nurse accused them of torturing the patient. This made the physician realise the limitations of the life-saving mode. The critical view on medicalisation is contrasted by Dr Bhargava, who argues that specialists and further treatment options bring hope for the families. This conflict – whether to maintain hope or letting an individual die 'naturally' – creates the core of this documentary as well. The conflict is played out in the trajectories of two patients, Donna and Selena, whose families make opposite choices. Donna's family decides to remove the ventilator and say their goodbyes before Donna passes away a day later. Selena's family decides to continue life-sustaining treatment where Selena is surgically attached to the ventilator before dying about six months later. While the documentary appears to represent fair and balanced arguments for both sides, affective images and attachment with the dying patients align the viewer with the narratives of demedicalisation and acceptance of death.

The documentary introduces Donna strapped to a hospital bed, with a ventilator helping her breathe. The scene starts with the peeping sound of the ECG machine and the whooshing of the ventilator, which guide the viewer to pay attention to the presence of medical technology. The sounds diminish when Donna's husband starts talking to her in a soothing way. The husband is worried that the only functioning thing is the ventilator, and he admits to the doctors that he had promised Donna he would do everything he could, but that reality is here now. When Donna is able to signal that she wants the breathing tube removed instead of being connected to the machines, the husband tearfully whispers, 'You did the right thing.' Donna's part of the film finishes with her smiling after the removal of the tube and telling everybody to calm down. Both Donna and the family appear to accept the approaching death, even when they are saddened by the loss. Also, Donna has autonomy to decide on her treatment, which allows everybody to say their goodbyes without intervening medical technology. Donna's demedicalised death is pictured as comforting for everybody involved.

Selena's case contrasts the death acceptance narrative. Her response to any stimulus is very limited, which means that all care decisions are made by surrogate caregivers, mainly her daughter and brothers. To highlight the patient's lack of autonomy, the camera rarely visits her bedside. Consequently, Selena becomes part of the film's background. The visual and narrative focus is on the family members who struggle to accept the physicians' estimation that Selena will not wake up. The family is against stopping the treatments because of their spiritual views and trust in the medical profession. While Dr Zitter admits that seeing such critical situations daily has dwindled her optimism, Selena's daughter continues to look for a miracle. For her, Selena's survival of CPR (cardiopulmonary resuscitation) is a sign that her mother has chosen to stay. Selena's family equals medical technology with life, and due to their religious beliefs, with God's will. One of the brothers argues that living is a sign of God's powers, and if it were God's will, Selena would die regardless of medical interventions. The family likens the removal of medical technology to committing a murder. In Selena's story, technological optimism and religious beliefs lead to a medicalised death.

Rhetorical, narrative and aesthetic choices create judgements of these two choices. Rhetorically, Dr Zitter, who is frustrated by medicalised deaths and whose voice and experiences are given most time and space in the narration, becomes the primary representative of the ICU. Narratively, the endings where

Donna's family is rewarded with reassuring goodbyes and Selena dies being hooked to a machine without any agency, add emotional argumentation for the undesirability of medicalised death. Donna's case speaks for quality of life and agency of the patient, while Selena represents quantity of life and lack of agency. And aesthetically, Dan Krauss, the director of the film, draws from *cinéma vérité* and observational traditions to build authenticity that supports the trustworthiness of the demedicalisation argument.

In another media interview, Krauss idolises observational modes of film-making and argues that in *Extremis* he wanted to 'do something that was pure' (White 2017). 'Pure' connects to the *cinéma vérité* tradition, where filmmakers understand observational modes as representing honesty and authenticity in ways that could provide a 'pure', or an objective, view of the documentary's subject (Hall 1991). *Cinéma vérité*, which emerged in Europe and North America in the 1960s has highly influenced the making of social issue documentaries (Borum Chattoo 2020, 29), including the style of early medical documentaries, such as Frederick Wiseman's *Hospital* (1970). Here, the ambient sound as well as the images of medical technologies give an impression of unmediated reality, while institutional scenes of rushing doctors convey a sense of authenticity (Ostherr 2013, 154–9). The arrival of lighter, portable cameras and sound equipment allowed filmmakers to access lived experience easily, which led them to favour a 'fly on the wall' approach. They recorded and observed, typically with a hand-held camera, and brought these moments to the viewers without voiceover commentary, added music or sound effects, as if to emphasise the 'real' feeling of the films (MacDougall 2018, 1–2; Hall 1991). Despite the values of 'pureness', 'authenticity' and 'real', all documentaries are recorded from a perspective. As David MacDougall (2018, 5–6) argues, documentary filmmaking is never neutral observation, but participant observation. In this case, observational aesthetics add a feeling of trustworthiness and verifiability of the arguments.

Extremis uses observational techniques to continue the tradition of authenticated medical life of hospitals. The hand-held camera creates an awareness of 'being there'. And while the opening titles, closing titles and the two montage sections of daily lives at the ICU have added non-diegetic sounds, the sections that focus on Selena's and Donna's stories create a soundscape of recorded dialogues, medical equipment noise and the background buzz of a busy ICU ward. The unfiltered sounds of medical technology emphasise the authentic mediation of hospital space, but they also guide the viewer to pay attention to the medical technology to which the patients are attached and whereby their lives are artificially prolonged. The sounds and images of the medical devices suggest artificiality of life-continuing treatments, illustrating the criticism in Dr Zitter's reflection of the medical profession's problematic relationship with death and dying.

Together, the rhetorical, narrative and aesthetic solutions challenge the authoritative role of medicalisation. In addition, comparison of Donna's and Selena's stories actualises questions of the benefits of death acceptance and the negative consequences of death denial. The comparison is familiar from (fictional) medical programming. Based on American, Australian and British medical dramas, Jennifer Freytag and Srividya Ramasubramanian recognise 'bad' and 'good' deaths. Bad deaths are those where the patient (or their caregiver) refuses treatment and takes the blame for death, or where medical professionals make a mistake, which becomes a teaching opportunity for the professionals while ignoring the patient's perspective. Good deaths are heroic narratives of sacrifice (organ donations) or end-of-life moments where the dying person accepts their death and offers wisdom and advice for the living. Thus, if a patient must die in a medical drama, death acceptance is a dignified and comforting choice that makes death meaningful (Freytag and Ramasubramanian 2019).

In *Extremis*, Donna and the family embrace demedicalised death. Their moment of goodbyes is meaningful and dignified, and a sign of 'good death'. In contrast, in Selena's case, the family opposes the medical professionals' evaluation of the situation. As such, the family also 'takes the blame' over the medicalised death that Selena goes through in the following six months. However, as Freytag and Ramasubramanian (2019) argue, the grand narratives of medical programming favour the existence of institutionalised medical systems, which marginalise the social, cultural and spiritual aspects of dying. Selena's family's religious beliefs are contrasted with the medical knowledge and authority in ways that encourage the viewer to question their choices. Thus, in challenging the practices of medicalised death, the documentary frames medicalisation as arising from the patients' and families' unrealistic expectations, whereas the medical professionals appear as responsible and humane users of medical knowledge and technology. The documentary thus continues to maintain the medical field's authority to evaluate the best possible dying process for the patients.

QUESTIONS OF AGENCY

In ICU care, where hard decisions are an integral part of the work, *Extremis* is not the only film that stands for the death acceptance storyline and shows consequences of death denial in a critical light. *Facing Death* (Navasky and O'Connor 2010), an hour-long television documentary, also focuses on end-of-life care choices when patients and their families have to choose when to stop or continue aggressive medical procedures. Compared to the observatory mode of *Extremis*, *Facing Death* takes an expository approach, where a voiceover narrator frames the debates on ethical and moral issues of end-of-life care (Nichols 2017, 107–8). At the beginning of the film, the narrator states that many Americans die in hospital after prolonged illnesses, which, due to medical advances, are treated with expensive and aggressive interventions. From this starting point, various medical professionals voice their views, and once again, the documentary seemingly represents a balanced view on the topic.

The views that support medicalisation explain treatments as the right of an individual and as a medical institution's responsibility to sustain life. A professor at Harvard University, Dr Groopman, favours modern medical science and says that treatment should never be reduced to expenses or statistical probabilities, because if there is a chance to defy expectations, an individual's life is worthy of a potential medical failure. Physicians working with bone marrow transplants express slightly more hesitant views but they understand the patients' hope for treatment. They follow the patients' wishes to try out further treatment options even when they recognise potential suffering from treatments which have low odds of working. Dr Keren, for example, confesses that after the death of a patient, the physician questioned whether they had provided any quality of life. Perhaps accepting the situation would have given some comfort, if not for the patient then for those around them. These voices represent the high-tech medical options that, despite their risks, can turn to success stories, which encourages the physicians to support patients' hopes for cure.

The ICU doctors of *Facing Death* express the most critical views on medicalised death. Many of them feel that intensive care is misused; their efforts postpone impending death in cases where underlying diseases cannot be removed or fixed. For example, Dr Muller argues that medical technology has complicated end-of-life decisions with the question of 'what if'. This uncertainty has led patients and their families to expect technology to save lives, even when the trade-off can be devastating, and patients might not have the lives they want after invasive and aggressive treatments. Dr Nelson calls these patients 'broken survivors of intensive care', who suffer when families must choose between allowing and not allowing life through technology. Decision-making is often especially difficult at the ICU, where most patients are sedated and unable to express their views. Dr Nelson, for example, sees the patients as 'vulnerable' and 'voiceless', dependent on their families who are struggling to let go. Thus, while the potential of technology plays a key role in these argumentations, the documentary also highlights the question of patients' agency, which offers affective arguments to accompany the rational arguments of the medical staff.

Agency can be defined as an individual's ability to act freely, to make choices and impact the world around them (Giddens and Sutton 2017, 23), and is often connected to such terms as self-determination, autonomy and empowerment. *Facing Death* introduces seven patients: Albert, John, Norman, Condolena,

Robert, Diane and Martha. The patients stand as illustrative examples to the argumentations of the physicians, and their main function is to give depth to the debates over potentials and limitations of medicalised death. This also shows in the on-screen time allocated to the patients, who appear on-screen for 12:31 minutes out of the total length of 53:40 minutes. Divided between the seven patients, this gives most of them less than two minutes of on-screen visibility. Consequently, the viewer does not learn their personal stories beyond medical questions.

Most on-screen time is dedicated to transplant patients who can express their agency. Albert is having complications from transplants, but he is unable to accept that he cannot be treated, and at the end, interventions cause him to have a seizure, and he dies a week later without being able to communicate with his wife. Here, the inability to accept death becomes unwanted, or even 'bad' death. Similarly, Norman is afraid of dying, but he is growing tired with the treatments and hospitalisation. After struggling to decide, the family chooses comfort care, and Norman dies from complications two days later. The physician evaluates that the treatments did not prolong his life, but did make his death more difficult. In comparison, John, who is in a rather similar situation, represents the potential of a good death. John is undergoing further aggressive cancer treatments, but his wife is tormented by the negative consequences of treatments. When John's condition deteriorates, a doctor asks them to consider the quality of life. After an emotional struggle John accepts hospice care (or, in other words, accepts his impending death), and he dies a day later.

The filmed ICU patients have limited agency in the documentary. Unreactive Robert shows what heavy sedation does to a person when the treatment prolongs life but is painful. Condolena, Diane and Martha become examples of what it means to be mostly sedated and attached to a ventilator. There is very little room for patients' agency, which has been discussed in the ICU context in general (Laerkner et al. 2017). In all these cases, aggressive treatments and medical interventions have unwanted consequences, even if they comply with the requests of the patients or their families.

The aesthetic choices in the filming and editing of *Facing Death* highlight questions of agency. In several shots, Condolena, Robert, Diane and Martha are in the background, almost unrecognisable beneath tubes attached to medical devices. The physicians and family members are at the front as active participants debating and making decisions on behalf of the patient. The spatial use of imagery strips the patient of agency and gives it to others, people and machines. When mechanical ventilation assists or replaces the breathing of the patients, the respiratory machines are made the main visual elements of the documentary; images focus on medical technology instead of the patients (see also Hakola 2022). As such, *Facing Death* represents, and gives voice to, medical technology. It takes space on-screen, its mechanical sounds can be heard, and it receives agency in the scenes with unresponsive ICU patients. Medical technology becomes an active agent in the narrative.

Objects can, in fact, have agency as they carry meanings, originate action, shape various practices and participate in constructing the social world (Latour 1996; Cooren 2010). In an ethnographic ICU study, Letizia Caronia and Luigina Mortari (2015) found that everyday objects, structures of space and medical technology had a more important role than merely providing a background for medical care. For example, when entering the patient's space, members of medical staff did not look at the patient first, but at the monitor which gave 'a specific representation of the patient's body, its boundaries and meaningful clues' (Caronia and Mortari 2015, 403). Both the diagnosis and the caregiving were shaped by technology. The ways in which monitors and other medical technology communicated messages to the caregivers could be seen as speech acts, declare Caronia and Mortari (2015). In other words, the medical technology has a voice which impacts the treatment of the patient.

In one of the scenes of *Facing Death*, the camera focuses on a close-up of the illuminated monitor of the medical device that measures oxygen levels and the breathing rhythm. Slowly, the camera pans to the breathing tube and follows its regulated movements. The impact is almost hypnotic. Then, the image slightly refocuses, giving a glimpse of the patient at the end of the tube (Figure 2.1). Even here, the face remains out of focus, unrecognisable. This image contrasts the blurred image of the person with medical technology, the breathing mask and its timely movements, which are in focus. This moment

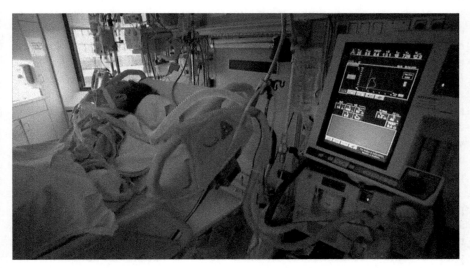

Figure 2.1 The shot focuses on the breathing machine in the documentary *Facing Death* (Navasky and O'Connor 2010).

frames medical technology as overtaking the subjectivity or agency of the patient: instead of an individual, one is dealing with a machine. This visual allegory prompts the question as to whether the medical options provide meaningful life and whether the families should let go and deal with the loss instead of seeing death as a (medical) failure.

In most cases, breathing tubes are eventually removed and the ICU patients die soon after. Only Martha is successfully taken off the ventilator, which encourages the family to continue treatments. However, a day later, Martha is back on the ventilator, where she remains a year later, unable to speak. The question whether the patients can breathe on their own builds narrative tension to the film, and the removal of breathing technology closes each of these stories (Hakola 2022). The visual emphasis of medical technology could support the medicalisation view, its ability to keep a person alive, yet in this documentary, technology connects to overmedicalisation that takes over the agency of the person. This aesthetic and affective choice supports a critical view on medicalisation of death, even when the interviewed physicians represent both sides of the debate.

TOWARDS DEMEDICALISED DEATH

Edge of Life, *Extremis* and *Facing Death* explain overmedicalisation with the availability and overuse of medical technology, but also with cultural expectations of what are regarded as omnipotent medical interventions. And while these documentaries are critical of medicalised death, they follow in the footsteps of medical programming where life-threatening illnesses are discussed in relation to treatment options, life-sustaining interventions and the possibility of dying. In such programming, discussions on hospice and palliative care are rarely or only briefly mentioned (Houben et al. 2016; Drukarczyk et al. 2014). *Being Mortal* (Jennings 2015), which is based on Dr Atul Gawande's eponymous book, shifts the discussion on overmedicalisation beyond the context of hospitalisation. The documentary describes his journey of learning to deal with dying patients, and as part of his learning process he talks to different doctors working with palliative care. These discussions, he hopes, will open himself, and through his example, others, to have discussions about death, dying and palliative care.

At the beginning of the film, Gawande reunites with the husband of his late patient. Together, they reflect on the desperate search for the cure and how, after the death of the wife, both regretted some actions and experimental therapies that took away precious time that could have been spent together with the family. Gawande was aware of the dire situation and admits that he avoided talking about death because in his understanding, medical competence equalled the capability to fix problems, but also because he sought to avoid

MEDICAL DOCUMENTARIES

emotional discussions on death that, by design, uncomfortably move beyond scientific rationality. It seemed easier to continue treatments, even though they shortened, and decreased, the quality of the patient's life. This case inspired Gawande to learn how to speak about the end of life with patients (Frontline, PBS, 2015; Jennings 2015). Reflective meetings of this kind are rare in medical programming, where the stories rather stress the time of hospitalisation. The importance of preventive measures, care of chronic conditions, follow-up on long-term impacts of aggressive interventions and the need for palliative care are commonly excluded (Hetzler and Dugdale 2018, 767; van Dijck 2005, 14; Ostherr 2013, 201–2; Houben et al. 2016).

During the film, Gawande meets with Doctor Lakshmi Nayak and her patient Bill who is not ready to give up hope. While respecting Bill's stance, Nayak prepares him and his wife for the worst-case scenario. On-screen, the learning experience is visually emphasised: in the office, Gawande and Nayak are watching recorded material from a patient meeting. While the scenes are rolling, Nayak explains her course of actions by wanting to maintain some options for the scared family. When Bill's condition deteriorates, doctors convince him to consider hospice, which is a difficult topic for him and his wife to discuss. From these scenes, Gawande learns about a tactful approach to bringing the subject of death into the discussion.

With another doctor, Kathy Selvaggi, Gawande learns that meeting with patients is about listening. He learns to ask how the patients understand their situation and what their priorities are. Gawande follows Selvaggi's meeting with Norma, whose cancer treatment is not working. Selvaggi tells Norma that now is the time for hard questions, and for making the best out of the time that is left. The patient hopes for a miracle all the same. Selvaggi confides in Gawande that medicine is the easy part of the equation. It is the discussions on hospice care that are harder. In Norma's case, the doctor slowly adds hospice care to the discussions and asks how Norma feels about her situation. 'I think we are coming close,' she says, to which the doctor replies: 'I worry about the same thing. We take care of you here.' Gawande learns from this that there are no natural moments for difficult conversations, but it is crucial to have them. If one waits until there is a crisis, it is too late, and the patient might end up in similar situations as in ICU documentaries where their own agency in decision-making is bypassed.

While both Norma and Bill struggle to accept they are dying, their final choices to accept comfort care is celebrated as person-oriented care, where the focus is on the person, not on the illness. This compares to Shlomith Rimmon-Kenan's discussion on illness narratives, where the medicalised approach turns the focus on 'case reports', where illness rather than the patient is assigned the role of the protagonist and where the story of illness is told through 'the voice of medicine' (Rimmon-Kenan 2002, 11). In other words, the decision to

45

demedicalise death turns the focus back onto the person and to their voice and experience.

This point is stressed in Gawande's last meeting with Doctor Robert Soiffer, who has a more traditional, treatment-oriented approach. However, one of his patients, Jeff, is clear about his priorities: after three years of treatments, he wants to die at his farm, surrounded by family and friends. On his deathbed, he tells the filmmaker that his final days have been 'some of the best days of my life'; even while his mind and body have rapidly declined, 'I'm still a happy guy' (Jennings 2015). Similarly, his wife witnesses that while Jeff's world is reduced to a bed by a window, his relationships grow deeper towards the end. With Jeff, the camera moves out of the hospital environment. The visual contrast is significant. Instead of reclining under harsh fluorescent lamps in an impersonal hospital room, Jeff watches his yard and natural light through the window. His death is framed by the cosy and comforting space and atmosphere. To Gawande, Jeff's case is a testimonial of the benefits of stopping medical interventions in time. Death acceptance and demedicalisation of death enable Jeff's agency, give him time with family and friends, and increase the quality of the end of life.

The documentary's narrative viewpoint remains institutional; it is about a doctor learning about end of life through (medical) case studies. In a podcast on the documentary, Gawande sees that his exploration changed him and made him a better physician. He learned to consider not only the benefits and risks of the medical treatments, but to discuss the patients' goals and values, and how these could be taken into consideration when treating terminal illnesses (Frontline, PBS, 2015). However, these experiences are intended to be more than a personal transformation story. The viewer is invited to change together with the physician, who admits that the medicalised vision obstructs accepting death as a part of life. The film invites the viewer to share the responsibility; the medicalised hopes and expectations are part of western culture, and the change of attitudes should not be limited to medical professionals. It should include everyone. If the demedicalisation narrative replaced medicalised practices, end-of-life experiences could improve both for the dying and their families.

The educational aspect is also noticeable in a short documentary *Dying in Your Mother's Arms*, which follows the work of children's palliative care doctor Nadia Tremonti. The film begins with an interview, Tremonti facing the camera. She had consulted her colleagues about a case where the family struggled to understand the situation of their child. Tremonti recalls asking the physicians who refused to use the word death: 'Do you think the reason the family is confused about how serious this is because you can't even say it?' (Beder 2020) The documentary places Dr Tremonti into a teacher's position. She is filmed giving lectures to other professionals, while in voiceover she explains the benefits of palliative practices. In addition, her compassionate

MEDICAL DOCUMENTARIES

and open discussions with the mother of a dying baby provide an example of how to deal with difficult encounters and discussions. The structure of the film, similarly to *Being Mortal*, emphasises that other medical professionals, as well as the viewers, can and should learn from her expertise to understand the benefits of demedicalised death. Tremonti's work with the mother and her baby emotionally and affectively proves how focusing on loving touches and the intimacy of the last moments create a 'good death' in comparison to technological interventions.

CONCLUSION

Medical documentaries on the end of life reveal how all parties involved, the physicians, the patients and their families struggle with end-of-life care decisions. These struggles are traced back to medicalisation practices, where medical professionalism and technology, and their mediated representations, have created expectations that life-threatening and terminal illnesses can be cured. In their criticism of the omnipotence of the medical field, end-of-life documentaries appear to turn around the cinema's appreciative solidarity with modern medicine. Yet, it is not the patients but rather the physicians who recognise the disadvantages of overmedicalisation and call for a change of attitudes. Thus, these documentaries' institutionalised perspectives both renew and uphold the practices of medical documentaries and programming. They question the overtly technological aspects of end-of-life care (instead of acute care) but idealise the authority of medical professionals.

To refine their arguments in favour of a change in sociocultural attitudes and medical practices, these documentaries represent physicians' arguments for and against medicalisation. Despite the apparent balance of rhetorical and verbal arguments, the films' ethical claim is created on the affective and (audio) visual level of the narration. The viewers are scared by the affective visuals of medicalised images, where a person's autonomy is assumed by impersonal machines. The occasional positive image emphasises the benefits of demedicalisation, Jeff on his deathbed in the comfort of his home or the ability of the mother to hold a dying baby in her arms. These images build visual and affective comparisons between death acceptance or 'good death', and death denial or 'bad death'. Consequently, the documentaries suggest that death denial and medicalisation strengthen death anxiety, which decreases the potential for well-being.

The purposeful use of affective visuals also makes clear what Lisa Downing and Libby Saxton (2010) mean by visualised ethics. They argue that in a contemporary society saturated with images, ethics also functions more on the visual than the verbal level. For them, the question is not what ethics is, but what 'ethics does', which encourages us to study how films as visual

47

objects participate in making ethical statements. They also suggest that ethics is created in an encounter between the viewer and the film; the film can encourage the viewer to challenge the existing practices and norms when confronted with ethical questions (Downing and Saxton 2010, 1–3).

Medical end-of-life documentaries represent medicalised death as the main ethical question of which the viewer is expected to create an opinion. The most interesting ethical debate takes place on the visual level illustrating cautionary tales of medicalisation. These images urge the viewer to re-evaluate the benefits and limitations of medicalisation of death. As such, the visual ethics of these documentaries confront the viewer with 'behind the scenes' access to medical care, on which, as investigative approaches suggest, our values and attitudes need readjusting. Thus, the ethics of documentaries go beyond questions of objectivity or balance of spoken arguments, reaching out to engage the viewer towards attachment with represented images. Documentaries that advocate change show that ethics is only partially about whether filmmaker's creative processes create a reliable representation of the chosen topic. It also includes the viewer's responsibility to feel, think, evaluate and to be open to change.

References

Ariès, Philippe. 1975. *Western Attitudes toward Death: From the Middle Ages to the Present*. Translated by Patricia M. Ranum. First published 1974. Baltimore, MD: Johns Hopkins University Press.

Aufderheide, Patricia. 2008. *Documentary Film: A Very Short Introduction*. Oxford: Oxford University Press.

Austin, Thomas. 2012. *Watching the World: Screen Documentary and Audiences*. Manchester: Manchester University Press.

Bauman, Zygmunt. 1992. *Mortality, Immortality and Other Life Strategies*. Stanford, CA: Stanford University Press.

Beder, John. 2020. *Dying in Your Mother's Arms*. Documentary, Short. The New York Times.

Borum Chattoo, Caty. 2020. *Story Movements: How Documentaries Empower People and Inspire Social Change*. New York: Oxford University Press. https://doi.org/10.1093/oso/9780190943417.001.0001.

Brylla, Catalin, and Mette Kramer. 2018. 'A Pragmatic Framework for the Cognitive Study of Documentary'. *Projections* 12 (2): 159–80. https://doi.org/10.3167/proj.2018.120216.

Caronia, Letizia, and Luigina Mortari. 2015. 'The Agency of Things: How Spaces and Artefacts Organize the Moral Order of an Intensive Care Unit'. *Social Semiotics* 25 (4): 401–22. https://doi.org/10.1080/10350330.2015.1059576.

Charles, Mathew. 2013. 'News, Documentary and Advocacy Journalism'. In *Journalism: New Challenges*, edited by Karen Fowler-Watt and Stuart Allan, 384–92. Poole: CJCR: Centre for Journalism and Communication Research, Bournemouth University.

Conrad, Peter. 2007. *The Medicalization of Society: On the Transformation of Human Conditions into Treatable Disorders*. Baltimore, MD: Johns Hopkins University Press.

Cooren, François. 2010. *Action and Agency in Dialogue: Passion, Incarnation and Ventriloquism*. Amsterdam; Philadelphia: John Benjamins Publishing Company.

Dijck, José van. 2005. *The Transparent Body: A Cultural Analysis of Medical Imaging*. Seattle; London: University of Washington Press.

Downing, Lisa, and Libby Saxton. 2010. *Film and Ethics: Foreclosed Encounters*. London; New York: Routledge.

Drukarczyk, Laura, Carsten Klein, Christoph Ostgathe, and Stephanie Stiel. 2014. 'Life Threatening Illness in Popular Movies-a First Descriptive Analysis'. *SpringerPlus* 3 (1): 411. https://doi.org/10.1186/2193-1801-3-411.

Eitzen, Dick. 2007. 'Documentary's Peculiar Appeals'. In *Moving Image Theory: Ecological Considerations*, edited by Barbara Fisher Anderson and Joseph Anderson, 183–99. Carbondale: Southern Illinois University Press.

Elias, Norbert. 2001. *The Loneliness of the Dying*. First published 1985. New York: Continuum.

Field, David. 1994. 'Palliative Medicine and the Medicalization of Death'. *European Journal of Cancer Care* 3 (2): 58–62. https://doi.org/10.1111/j.1365-2354.1994. tb00014.x.

Freytag, Jennifer, and Srividya Ramasubramanian. 2019. 'Are Television Deaths Good Deaths? A Narrative Analysis of Hospital Death and Dying in Popular Medical Dramas'. *Health Communication* 34 (7): 747–54. https://doi.org/10.1080/1041023 6.2018.1434735.

Froemke, Susan, and Matthew Heineman. 2012. *Escape Fire: The Fight to Rescue American Healthcare*. Documentary. Aisle C Productions, Our Time Projects.

Frontline, PBS. n.d. 'Inside "Being Mortal" with Atul Gawande and Tom Jennings'. Frontline. Film Audio Track. https://soundcloud.com/frontlinepbs/inside-being-mortal?utm_source=www.pbs.org&utm_campaign=wtshare&utm_medium=widget&utm_content=https%253A%252F%252Fsoundcloud.com%252Ffrontlinepbs%252Finside-being-mortal. Last accessed 7 November 2022.

GBH. 2018. 'FRONTLINE Journalism Fund'. WGBH Educational Foundation. 13 April 2018. https://www.wgbh.org/support/directed-giving/frontline-journalism-fund. Last accessed 20 May 2022.

Giddens, Anthony, and Philip W. Sutton. 2017. *Essential Concepts in Sociology*. Second edition. Malden, MA: Polity.

Hakola, Outi. 2022. 'Breathing in Mortality: Demedicalization of Death in Documentary Films'. *Journal of Somaesthetics* 8 (1): 30–44.

Hall, Jeanne. 1991. 'Realism as a Style in Cinema Verite: A Critical Analysis of "Primary"'. *Cinema Journal* 30 (4): 24. https://doi.org/10.2307/1224885.

Harrison, Natalie. 2014. 'Life and Death in Hollywood'. *The Lancet Oncology* 15 (6): 568. https://doi.org/10.1016/S1470-2045(14)70210-4.

Heineman, Matthew. 2021. *The First Wave*. Documentary. National Geographic Documentary Films, Participant, Our Time Projects.

Henderson, Lesley. 2010. 'Medical TV Dramas: Health Care as Soap Opera'. *Socialist Register* 46: 198–215.

Hetzler, Peter T., and Lydia S. Dugdale. 2018. 'How Do Medicalization and Rescue Fantasy Prevent Healthy Dying?' *AMA Journal of Ethics* 20 (8): E766-773. https://doi.org/10.1001/amajethics.2018.766.

Houben, Carmen H. M., Martijn A. Spruit, Emiel F. M. Wouters, and Daisy J. A. Janssen. 2016. '"Am I Dying Doctor?": How End-Of-Life Care Is Portrayed in Television Medical Dramas'. *Journal of Palliative Care & Medicine* 6 (1). https://doi.org/10.4172/2165-7386.1000247.

Jennings, Thomas. 2015. *Being Mortal*. Documentary. Frontline, PBS.

Kemmitt, Alicia. 2007. 'Documentary Stories for Change: Viewing and Producing Immigrant Narratives as Social Documents'. *The Velvet Light Trap* 60 (1): 25–36. https://doi.org/10.1353/vlt.2007.0018.

Krauss, Dan. 2016. *Extremis*. Documentary. Netflix.

Laerkner, Eva, Ingrid Egerod, Finn Olesen, and Helle Ploug Hansen. 2017. 'A Sense of Agency: An Ethnographic Exploration of Being Awake during Mechanical Ventilation in the Intensive Care Unit'. *International Journal of Nursing Studies* 75 (October): 1–9. https://doi.org/10.1016/j.ijnurstu.2017.06.016.

Latour, Bruno. 1996. 'On Interobjectivity'. *Mind, Culture, and Activity* 3 (4): 228–45. https://doi.org/10.1207/s15327884mca0304_2.

Lofland, Lyn H. 1978. *The Craft of Dying: The Modern Face of Death*. Beverly Hills, CA: SAGE Publications.

Luers, Erik. 2021. '"Burnout and Fatigue and a Loss of Sanity": Matthew Heineman on Making COVID-19 Documentary "The First Wave"'. *Filmmaker Magazine* (blog). 13 December 2021. https://filmmakermagazine.com/112666-matthew-heineman-covid-19-documentary-first-wave/. Last accessed 28 June 2023.

Lupton, Deborah. 1995. 'G.P.: A Postmodern Medical Drama?' *Australian Journal of Communication* 22 (2): 108–20. https://www.researchgate.net/publication/28634 6215_GP_A_Postmodern_Medical_Drama. Last accessed 31 August 2023.

MacDougall, David. 2018. 'Observational Cinema'. In *The International Encyclopedia of Anthropology*, edited by Hilary Callan, 1–10. Oxford: John Wiley & Sons, Ltd. https://doi.org/10.1002/9781118924396.wbiea1535.

Nash, Kate, and John Corner. 2016. 'Strategic Impact Documentary: Contexts of Production and Social Intervention'. *European Journal of Communication* 31 (3): 227–42. https://doi.org/10.1177/0267323116635831.

Navasky, Miri, and Karen O'Connor. 2010. *Facing Death*. Documentary Frontline, PBS.

Nichols, Bill. 2017. *Introduction to Documentary, Third Edition*. Bloomington: Indiana University Press.

Ostherr, Kirsten. 2013. *Medical Visions: Producing the Patient Through Film, Television, and Imaging Technologies*. Oxford; New York: Oxford University Press.

Painter, David Lynn, Alison Kubala, and Sarah Parsloe. 2020. 'Playing Doctor on TV: Physician Portrayals and Interactions on Medical Drama, Comedy, and Reality Shows'. *Atlantic Journal of Communication* 28 (5): 322–36. https://doi.org/10.1080/15456870.2020.1691002.

Plantinga, Carl. 2013. '"I'll Believe It When I Trust the Source": Documentary Images and Visual Evidence'. In *The Documentary Film Book*, edited by Brian Winston, 40–7. London: British Film Institute.

Quinlan, Christina. 2009. 'Media Discourses on Autonomy in Dying and Death'. *Irish Communication Review* 11 (1). https://doi.org/10.21427/D7XM8T.

Rimmon-Kenan, Shlomith. 2002. 'The Story of "I": Illness and Narrative Identity'. *Narrative* 10 (1): 9–27.

Sadler, John Z., Fabrice Jotterand, Simon Craddock Lee, and Stephen Inrig. 2009. 'Can Medicalization Be Good? Situating Medicalization within Bioethics'. *Theoretical Medicine and Bioethics* 30 (6): 411–25. https://doi.org/10.1007/s11017-009-9122-4.

Saito, Stephen. 2017. 'Interview: Director Dan Krauss on the Difficult Decisions Behind "Extremis"'. The Moveable Fest. 4 January 2017. https://moveablefest.com/dan-krauss-extremis/. Last accessed 19 May 2022.

Semino, Elena, Zsófia Demjén, and Jane Demmen. 2018. 'An Integrated Approach to Metaphor and Framing in Cognition, Discourse, and Practice, with an Application to Metaphors for Cancer'. *Applied Linguistics* 39 (5): 625–45. https://doi.org/10.1093/applin/amw028.

Semino, Elena, Zsófia Demjén, Jane Demmen, Veronika Koller, Sheila Payne, Andrew Hardie, and Paul Rayson. 2017. 'The Online Use of Violence and Journey Metaphors by Patients with Cancer, as Compared with Health Professionals: A Mixed Methods Study'. *BMJ Supportive & Palliative Care* 7 (1): 60–6. https://doi.org/10.1136/bmjspcare-2014-000785.

Styles, Ruth. 2014. '22-Year-Old Man Who Overcame Traumatic Brain Damage'. *Daily Mail*, 28 March 2014, sec. Femail. https://www.dailymail.co.uk/femail/article-2591559/Incredible-story-22-year-old-man-odds-MILLION-one-revealed-heart-warming-Louis-Theroux-film.html. Last accessed 3 November 2022.

Tabernero, Carlos. 2018. 'The Changing Nature of Modernization Discourses in Documentary Films'. *Science in Context* 31 (1): 61–83. https://doi.org/10.1017/S0269889718000066.

Theroux, Louis. 2014a. *Edge of Life*. Documentary. BBC.

———. 2014b. 'Q&A with Louis Theroux on "Edge of Life"'. Facebook Event. https://m.facebook.com/LouisTheroux/photos/qa-with-louis-theroux-on-edge-of-life1-edge-of-life-is-a-very-emotive-film-why-d/530128420438345/. Last accessed 4 November 2022.

Walter, Tony. 2020. *Death in the Modern World*. London: SAGE Publications.

White, Tom. 2017. '"Extremis" Takes an Emotional Journey Through the End of Life'. International Documentary Association. 14 February 2017. https://www.documentary.org/online-feature/extremis-takes-emotional-journey-through-end-life. Last accessed 19 May 2022.

Wiseman, Frederick. 1970. *Hospital*. Documentary. Osti Films.

Zimmermann, Camilla, and Gary Rodin. 2004. 'The Denial of Death Thesis: Sociological Critique and Implications for Palliative Care'. *Palliative Medicine* 18 (2): 121–8. https://doi.org/10.1191/0269216304pm858oa.

3. HOSPICE DOCUMENTARIES

Responsibility to Care

In 1965 Cicely Saunders, founder of the modern hospice movement, wrote: 'I am sure the most important foundation stone we could have comes from the summing up of all the needs of the dying which was made for us in the Garden of Gethsemane in the simple words "Watch with me"' (Saunders 2005, 1). Saunders refers to the hospice movement philosophy of holistic care for the terminally ill, shifting the focus from finding a cure to supporting the patient physically, emotionally, spiritually and socially.

For a film scholar, the phrase 'watch with me' offers an entry to hospice documentaries, which are commissioned by, or produced in collaboration with, the hospice organisations. In these documentary films, 'watch with me' turns into an invitation to enter the hospice spaces and the stories of dying people. In the western countries, these are often deemed to belong to the private sphere. The documentary camera allows the viewer to join the watch and to learn from these encounters. As many viewers have little experience of hospices in their everyday lives, watching also turns towards the hospices' daily practices. This direction of gaze is purposeful; through these films, hospices raise awareness of their work and of mortality. 'Watch', thus, summons the viewer's activity, and the agency of 'with me' refers to the hospice's institutional framing of end of life.

Hospices are not a new idea. While many churches, for example, have a long history of caring for the sick and dying (Tatko 2017; Milićević 2002), the modern hospice movement has branded this form of care. Saunders, a nurse,

52

social worker and physician, actively advocated holistic care for the terminally ill in the 1960s, and in 1967 established St Christopher's hospice in London to develop treatments of dying patients (Clark 2005, viii). These practices turned into a movement that spread quickly around the world (Bennahum 2003, 3–7; Kim 2019; Zeugin 2021, 98; Centeno and Rhee 2019). From the beginning, the hospice movement has presented itself as an alternative to medicalised death by offering a human-centred, 'natural' death (Hall 2017, 232–5).

Since the 1990s, the hospice movement has institutionalised: hospice practices and management as well as palliative medicine have been standardised. Institutionalisation has helped to raise resources and political acceptance, but has also burdened the movement with a stigma of its own (Abel 1986; James and Field 1992; Zeugin 2021, 98; Graven and Timm 2021). Alongside medicalisation, the institutionalisation and professionalisation of death, confining death to specialised institutions to be dealt with by professionals, have been blamed for the modern subjects' assumed alienation from death and dying (Elias 2001; Ariès 1975; Bauman 1992). While death awareness movements, and by extension the hospice movement, oppose this alienation, the institutionalisation turns into a paradox. Camilla Zimmerman and Gary Rodin (2004) describe this as a cultural struggle on whether hospices are seen as distancing institutions or society's way to prepare for death in ways that allow a 'natural' dying process, reduce suffering and provide quality of life. The hospice documentaries' invitation to watch provides an interesting outlook to the paradox of institutionalisation. The viewers are invited to see for themselves whether hospices reproduce negative connotations related to institutionalised death or whether they embrace the awareness of mortality and provide an alternative for the care of the dying.

This chapter is dedicated to documentaries produced by hospice institutions, such as *Except for Six* (Burnell 2008), which was commissioned by the Hospice of Michigan in the United States, and *The Light Inside* (Hicks 2015), a commission by Hospice Peterborough, Canada. In addition, I will discuss films produced in close collaboration with hospices. These films, which tell the story of the hospices, include *Last Days of Life* (Persson 2013), a documentary of a hospice in Uppsala, Sweden; *End Game* (R. Epstein and Friedman 2018) filmed in collaboration with the Buddhist Zen Caregiving Project (also known as the Zen Hospice Center) and the palliative ward at the University of California Medical Center in San Francisco (UCSF), and produced by Dr Shoshana Ungerleider, a hospice and palliative care physician and advocate (Sidewinder Films); *Here & Now* (Banci 2018), a short documentary filmed in collaboration with La Casa di Iris hospice in Italy; and *Les Pal·liatives* (Gispert and Valls 2018), a documentary about the Catalonian PADES (home hospice programme) team in Barcelona's Nou Barris district. What is shared by each of these documentaries is the institutional framing, the perspective of the hospices and their staff, accompanied by the stories of the dying patients. I argue that the movement between these perspectives – institutional and personal – creates an image of hospice as a form of care that can become institutionalised without losing compassion, responsibility and value of individual autonomy.

ETHICS OF CARE

'Hospice philosophy' is often construed as differentiating hospices from other medical care institutions. The philosophy stems from Cicely Saunders's understanding of 'good care' for the dying patients, where the patients' individual needs are met with compassion (Saunders 2005; Graven and Timm 2021, 326; Clark 1999). The short documentary *Here & Now* emphasises this philosophy, finishing with these words on a black screen:

> La Casa di Iris is an Italian hospice that provides help to terminally ill people and their families through palliative care, compassion and love. Day after day this little community brings dignity, respect and peace to one of the most natural aspects of life: death. (Banci 2018)

This description sums up the previous scenes of daily life at the hospice – families visiting the patients with their pets, the staff getting ice cream for a patient outside mealtimes, and a staff member and patients playing cards together. The documentary portrays hospice as a form of care and a philosophy rather than a bureaucratic institution. The scenes contrast hospice with Max Weber's influential ideas of institutions as part of bureaucratic states with formalised, normative and hierarchical processes that aim for efficiency and order. In the Weberian tradition, the idealisation of efficiency has left little room for individual desires or emotions (Weber 2013). When hospices are portrayed as places where the staff have time to 'waste' with patients, efficiency is replaced by affective relationships, and this, in turn, creates an image of a unique institution with a unique ethical approach to care.

In the context of hospice and palliative care, the 'ethics of care' approach builds on this contradiction between hospices and traditional medical institutions. Ethics of care is a feminist approach to moral theories, an alternative to classical theories that emphasise (male) rational reasoning and universal, objective rules for an unemotional agent who makes moral decisions based on logic (Gilligan 1982; Noddings 1984, 1–6; Tronto 2020, 25–60). The unemotional moral agent aligns with Weberian institutions and with the four principles of traditional medical ethics: beneficence, non-maleficence, autonomy and justice (Lawrence 2007). In comparison, ethics of care builds on a (feminine) approach that emphasises context and takes compassionate practices (care) and emotions (compassion) as its moral guideline. Here, 'care' includes two connotations of the verb – care as an act and as a value, an emotion. In the context of caring for the elderly and terminally ill, the benefits of the ethics of care approach have been recognised (De Panfilis et al. 2019; de Vries and Leget 2012). Ludovica De Panfilis and others argue that the values in the ethics of care approach, such as compassion, trust and responsibility, the context and quality of the caring relationship and respect of individuality meet the needs of the dying people who often struggle with quality of life, dignity, emotions and existential issues (De Panfilis et al. 2019, 2–3).

Ethics of care discussions involve various traditions, and here I turn to the question of responsibility, which is contrasted with obligation. Carol Gilligan, an influential figure in the ethics of care approach, sees that the expression of care is 'fulfilment of moral responsibility'. This responsibility directs itself towards relationships and embraces reciprocity (Gilligan 1982, 73). Whereas traditional ethics treats moral choices as obligation, assuming separation between individuals, Steven Edwards contends that Gilligan's demand for responsibility-based ethics expects involvement with others. He exemplifies the difference: 'Instead of asking, "what, if any, obligations do I have to help that person?" one asks "How can I help?"' (Edwards 2009, 234). Thus, ethics of care builds on interpersonal relationships, acts of communication and a sense of responsibility towards others.

These principles are exemplified by the documentary *Here & Now* on La Casa di Iris in Italy. The hospice staff go beyond the roles of providing physical care and answering the needs of the patients. A staff member talks about Carlo, an artist and a patient. While others continue to play cards, Carlo is wheeled into the common room, and the camera moves to follow his encounter with the hospice staff. Three staff members come to see his pictures being hung on the bulletin board. Together, the staff members examine the pictures, compliment them and ask Carlo to paint more of them. Carlo smiles and laughs with them (Figure 3.1). The moment communicates warm and reciprocal relationships. There is value in the emotional support whereas the efficiency of care acts is not even hinted at.

In the context of documentary film, ethics of care has meanings beyond mediating hospice care practices for the viewer. The ethics of care approach shares key elements with Vivian Sobchack's (2004) thoughts about aesthetics and ethics as ethical care, which builds on the viewer's responsibility and recip-rocal relationship with the film. For Sobchack, the film-viewing experience is grounded in senses, where the aesthetics evokes the viewer's 'sense-ability', a corporeal connection to the materiality of film as an object. These sense-making capabilities require the viewer's response (to feel, to embody, to think) to the images, and this corporeal and cognitive 'response-ability' also includes ethical aspects. The viewer's responses to a film's materiality can evoke 'ethical care and consciousness and, perhaps, responsible behaviour' (Sobchack 2004,

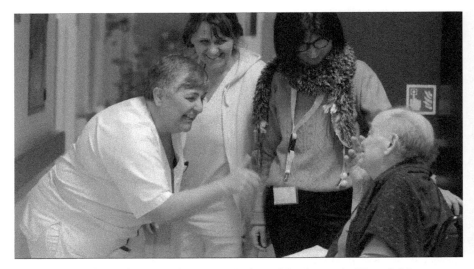

Figure 3.1 Staff members complimenting Carlo on his pictures in *Here & Now* (Banci 2018)

227, 241, quote from 135). Thus, by arguing that the viewer's ability to respond to the aesthetics is ethically charged, Sobchack connects ethics to responsibility, a theme familiar from the ethics of care approach. The connection between these approaches is further deepened by highlighting the role of relationships. Ethics of care emphasises intersubjectivity, whereas Sobchack (2004, 232–4) prefers the neologism of interobjectivity, which tempts us to recognise that connections are created not only to other people, but also to material objects (such as films).

The similarities between ethics of care as a moral theory and ethical care as the viewer's connection to a film's materiality bring us back to 'watch with me'. Hospice documentaries invite the viewer to witness hospice care and the patients' dying experiences, and by doing so, they can prompt ethical responses in the viewer. The reciprocity in the relationship between the film and the viewer ties ethics both to the filmed content and to the viewer's (responsible) responses to this content.

The connection between aesthetics and ethical approaches – both at the level of hospice work and the level of the viewer's experience – is visible in the Swedish documentary *Last Days of Life* (Persson 2013), based on the practice of ethics of care in a hospice in Uppsala. The opening scenes capture glimpses of patients in their rooms with their families, staff members walking in the corridors, a nurse lighting a candle (signifying someone's death) and a body being transported from the hospice. After the credits, action starts by introducing Kerstin, a patient. She is standing in the social space of the hospice, and is supported by two nurses, one on each side. Kerstin complains about the pain she is in, and a nurse leaves to get her pain medication. The short interaction refers to the importance of pain relief (whether physical or emotional pain) in the hospice practices, which allows the bodies to become social again (Graven and Timm 2021, 330). The benefit of this practice is visible in the image of Kerstin and a nurse on the sofa, waiting for the medication, amiably chatting and laughing. The help with the pain enables Kerstin to make the best use of social spaces and activities at the hospice.

After Kerstin is escorted to her room, the editor cuts to a close-up of clasped hands, old and young. The image of 'holding hands' has become symbolic of caring for the elderly and terminally ill, signifying as it does intersubjective connection and comfort. In cinema, as Emma Wilson (2012, 111–12) points out, comforting touches are powerful means to express unspoken meanings and emotions because these kinds of haptic images of mortality can convey love and compassion, or in other words, ethics of care. The camera framing expands, revealing the context as the nurse massages Kerstin's hands while having a conversation. This moment of chatter and laughter builds everyday interaction, but also shows that the nurse has the time and the willingness to be present at the patient's side. This highlights another element that Graven and Timm (2021, 331) recognise from hospice practices – the importance of being present and caring according to 'hospice time', instead of institutional time. The care is paced in such a way that nurses have time for patients without appearing busy. Indeed, the moment between the nurse and Kerstin avoids any sense of rushing; it is presented as a meeting of two people. The connotation is enhanced by an image where the two sit next to each other on a bed, instead of the patient being on the bed and the nurse in a visitor's chair. The two share more than a space in the hospice room, they share an intimate piece of furniture.

Kerstin confirms the meaning of this moment when she starts talking about her emotions. The camera records a close-up of her face, highlighting the sincerity of her emotions when she tells the nurse that 'it's nice to have someone to talk to. You're very good at that here. That's the truth.' Kerstin emphasises the support provided by the hospice, and the camera pans out from a close-up to a mid-shot that includes the nurse in the framing. The viewer witnesses the two looking at each other, sharing a moment. The moment communicates a feeling of 'being safe', or a feeling of being looked after, a third aspect of Graven's and Timm's (2021, 302) understanding of how the hospice philosophy translates into care practices. Kerstin's positive feedback is a sign of her feeling safe to talk about emotions. These subtle ways in which the film reflects the ethics of care through aesthetics build a warm and welcoming atmosphere for the viewer. While dealing with a challenging topic (death), the documentary creates a safe and caring space to connect with the filmed subjects, the images and the hospice. This ethos prevails throughout the film. The staff are present and interact with the patients. The care takes place in everyday encounters of shared moments and support. Medical treatment is almost absent; the focus is on the affective nature of care. The decision to bypass physical and medical care is a conscious choice that directs the attention to reciprocal relationships.

From the perspective of carers, ethics of care connects with affective labour. This term, popularised by Michael Hardt (1999), translates into non-material work that produces or manipulates affects, such as well-being, comfort and excitement. Johanna Oksala (2016, 290–1) argues that affective labour takes place in un-commodified work, such as taking care of the terminally ill at home, and in commodified work, such as nursing. Due to the affective labour's connotations with domestic work, traditionally performed by women, this often-invisible work has been seen as feminised and underappreciated. Nowadays, affective labour is recognised as a productive part of social reality, and as such, the emotional capacities of the carers are recognised along with their technical skills (Oksala 2016, 285–91). At the core of affective labour is hospice and palliative care that asks the carers to be present, support and comfort, to provide human contact and interaction, and to produce relationships and emotional responses. Thus, similarly to ethics of care, affective labour does not magically or 'naturally' appear, and as such, it has become a marketed product of the hospice institutions (Hakola 2021).

While they approach the end of life from an institutional perspective, hospice documentaries also shed light on the practices of affective labour. In *Last Days of Life*, Anne, a nurse, keeps the patients company, helps them to have a bath, eat and take their medications, but also just sits with them. There is warmth in her presence, and she either smiles or looks supportively at the patients. Outside the patients' rooms, the viewer is privileged to her thoughts and feelings. In a scene, she exits the room of a withdrawn patient. In the corridor, she faces the camera and reflects on her experiences:

> First, I go into one room and see someone who's not doing well, who's in pain, maybe someone who's closer to death than someone else, and then I have to go to the next room and talk about something different. Then I have to take a few deep breaths before I go in. But it's important to show these patients that might not need me that much and can take care of themselves that I'm still here and I'm interested. (Persson 2013)

While talking, Anne gazes slightly off the camera, but when she assesses someone being close to death she looks directly at the camera. The difference is striking. She is comfortable in recognising the situation of the patients, but reflecting her own thoughts and feelings requires a distance from the viewer. When she starts to speak about the importance of being present, the framing changes from medium close-up to a mid-shot. This slight distancing highlights the institutional reflection of the situation – the hospice philosophy. In this case, she also gazes towards the camera, showing her acknowledgement of the expectations and importance of the job. The personal and hospice philosophy mix, creating both institutional expectations and individual experiences.

By being able to follow Anne's (and other hospice staff's) work and feelings and see how positively their care is received by the patients, the viewer can be impressed by the benefits of ethics of care. The inclusion of the staff perspective helps the viewer to understand what ethics of care means in practice. In addition to the staff's affective labour, the documentary also produces affective labour, because the film's materiality has a similar ability to produce and manipulate emotions. The careful planning of the images that mediate and communicate compassion, responsibility and reciprocal relationships extends the ethics of care towards the viewer. The created aesthetic is comforting, supportive and peaceful; the images create a safe and caring space for the viewer's responses. In a reciprocal relationship, the viewer is requested to care, to 'watch with me' and respond to the represented images in a responsible way.

In the ethical processing of film's materiality, Sobchack gives a specific role to documentary expressions. She argues that documentary images that are 'charged with real' make the viewer conscious of extra-cinematic social and cultural aspects, where previous knowledge and experiences inform the viewer's relationship with the images, and prompts not only aesthetic evaluation, but ethical judgment, or 'ethical care of knowledge'. In other words, documentary spaces are ethically invested and request response-ability and responsibility (Sobchack 2004, 222). By inviting the viewer into the everyday lives of hospices, their staff and patients, the hospice documentaries request ethical responsibility over witnessing, but also responsibility to become aware (and appreciate) the work that hospices do.

RAISING AWARENESS OF HOSPICE CARE

Hospice documentaries, by definition, desire to raise awareness of hospice care work, practices and philosophy, underpinned by and culminating in the ethics of care approach. The hospice movement's roots are in social activism that strives for public, legislative and political recognition (Bennahum 2003). This is where storytelling by audiovisual materials can serve to increase public visibility. For example, a representative of the Hospice of Michigan sees their film *Except for Six* as a tool to 'tell our story better' (Serba 2008), and the Spanish documentary, *Les Pal·liatives* was supported by 'la Caixa' Foundation's social programme of promoting and raising awareness of the meaning of palliative care (CCMA 2018). In the case of *The Light Inside*, a documentary commissioned by Hospice Peterborough in Canada, I had a chance to interview

David Kennedy, bereavement coordinator at the hospice who also appears in the film, and the film's director Neil Hicks. Both highlight the film's importance as an awareness tool. The film was connected to the hospice's fundraising goals, but instead of just asking people for money, the hospice team wanted the film to show what they do and what their work means. Hicks, for example, wanted 'to tell their story in such a way that allowed the community to understand, number one, hey, we are here, hospice exists, and hey, number two, we play an important role in the community' (Hicks 2019).

Hospice documentaries raise awareness by balancing the aims of not wanting to be seen as an institution and the desire to manage public relations in favour of the hospice movement. This struggle turns into another balancing act of weighing the documentaries' informational and affective aspects. The informative aspects seek to increase the public understanding of hospice work and to decrease negative connotations and misunderstandings. Particularly, the hospices have struggled with a reputation of being 'places to die'. While death often causes anxiety, many people avoid thinking about it, and by extension, they have not wanted to learn about hospice work (Hickey and Quinn 2012; Friedman, Harwood, and Shields 2002). To alleviate such hospice-related fears, the documentaries have become tools to open the doors symbolically and literally to the hospice and welcome the public to follow the daily activities that aim to support quality of life. Here, the opening of the doors and allowing the camera inside becomes an informative act, yet the meanings attached to these places emphasise affects in which the viewer can hopefully find comfort.

Thus, the first balancing act between being informative and affective negotiates the uses of place and space. Place can be seen as locations and sites that are defined by human experiences, whereas spaces are more abstract and occur in time as part of human activities (Seamon and Sowers 2008). In hospice documentaries, hospices are described as spaces for ethics of care. The actual place does not matter, and often the buildings are not filmed from the outside. This is highlighted in the Spanish documentary *Les Pal·liatives*, which introduces the 'Catalonian model' for home hospice care. The care workers visit hospice patients, and between meetings, they talk about their own experiences of hospice care. The camera follows them through the doors to a new home where the care workers chat with the patients and their families. These chats include checking up on the patients' physical state, but also their emotional and social well-being. Furthermore, the visits build relationships and create a sense of being taken care of by a community. The presence of the hospice workers carries a sense of safe space and ethics of care, and thus extend hospice space to the personal spaces of the patients. Instead of a physical place, what matters are the activities, the care that these spaces enable and offer.

Given that hospice homes can convey a sense of infrastructure, the documentaries shot in them have the added struggle of dealing with the stigma of institutionalisation. Research has highlighted that hospice buildings wish to communicate hospice philosophy, including 'homeliness' and community aspects where people can spend time together with their families, friends, other patients and staff members, and to provide access to nature, such as gardens and natural light. Both outside and inside spaces balance privacy and ideals of community to avoid a sense of institutionalisation, or as McGann articulates, 'incarceration' (McGann 2016; Graven and Timm 2021, 333). In *The Light Inside*, for example, the camera visits different rooms at the hospice and shows spaces for community, such as a room for group meetings and sitting rooms. The homelike furniture, with plush sofas, chairs, curtains and fireplaces create a space that brings elements from private spaces (home) and public spaces (community) together. By inviting the viewer to cinematically visit these spaces, the informative yet affective spatial descriptions familiarise and normalise hospice spaces, and consequently, hospice as a form of care.

The ultimate institutional place/space comparison happens between hospitals and hospices. The patients, such as Ron in *Except for Six*, visit hospitals to receive medical care, but these are short and efficient visits that focus on medical aspects. The hospice as a space for care, in comparison, builds on compassion, company and lack of urgency. This distinction corresponds to the description of medical documentaries (Chapter 2), where the sense of authenticity and space for medicalised death were generated by hurrying doctors and medical technology. Christina Quinlan, similarly, has noted that public images, such as media representations, deal with institutionalised death by contrasting hospital and hospice deaths. The hospitals are pictured as places where technical and institutional approaches take precedence, whereas hospice space is seen as dedicated to the personal (Quinlan 2009). In *Except for Six*, for example, Professor Henry Holstege finds the main difference in the hospices' human-centred approach:

> You have people here who understand the dying process, you have people who are very empathetic, you have people who take their time to try to bring out the emotions. You have people to dialogue and talk. That's why hospice is such a wonderful advancement in regard to palliative care and the dying process. (Burnell 2008)

Here, hospice becomes 'a good institution' because it openly acknowledges death, opposing its medicalisation. Also, the human-centred approach, where caring takes place in reciprocal relationships, defies the Weberian understanding of institutionalism. Consequently, the documentaries tend to promise that if the viewer becomes aware of this 'good institution', more people could benefit from these services.

The second balancing act between informative and affective approaches takes place through the narrative perspective, where the institutional perspective is balanced by the hospice patients' personal stories. This sequence is especially visible in *Except for Six*, a film commissioned by the Hospice of Michigan. The film has a dialogical structure: interdisciplinary hospice experts explain what a hospice is, followed by the hospice patients' experience. The expert interviews have an educational tone, which is stressed in the spatial aspects. The experts are interviewed in their offices, or, in the case of physician Robert J. Zalenski, in his classroom at Wayne State University. In her interview, National Hospice leader Dottie Deremo describes hospice as a supportive model with well-toned structures and practices that aim for holistic and affective care. The patients' perspectives complement the institutional message by representing the lived experiences of care. Ron, a 69-year-old cancer patient, becomes the main filmed subject, whose journey from day twenty-seven at the hospice is followed until his death. In an interview for the Michigan Live news site, the film's director Matthew Burnell declares that in their desire to raise awareness of end-of-life care, they 'decided to follow elderly people through hospice care to help people better understand the process' (Serba 2008). This comment supports the perspective that while Ron's story adds emotional depth to the story, Ron becomes an example in a story about hospice, not the other way around.

In setting the scene, the experts agree that hospice care is not to be feared. This care helps terminally ill people to live their remaining lives to the fullest. From this philosophical perspective, the film moves towards practices, where Deremo explains the role of each interdisciplinary staff member – physicians, nurses, social workers, spiritual care providers and volunteers. In each case, Deremo's talk is given a rhythm with scenes of staff members meeting with Ron and other patients. The staff help Ron to take his medication, converse with him and follow his physical condition. Their work represents ethics of care in practice, and includes comforting touches, hugs and caresses, as well as laughing, storytelling and reciprocal relationships. Deremo's abstract description about creating a 'sacred space' for the dying and their families is seconded by Ron, who admits that at first, he resented the idea of hospice, because it is 'not for the living', but he reconsidered after realising that hospice helped him to live with his diagnosis and enabled him to stay at home. Indeed, Ron is shown working with his cars and playing with his grandchildren. The film uses Ron's affective experiences to support the institutional and informative message of the hospice experts that hospice is about improving the quality of life.

In the case of *The Light Inside*, director Neil Hicks emphasises that to support the film's message it was extremely important to have real people tell their stories and voice their support for their local hospice. Hicks argues that finding these people also gave them an opportunity to give back to the hospice, to show how meaningful this form of care had been for them (Hicks 2019). The film tells the stories of two families battling with end-of-life issues. First, cancer patient Patti and her husband are trying to deal with the life-threatening illness. Second, parents Kathy and Gregg are mourning the sudden loss of their child. The structure of the film presents hospice as a support in this struggle. At the beginning of the documentary, both families share on camera their battle and need for help. Both are filmed in their homes, and Patti is also filmed in hospital receiving chemotherapy. The section ends with Kathy and Gregg narrating how overwhelming it was to lose their son and to deal with everyday life, and how that feeling of disconnection was 'an ugly place to be, because we did not know what to do'. From the home interview, the scene fades to black, and an intertitle appears on the screen: 'A place to turn to'.

The second section starts by introducing the local hospice. The camera travels through the streets of Peterborough, making the physical and geographical places familiar to the community a meaningful part of the narration. The gaze turns from the main street to a church tower, and from there to the driveway of the hospice building. The door opens, both literally and symbolically, and the viewer is allowed into the hospice. Here, the viewer also meets the staff of the hospice. A volunteer coordinator talks about the philosophy and values of care and how these, together with the people working there, make the place special and real. David Kennedy, the hospice's bereavement coordinator, promises that they help people struggling with death and dying, and while they cannot give any ultimate answers, they provide support so that 'you don't have to feel alone'.

Through Patti and Kathy and Gregg, the viewer visits the support groups and witnesses the help the hospice staff provide. This section alternates between the testimonial aspects and the institutional explanations of how the hospice helps. Patti's husband laments that not many people understand what they are going through, but the hospice helps to ensure that there is still life left. Both Kathy and Gregg say how important it was to know that they were not alone, and how the hospice gives them tools to help with the grief. These testimonials are supported by David's narration of how one needs to learn to live with grief, how death and dying cannot be put aside. One can find ways to deal with them and see how encountering death can make people appreciate life more. The film ends with Kathy and Gregg confirming that they have learned how their loss and sorrow can include life that honours their son. From this interview, filmed outdoors where the family is enjoying winter activities, the screen fades to black with the words, 'When the unthinkable happens, you are not alone.' In this video, the educational aspects are carefully woven together with the message that hospice provides tools and hope in difficult situations.

In a way, the structure of this short documentary conveys a sense of rescue. Hicks, the film's director, recognises the dual structure of the film (from problem to solution), but instead of straightforward rescue, he sees it as a message of support:

> One of the concerns we had was making sure that to be honest about the story and to be honest about the role that hospice plays is to celebrate the role that they do play, but to not overstate it to the extent that it becomes inauthentic. Hospice didn't fix these problems, nor did it fix these brutal situations that these families were in, but hospice did provide a support structure that was very important during these moments in time. (Hicks 2019)

Here, Hicks's insight into the planning of the film shows how affective storytelling elements add value to the informational needs related to awareness. Indeed, according to research done on social issue documentaries, human-centred stories are less likely to create rejection or counter-arguments than are informational or educational rhetoric, not least because these stories are seen as more engaging, less ideological, easier to comprehend, better at addressing emotional or existential issues, and are better remembered than informational messages (Borum Chattoo and Jenkins 2019; D. Epstein, Farina, and Heidt 2014; Hoeken and den Ouden 2019). In addition to raising awareness more effectively, balancing the information with stories allows hospice documentaries to focus on hospice philosophy without emphasising institutional aspects. The informative aspects easily connect to the sense of institution, whereas affective elements mediate a public image of hospices as spaces for care. At best, the message of care communicated by these documentaries invite interpretations that serve to alleviate the fears and negative connotations that the viewer might have about hospices.

Raising Awareness of Mortality

While hospice documentaries aim to increase awareness of the hospice movement, this aim intertwines with a wider context, the death awareness movement. Indeed, in their empirical work with hospices, Graven and Timm (2021, 329) found that the death awareness serves as a significant philosophical support for hospice staff. Similarly, while making hospice care visible, hospice documentaries also raise death and dying into the public discussion. This is visible in the closing words of the Netflix-distributed *End Game* (R. Epstein and Friedman 2018), a documentary that was nominated for an Academy Award in the category of Best Documentary (Short Subject). The film closes with the words of palliative care physician B. J. Miller: 'We are wired to run away from death. But dying is a part of life.' As such, the documentary aims to normalise death alongside hospice care. In an interview for an international documentary association, directors Rob Epstein and Jeffrey Friedman continue with this theme. Epstein argues that making the film was important because people do not want to think about death:

> It's a very hard thing to wrap your mind around. It's too scary. That was one of the reasons why we wanted to make this film—to make it less so. And that's what we were experiencing as we were doing the research and conceptualizing the project—witnessing these people whose job it is to alleviate suffering and to make death less scary. (Kurie 2019)

This film also builds from an institutional perspective. Epstein says that they shadowed the two doctors and met all the patients in the film through them (Kurie 2019). Thus, while the patients' stories are heartfelt, their stories are framed by the work of the care teams, who do their best to help them to deal with difficult situations. Epstein also considers that the patients and their families wanted to be part of the film because of their appreciation for end-of-life care: 'They were so appreciative of the palliative care that they were getting and understanding its value, that they wanted to be part of demystifying and educating others through their experience to help alleviate the suffering of others' (Kurie 2019).

The filmmakers follow two palliative care teams. One is led by Dr B. J. Miller, a palliative care physician at the Buddhist Zen Caregiving Project (also known as the Zen Hospice Center) in San Francisco. The other is Dr Steven Pantilat at the University of California San Francisco Medical Center, a hospital-based palliative ward. In this film, the hospital and hospice environments are set next to one another, but unlike in many hospice documentaries, the hospital institution is not demonised, but appreciated. In fact, the film starts from a scene where Pantilat discusses one of the main characters, 45-year-old Iranian-American Mitra, who is dying but whose family struggles to accept the situation. With his palliative team, Pantilat wonders if the family would be open for a hospice referral, but the chaplain of the team comments that the family equates hospice with death, which they are not ready to accept. Thus, the team continues to treat Mitra and the family at the hospital, and they do this with similar ethics of care as in the hospice institutions. Here, palliative care within a hospital creates a similar space for care as do hospices.

End Game acknowledges the difficult emotions of the patients and their families and observes staff trying to help patients and families deal with these difficult emotions. This follows from what Graven and Timm have found in the rhetoric of hospice workers. At first glance, the hospices' desire to avoid the stigma of being 'places' for death but wanting to be open about death can appear contradictory. However, as Graven and Timm argue, for hospice workers the openness refers to the emotional aspects of the dying process, not about being dead. Hospice staff create opportunities 'for patients to express emotions such as grief, anxiety, and to share memories and thoughts about what is important at the end of life' (Graven and Timm 2021, 329). Awareness of death thus translates into being allowed to experience complex emotions.

This is evident in a dialogue that Miller has with Thekla, one of the patients. In their previous meeting, Miller had asked Thekla to think about dying, to try to make death a bit less unknown. Thekla says that she has failed the assignment. Because she loves to live, accepting dying or death feels impossible and scary. Miller is understanding, yet continues to encourage Thekla to acknowledge her situation, and that perhaps it might be better to get used to the idea of death at some level. If nothing else, Thekla could hold onto an idea that one does not know what death is. Perhaps it would not be as bad as Thekla imagines. Thekla thinks about this, and admits: 'It could be terrible, but it could be wonderful.' Miller takes this as a cue to continue and argues that based on his experience, whatever we encounter after death, it will not be too horrible. When Thekla questions this, Miller turns to near-death experiences which people have described in positive terms. Thekla concedes that there might be some truth to these experiences (R. Epstein and Friedman 2018). In this exchange, Thekla does not experience sudden enlightenment. Her fears are heard and taken seriously, and at the same time, Miller tries to suggest ways to alleviate them.

Similar encounters between hospice and palliative care experts and patients structure the narration. The staff allow patients to feel mixed emotions and are not afraid to have difficult discussions. They offer the patients support to deal with the emotional upheaval of, and difficulty accepting, forthcoming death. Their expertise makes hospice and palliative care specialist work, something that separates commodified affective labour from non-commodified care work. For example, in the case of Mitra, the viewer witnesses a scene where she is anxious and struggling. She cries and shouts, letting out her frustrations, fears and anxiety. The family members start crying because they are upset about Mitra's uncontrollable responses and suffering. Mitra cries that she does not even know what she is anxious about. There is no clear problem that could be solved. Mitra's mother admits on camera that this causes anxiety in her as well and she feels that she is suffering and at the limits of her ability to cope. In situations like this, ethics of care is offered as additional support, something that can be managed by professionals rather than on your own.

In their desire to alleviate fears, hospice documentaries encounter both emotional and physical aspects of dying. During the filming, the patients get weaker and more fragile. While these films do not show moments of death, they include scenes both before and after. The final section of *Last Days of Life*, for example, shows Kerstin struggling to sit up and stand up, yet her desire to do so has not vanished. From these struggles, the film cuts to a shot in the hospice corridor. A nurse exits the room and lights a candle. The camera moves closer and records from the doorway Kerstin's family standing by her bed before they collect their belongings and leave. The camera follows their quiet parade, while Cornelis Vreeswijk's ballad about a beautiful dance between a young, vibrant woman and an older man plays in the background (Vreeswijk 1986). The camera then moves into the room and stays at Kerstin's bedside. Her now still body – an opposite to her vibrant personality – and flowers in her hand create a peaceful, yet sad image that remains until the film closes.

This, and similar scenes in other hospice documentaries, are reminders of the destination of the hospice journey. Such scenes also require the viewer's 'response-ability'. Sobchack argues that the viewers have a responsibility to justify why they watch real events, those in particular that are about death and dying. Based on her own reactions to seeing a rabbit's death on-screen, Sobchack views these on-screen images of dying as material reminders of being both a mortal and a moral being. In other words, watching requires responsibility, which includes becoming aware of one's own mortality (Sobchack 2004, 222–3). Thus, while hospice documentaries build understanding and awareness of what hospices do, they also demand that the viewers acknowledge mortality instead of running away from it. These documentaries build an image where death and dying is everybody's business, and that hospices refuse to be institutions where death can be hidden away.

Conclusion

Hospice documentaries approach end of life through the care provided by hospice and palliative care institutions. By giving examples of everyday work and life at the hospices and by opening the hospice doors, the documentaries make it known that these are welcoming and communal places which embrace life. Raising awareness is a reciprocal relationship. The hospices have a responsibility to care for the dying, and the viewer is invited to share this by watching and becoming aware of their work, and consequently, by wanting to support this form of care. In the context of end-of-life documentary films, Anna Elsner (2020, 2) argues that the process of dying is always 'inseparable from the question of how we care for the dying'. This, for Elsner, includes the staff and the filmmakers, but in ethical film viewing, it needs to extend to the viewer as well. Caring for the dying is everybody's responsibility.

When the viewers are included in ethics of care, hospice documentaries provide the ultimate reasoning to why hospices are 'good' institutions; as spaces for ethics of care, they should not be seen as 'traditional' institutions, but as alternative societal structures that include everyone in society, a way for the community to manage supporting the dying. Thus, request for responsibility turns into a promise. When hospice documentaries promise to support the dying person and their families, they promise that one day the viewer may be on the receiving end of ethics of care. By watching with the filmmakers, the viewer is promised that good end-of-life care can be one reason why one should not be so afraid of dying and death.

References

Abel, Emily K. 1986. 'The Hospice Movement: Institutionalizing Innovation'. *International Journal of Health Services* 16 (1): 71–85. https://doi.org/10.2190/RQBV-J2PG-VFNM-1H97.

Ariès, Philippe. 1975. *Western Attitudes toward Death: From the Middle Ages to the Present*. Translated by Patricia M. Ranum. First published 1974. Baltimore, MD: Johns Hopkins University Press.

Banci, Virginia. 2018. *Here & Now*. Documentary, Short. Bournemouth Film School.

Bauman, Zygmunt. 1992. *Mortality, Immortality and Other Life Strategies*. Stanford, CA: Stanford University Press.

Bennahum, David. 2003. 'The Historical Development of Hospice and Palliative Care'. In *Hospice and Palliative Care: Concepts and Practice*, 1–11. Boston, MA: Jones and Bartlett.

Borum Chattoo, Caty, and Will Jenkins. 2019. 'From Reel Life to Real Social Change: The Role of Contemporary Social-Issue Documentary in U.S. Public Policy'. *Media, Culture & Society* 41 (8): 1107–24. https://doi.org/10.1177/0163443718823145.

Burnell, Matthew. 2008. *Except for Six*. Documentary. Hospice of Michigan; Visioneer Films.

CCMA. 2018. 'S'estrena la coproducció de TV3 "Les pal·liatives", a "Sense ficció"'. *CCMA*. 29 October 2018. https://www.ccma.cat/premsa/sestrena-la-coproduccio-de-tv3-les-palliatives-a-sense-ficcio/nota-de-premsa/2883690/. Last accessed 19 November 2022.

Centeno, Carlos, and John Y. Rhee. 2019. 'Organization of Palliative Care in Different Parts of the World'. In *Textbook of Palliative Care*, edited by Roderick Duncan MacLeod and Lieve Van den Block, 37–75. Cham: Springer International Publishing. https://doi.org/10.1007/978-3-319-77740-5_6.

Clark, David. 1999. '"Total Pain", Disciplinary Power and the Body in the Work of Cicely Saunders, 1958–1967'. *Social Science & Medicine* 49 (6): 727–36. https://doi.org/10.1016/s0277-9536(99)00098-2.

———. 2005. 'Foreword'. In *Watch with Me: Inspiration for a Life in Hospice Care*, edited by Cicely M. Saunders, vii–xii. Lancaster: Observatory Publications.

De Panfilis, Ludovica, Silvia Di Leo, Carlo Peruselli, Luca Ghirotto, and Silvia Tanzi. 2019. '"I Go into Crisis When …": Ethics of Care and Moral Dilemmas in Palliative Care'. *BMC Palliative Care* 18 (1): 1–8. https://doi.org/10.1186/s12904-019-0453-2.

Edwards, Steven D. 2009. 'Three Versions of an Ethics of Care'. *Nursing Philosophy* 10 (4): 231–40. https://doi.org/10.1111/j.1466-769X.2009.00415.x.

Elias, Norbert. 2001. *The Loneliness of the Dying*. First published 1985. New York: Continuum.

Elsner, Anna Magdalena. 2020. 'Landscapes of Care and the Enchantment of Dying in Edwin Beeler's *Die Weisse Arche* (2016)'. *Studies in Documentary Film* 14 (2): 147–60. https://doi.org/10.1080/17503280.2020.1725994.

Epstein, Dmitry, Cynthia Farina, and Josiah Heidt. 2014. 'The Value of Words: Narrative as Evidence in Policy Making'. *Evidence & Policy: A Journal of Research, Debate and Practice* 10 (2): 243–58. https://doi.org/10.1332/174426514X13990325021128.

Epstein, Rob, and Jeffrey Friedman. 2018. *End Game*. Documentary. Netflix.

Friedman, Betsy T., M. Kay Harwood, and Matthew Shields. 2002. 'Barriers and Enablers to Hospice Referrals: An Expert Overview'. *Journal of Palliative Medicine* 5 (1): 73–84. https://doi.org/10.1089/10966210252785033.

Gilligan, Carol. 1982. *In a Different Voice: Psychological Theory and Women's Development*. Cambridge, MA: Harvard University Press.

Gispert, Oriol, and Marta Valls. 2018. *Les Pal·liatives*. Documentary. La Lupa Producciones.

Graven, Vibeke, and Helle Timm. 2021. 'Hospice Philosophy in Practice—Toward an Authentic Death'. *OMEGA – Journal of Death and Dying* 83 (2): 325–42. https://doi.org/10.1177/0030222819852850.

Hakola, Outi. 2021. 'Advertising Hospice Care Services'. *Death Studies* 45 (9): 726–34. https://doi.org/10.1080/07481187.2019.1686089.

Hall, Lauren K. 2017. 'Rehumanizing Birth and Death in America'. *Society* 54 (3): 226–37. https://doi.org/10.1007/s12115-017-0129-6.

Hardt, Michael. 1999. 'Affective Labor'. *Boundary 2* 26 (2): 89–100.

Hickey, Deb, and Sharon Quinn. 2012. '"I Don't Want to Talk about It." Raising Public Awareness of End-of-Life Care Planning in Your Locality'. *International Journal of Palliative Nursing* 18 (5): 241–7. https://doi.org/10.12968/ijpn.2012.18.5.241.

Hicks, Neal. 2015. *The Light Inside*. Documentary, Short. Hospice Peterborough.

———. 2019. Personal interview by Outi Hakola.

Hoeken, Hans, and J. N. den Ouden. 2019. 'Narrative Health Communication'. In *Narratives in Research and Interventions on Cyberbullying among Young People*, edited by Heidi Vandebosch and Lelia Green, 61–74. Cham: Springer.

James, Nicky, and David Field. 1992. 'The Routinization of Hospice: Charisma and Bureaucratization'. *Social Science & Medicine* 34 (12): 1363–75. https://doi.org/10.1016/0277-9536(92)90145-G.

Kim, Chang Gon. 2019. 'The History of Hospice and Palliative Care in Korea'. *The Korean Journal of Hospice and Palliative Care* 22 (1): 1–7. https://doi.org/10.14475/kjhpc.2019.22.1.1.

Kurie, Peter. 2019. 'The Final Passage: "End Game" Offers a Lesson on Death and Dying'. International Documentary Association. 12 February 2019. https://www.documentary.org/online-feature/final-passage-end-game-offers-lesson-death-and-dying. Last accessed 10 January 2022.

Lawrence, Dana J. 2007. 'The Four Principles of Biomedical Ethics: A Foundation for Current Bioethical Debate'. *Journal of Chiropractic Humanities* 14 (January): 34–40. https://doi.org/10.1016/S1556-3499(13)60161-8.

McGann, Sarah. 2016. *The Production of Hospice Space*. London: Routledge. https://doi.org/10.4324/9781315553870.

Miličević, Nataša. 2002. 'The Hospice Movement: History and Current Worldwide Situation'. *Archive of Oncology* 10 (1): 29–31.

Noddings, Nel. 1984. *Caring, a Feminine Approach to Ethics & Moral Education*. Berkeley: University of California Press.

Oksala, Johanna. 2016. 'Affective Labor and Feminist Politics'. *Signs: Journal of Women in Culture and Society* 41 (2): 281–303. https://doi.org/10.1086/682920.

Persson, Nahid. 2013. *Last Days of Life* (*I Livets Slutskede*). Documentary. Sveriges Television AB; Real Reel Docs AB.

Quinlan, Christina. 2009. 'Media Discourses on Autonomy in Dying and Death'. *Irish Communication Review* 11 (1). https://doi.org/10.21427/D7XM8T.

Saunders, Cicely M. 2005. *Watch with Me: Inspiration for a Life in Hospice Care*. Lancaster: Observatory Publications.

Seamon, David, and Jacob Sowers. 2008. 'Place, and Placelessness, Edward Relph.' In *Key Texts in Human Geography*, edited by Phil Hubbard, Rob Kitchin, and Gill Valentine, 43–51. London: SAGE Publications.

Serba, John. 2008. 'Hospice Intends Film to Be "Awareness Tool"'. MLive. 1 September 2008. https://www.mlive.com/movies/2008/09/hospice_intends_film_to_be_awa.html. Last accessed 19 November 2022.

Sobchack, Vivian. 2004. *Carnal Thoughts: Embodiment and Moving Image Culture*. Los Angeles: University of California Press.

Tatko, Aleksandra. 2017. 'The Origins and Development of the Modern Hospice Movement in the Context of Ongoing Demographic and Social Changes in the World'. *Praca Socjalna* 2 (33): 155–74.

Tronto, Joan C. 2020. *Moral Boundaries: A Political Argument for an Ethic of Care*. First published 1993. New York; London: Routledge. https://doi.org/10.4324/9781003070672.

Vreeswijk, Cornelis. 1986. *Balladen Om Herr Fredrik Åkare Och Den Söta Fröken Cecilia Lind*. Vol. I Elfte Timmen. Max Records.

Vries, Maruscha de, and Carlo J. W. Leget. 2012. 'Ethical Dilemmas in Elderly Cancer Patients: A Perspective from the Ethics of Care'. *Clinics in Geriatric Medicine* 28 (1): 93–104. https://doi.org/10.1016/j.cger.2011.10.004.

Weber, Max. 2013. *Economy and Society: An Outline of Interpretive Sociology, Volume 2*, edited by Guenther Roth and Claus Wittich. First published 1922. Berkeley; Los Angeles; London: University of California Press.

Wilson, Emma. 2012. *Love, Mortality and the Moving Image*. London: Palgrave Macmillan. https://doi.org/10.1057/9780230367708.

Zeugin, Barbara. 2021. 'The Hospice Movement, Palliative Care, and Anthroposophy in Europe'. In *The Routledge Handbook of Religion, Medicine, and Health*, edited by Dorothea Lüddeckens, Philipp Hetmanczyk, Pamela E. Klassen, and Justin B. Stein, 98–112. London: Routledge. https://doi.org/10.4324/9781315207964-9.

Zimmermann, Camilla, and Gary Rodin. 2004. 'The Denial of Death Thesis: Sociological Critique and Implications for Palliative Care'. *Palliative Medicine* 18 (2): 121–8. https://doi.org/10.1191/0269216304pm858oa.

4. SPIRITUAL DOCUMENTARIES
Making Death Meaningful

> It *is* hard to die, and it will always be so, even when we have learned to accept death as an integral part of life, because dying means giving up life on this earth. But if we can learn to view death from a different perspective, to reintroduce it into our lives so that it comes not as a dreaded stranger but as an expected companion to our life, then we can also learn to live our lives with meaning. (Kübler-Ross 1975, 6)

The quote comes from psychiatrist Elizabeth Kübler-Ross, who was a driving force behind developing the international death awareness movement. In 1969, her classic book *On Death and Dying* (Kübler-Ross 2009) spoke against the medicalisation of death and approached death and dying through everyday experiences. The book gave visibility to death as a societal topic both among academics and the public. In this book, Kübler-Ross introduced her grief-stage theory according to which people adjust to terminal illness through five stages – denial, anger, bargaining, depression and acceptance. The model emphasises the importance of death acceptance in easing the emotional burden of everyone involved. Her later book, *Death: The Final Stage of Growth* (1975), from where the above quote is from, symbolically adds another stage to this personal growth. The book itself is a collection of essays by writers who discuss the ways in which different cultures, religions and philosophies have negotiated death acceptance, dealt with death anxiety and established the meaning of life and death. In this collection,

Kübler-Ross argues for the importance of creating a meaningful relationship with death.

In the field of psychology, Kübler-Ross's grief theory has become increasingly criticised. New grief theories do not consider death and loss to evolve in stages that lead to acceptance and personal growth, but place emphasis on individually varied emotional responses (McCabe 2003). Yet, the acceptance narrative continues to exert cultural influence. For example, Kübler-Ross's influence remains strong in spiritual approaches to the end of life. In this context, spirituality is an individual concept, which does not necessarily mean being part of an established religion, but it can be a philosophical approach to existential questions. Spirituality often becomes significant for the terminally ill and those approaching death. Studies have shown that it can help people to cope with end of life and add to their sense of quality of life (Stephenson, Draucker, and Martsolf 2003; Bovero et al. 2016), whereas some other studies have found that spirituality does not appear to diminish fears (Kates 2020). In the hospice movement, spiritual care is part of holistic care along with physical, psychological and social care. In practice, spiritual care includes supporting a person's religious beliefs and rituals, and it also recognises the individuals' desire to find meaning and purpose for life and death, validation for lived lives and ways to make suffering and pain understandable (Ferrell 2017).

The search for a meaning of life and death has also been contemplated in some end-of-life documentaries, which prioritise questions of how we should understand death's role in our lives. These documentaries suggest that anyone would benefit from thinking about the meaning of death, because the meaning-making process may alleviate death anxiety and encourage one to live more fully. In contrast to medical and hospice documentaries, which give institutional viewpoints on end-of-life care, spiritual documentaries adopt an institutional voice in guiding the viewer towards a meaningful death. In this chapter, I start by discussing the educational tone of spiritual documentaries with the help of two short films, *Lessons for the Living* (Henderson 2010), an American film, and *For One More Moment* (Timonen 2017), a Finnish documentary. I will then move to a close analysis of two American documentaries – *Solace: Wisdom of the Dying* (Adair 2008) and *Living Your Dying* (Pennybacker 2003) – and one from Switzerland, *Die Weisse Arche* (Beeler 2016). My argument is that these documentaries aim to transform spirituality from being a question of belief to a sphere of knowledge or truth which would endow spirituality with equal cultural appreciation bestowed upon the medical understanding of death. Because spirituality has the potential of alleviating death anxiety, these documentaries suggest that such cultural appreciation could benefit everyone, not only those in the midst of a dying process.

Searching for Spiritual Knowledge

The Finnish documentary *For One More Moment* centres on the interviews of three nurses of a hospice home in the Tampere region. Instead of introducing any patients, the documentary highlights the nurses' experiences of how their job has normalised death for them. The message is emphasised in the imagery of the scenes. While a few scenes are filmed in the hospice home, most take place outdoors. There is a scene of one of the nurses painting a picture by a lake, another saddling a horse, and the third sitting in a gazebo surrounded by trees. This symbolism serves as a testimony to how the nurses have learned to accept death as a natural part of life. Consequently, they have learned to appreciate the beauty of the last moments, and most importantly, to appreciate life.

In a review, film critic Pauliina Savola argues that this film's meaning is bigger than the thirteen minutes of its length. In that time, the film manages to crystallise images of life and death that have been shaped by decades of staff members' experience. These images, Savola writes, are not 'dark or gloomy, but full of warmth and hope. The message is important: before we die, it would be good to live. Today, not tomorrow' (Savola 2019, translated from Finnish). This reading relates to what director Jenny Timonen thinks about the tone of her film. In an interview for a local newspaper, Timonen says she wants the film to be hopeful, and that the viewer would 'sit quietly and think for a while when the film ends ... and when they leave, they would think about their own lives' (Kuusela 2017, translated from Finnish). The wisdom and experience of the hospice nurses teach the viewer to appreciate life and to respect death.

This is typical of spiritual end-of-life documentaries. The film has an existential message and something to teach. In many ways, these documentaries follow the same logic as Kübler-Ross's *Death: The Final Stage of Growth*. In the foreword the editors Joseph Braga and Laurie Braga frame the book as a tool to help the reader to 'learn' to 'find peace in life and death' through examining their emotional responses to others' knowledge and stories. By doing so, the readers might allow death to help them to find meaning for life and to become who they 'truly' are (Braga and Braga 1975, x–xii). In this framing, meaning-making connects to 'truth' as something that can be found. This chapter keeps returning to the word 'truth', mostly because it is repeatedly used in the context of spiritual and existential documentaries. 'Truth' appears to legitimate the factual claims that spirituality has an important role in everyday lives. Thus, I use 'truth' to accentuate the context of these arguments, while in my argumentation I prefer the terms 'knowledge' and 'testimony'. For me, 'truth' assumes an absoluteness, whereas knowledge refers to either practical or theoretical understanding of an issue and allows room for adjustments (Merriam-Webster n.d.), and testimony combines meanings of witnessing, 'firsthand authentication of a fact' and even 'public profession of religious experience' (Merriam-Webster n.d.). Both these terms emphasise lived experience and constructed viewpoint instead of assuming absolutes, and as such they are more in line with my understanding of documentary as an ethical space to explore mortality.

Yet, the idea that 'truth' is something to be found, remains well rehearsed in documentary contexts. Justin Wells, who works as a camera crew member in Hollywood productions and has studied both philosophy and fine arts, and has written about spirituality in documentary filmmaking. He argues that the 'truth' about the world and ourselves is always suppressed, something that remains in the margins of hectic everyday life. However, at their best, documentaries can offer a journey to explore the mysteries of life and the world, and as such, to reveal some parts of the philosophical, existential or spiritual 'truth' to the filmmaker and, in turn, to the viewer (Wells 2018). Here, documentary filmmaking is given a revealing role in the human enquiry to learn the 'truth' about meaning of life and humanity.

Many spiritual end-of-life documentaries, as the above example of *For One More Moment* shows, turn to the experts to find answers about life and death. This documentary was inspired by the filmmaker's encounter with hospice staff when her mother was dying. Awed by the staff's experience, she wanted to make a film about their expertise (Kuusela 2017). Similar experiences have inspired other spiritual documentaries as well. Lily Henderson, the director of *Lessons for the Living*, wanted to film hospice volunteers after her own experiences as a volunteer provided her with a transcendental experience on life and death. Thus, Henderson gives visibility to volunteering but her film also shows how death can ground a person, provide a holistic understanding of life and become a meaningful part of it (Henderson 2019).

Similar to *For One More Moment*, *Lessons for the Living* assumes that those who witness a lot of death and dying can gain knowledge that goes beyond everyday understandings of death and life. This is knowledge that has accumulated over the years and is based on experienced evidence. Documentary filmmaking can provide space for these testimonies in a way that enables the viewer to learn about death and dying. Even the name of the film reveals the importance of teaching potential, which is further highlighted by the opening quote from Kübler-Ross: 'We run after values that, at death, become zero ... That's what dying patients teach you' (Henderson 2010).

The short documentary is a collection of interviews of hospice volunteers in New York. They testify what they have learned from the dying people and how the volunteering has changed their thinking about life, death and dying. One of the lessons is to learn how to be in the presence of a dying person. The volunteers assure that these are meaningful and beautiful encounters, where they have learned to be present, to be compassionate and to prioritise the other

SPIRITUAL DOCUMENTARIES

over their own needs. Other lessons are related to the meaningfulness of death. As such, death encourages one to appreciate life and to find recognition for each individual existence. Says one of the volunteers: 'I think at the end people are who they are. All the masks are down. And they really are extraordinary.' In other words, by accepting that your life is limited, you can focus on being true to yourself.

Many volunteers in this documentary emphasise spirituality, even though they understand spirituality differently. The documentary introduces a priest, a shamanic healer and a follower of Buddhist religion, for example. Henderson, the director of the documentary, recognised that while she did not set out to make a spiritual film, many of her filmed subjects 'had this mystical tone', which 'sets into that world where everything is positive and light'. Thus, for her, the spiritual undertones of the interviews added 'polish' to the subject of death and dying, and therefore, the closing of the documentary provided a necessary balance to the testimonies of the meaning of death (Henderson 2019). The last person to be interviewed is Kathleen, a former volunteer, now a patient at a hospice ward. Unlike many others, she wants to avoid mystery. She argues that volunteering took the mystery out of death, and forced her to focus on the moment, the physical process, on something that is inevitable. For her, this matter-of-fact way of dealing with death encourages her to 'live today, as fully as I am able'. While Kathleen adds practical and physical aspects to accompany the mystical interpretations of death, even this practical view endorses the idea that death makes life meaningful.

In their desire to teach the viewer with their testimonies about the meaning of life and death, many spiritual end-of-life documentaries tend to follow the practices of expository documentary-making. Bill Nichols sees this as one of the oldest and still most prominent ways of creating non-fiction stories. The expository mode builds cognitive knowledge and rhetorical argumentation for a certain concept or perspective. In order to do so, these documentaries use voiceovers and interviews and list the experts' titles and affiliations to construct information that aims to reveal the 'truth' (Nichols 2017, 107–8). Similarly, spiritual documentaries use plenty of interviews, where the experts are given time and space to talk about their notions of death without interruption. This gives didactic importance to the spoken word. Images perform a supportive role, providing evidence (Nichols 2016, 75). The early documentary theorist John Grierson argues that while these kinds of documentaries would rather not be called lecture films, this is what they are. They rarely dramatise or aesthetically reveal. They describe and even expose. He gives these films value in education (and in propaganda), even if he finds that they do not make considerable contributions to the 'fuller art' of the documentary (Grierson 1966, 20). Due to such criticism, expository filmmaking has been partially displaced in the documentary field, whereas the observatory mode has increased its popularity

75

(Martin-Stone 2013). However, even the most speech-oriented documentaries express meanings on multiple levels and build meanings beyond what is said.

The tried and tested solution of spiritual end-of-life documentaries to use an expository mode further highlights these films' tendency to search for the meaningfulness of death. They suggest that there exists a 'truth' about death which needs to be discovered by careful examination to increase the quality of life. In this task, experts who have dedicated their professional and personal lives to these issues can help others to gain spiritual knowledge about life and death. Thus, the documentary films both showcase spiritual testimonies and participate in creating them.

In terms of showcasing spiritual knowledge, documentaries represent death and dying as transcendental themes. Erik Knudsen argues that documentaries can offer 'transcendental realism' by readjusting the focus from scientific, rational or material knowledge towards a holistic understanding of the world and its realities. He argues that because human experience has always included 'infinite, eternal, mystical and unconscious movements in existence', documentaries should also try to reach 'the very heart and soul of who we are and what we are' (Knudsen 2008, 3–4). Spiritual end-of-life documentaries rise to their transcendental challenge by exploring the meanings of life and death.

In terms of creating spiritual testimonies, documentaries can search for knowledge by various strategies. Sybille Krämer, for example, recognises a discursive and existential 'truth' from documentary expressions. The discursive approach highlights that the subjective 'truth' is not enough, but arguments need to be valid from a third-person perspective as well, and this validation is gained by careful rhetorical argumentation. Existential 'truth', then, has a performative dimension, where someone's personal experience or expertise (second-person perspective) can validate the 'truth' if the viewer believes in this authority (Krämer 2016, 30–2). Krämer only recognises these two ways of exploring 'truth' and does not consider whether there could be a first-person approach to 'truth'. Perhaps the first-person approach appears too subjective for a concept such as 'truth', whereas the concept of testimony gives more flexibility to explore this option as well. To continue from Krämer's dichotomy, I call this transcendental testimony (or 'truth', if this is what one prefers). In this argumentation, the viewer's personal experience with the film transforms their understanding of life and death, and the potential for this transcendental knowledge can be suggested through the film's aesthetics and narration. In the following analysis, I explore the different understandings of how the viewer's knowledge on spirituality of death is built through discursive (third-person), existential (second-person) and transcendental (first-person) narrative structures.

Discursive Testimony about Death

Solace: Wisdom of the Dying (2008) is created by Camille Adair, a hospice nurse, who felt that the end of life needed to be integrated into the healthcare field as a 'natural and sacred human process' (Camille Adair/Sacredigm Alliances, Llc n.d.). In an interview, Adair highlights the spiritual aspects as necessary for moving away from the medicalised, or 'pharmaceutical', approach to death and dying that has made western societies 'soulless'. Instead, she seeks elements from 'ancient traditions and ancient wisdom' that can bring attention back to the human experience and open our minds to 'the other realm' (Sitar 2012). The documentary-making inspired Adair to move into end-of-life and caregiving counselling, education and patient advocacy. She has produced an eleven-part video and multimedia project, the Solace Teaching Program, that discusses hospice and palliative care, aging, illness and dying, and is aimed primarily for people involved in caregiving or working in healthcare. In the programme, spirituality plays a prominent role in Adair's attempt to make healthcare more humane. These starting points show how spiritual knowledge is presented as an equal alternative to medical knowledge on death.

The narration of *Solace: Wisdom of the Dying* is framed by Adair's own voiceover. She uses voiceover moments to express her desire to manage the human suffering and grief that she encountered in hospice work. Her practice echoes Nichols's (2016, 59) argumentation that voiceover serves as 'moralising center around which a particular view of the world revolve[s]'. Similarly, Adair's voice guides us through the film. In her exploration of mortality, she supports her argumentation through interviews of various experts on the spiritual aspects of death. These professionals represent religious authorities, people working in healthcare fields, and various spiritual guides, such as end-of-life coaches. These people have been chosen to be interviewed due to Adair's recognition of their expertise in the field. Many have published books on end-of-life spirituality and have built companies or advocacy programmes to help dying people and their families.

For example, a major role in the film is given to Larry Dossey, a physician who praises the impact of spirituality on well-being and healing. In his book *Healing Words: The Power of Prayer and the Practice of Medicine* (Dossey 1993), he testifies that there is evidence of prayer's healing potential and it should be included in medical practices, a view that has faced considerable criticism for the way it takes a stand against science-based medicine (e.g. Baker 1994; Roberts 1995). In the documentary, Dossey talks about non-local consciousness, which makes all people connected, and how this consciousness ensures that death is a part of life, and that human consciousness continues after death. He claims that if science could accept this idea of continuing and flowing consciousness, the medical institutes could better approach questions of death and dying in patient encounters.

Religious authorities, such as Roshi Joan Halifax, founder of the Buddhist Upaya Zen Centre (Santa Fe, New Mexico), highlight natural death, but also discuss death's meaning in an individual's life. Halifax's book *Being with Dying: Cultivating Compassion and Fearlessness in the Presence of Death* seeks to help people to encounter death with courage, without fear, mainly by using their inner strength (Halifax 2009). In the documentary, she continues to discuss fear of death, which in the worst case can turn into morbid anxiety, but which, when prepared for, can turn into thrilling anticipation of what is to come. She also foregrounds the transformative role of suffering, which is seen as redemptive. Spiritual end-of-life coaches, such as Stephen Levine and Ondrea Levine, add to this view of seeing death as a rewarding experience: being conscious of our mortality can be gratifying and prepare us for dying. Death, they testify, can inspire people to look inwards and envision a greater reality after death; self-reflection can help us find the humanness and sacredness of end of life.

All the interviews focus on the teachable spiritual testimony that experts share and the viewer can absorb through speech acts delivered in front of the camera. The experts face the camera directly, their titles indicating the professional roles and institutions they represent and the books they have written. Their expertise is established through external validation, and their direct speech to the viewer emphasises that they are worth listening to. This narrative approach fits Krämer's understanding of validating testimony through discourse. For Krämer, discursive 'truth' requires outer validation, which is recognisable to a third person and which is typically located in a speech act. In other words, discursive 'truth' is rationally known and can be taught and learned (Krämer 2016, 30). The film's testimony is provided through 'talking heads', which turns spiritual knowledge into rational and cognitive argumentation. However, according to Catalin Brylla and Mette Kramer (2018), cognitive approaches to documentary viewing invite evaluation where the viewer assesses the film's truth claims by appraising whether the documentary appears trustworthy and whether the arguments resonate with their personal, cultural and societal understanding of the topic. This process, indeed, emphasises third-person validation in that the viewer becomes the third person to decide whether they can cognitively accept the testimony and whether they find these voices believable.

While the film is built around the experts' argumentative lessons, some personal experiences about death and dying are included. These snippets follow the experts' discursive testimonies to give them further validation. These subjective testimonies focus on personal growth and how suffering has helped people to find authenticity in life and their 'true selves'. Chris Calloway, a singer diagnosed with breast cancer, shares her experience of receiving help from chanting at the altar for hours at a time. It helped her to encounter her life situation, find wisdom in her own energy field and to gain a 'higher life condition'. Later, she also talks animatedly about finding power in spirituality (as opposed to materialism), where facing death is a way to find one's 'authentic' self and to appreciate each moment in life. Her words play at the very end of the film, when she cheerfully declares that death is a take-off to a new experience, and as such, death is framed as a transformative and positive experience, something to be looked forward to. Through these assurances, the documentary builds an image of death as a teacher in life; painful experiences make us better people, cultivate us. For that reason, suffering and pain also have a meaning. Through death acceptance, one can move beyond fear and emotional pain, and start enjoying the transformative passage to another existence, energy or consciousness.

While most of the film is based on rhetorical argumentation, the soundscape and imagery involved add a spiritual dimension to the film. By conceiving meditation and self-reflections as tools to gaining death acceptance, *Solace: Wisdom of the Dying* presents mindfulness practices as spiritual tools. Mindfulness can be seen as a theory and/or practice of a present-centred awareness that helps to manage anxiety, depression and stress. It has a background in Buddhism and meditation traditions, and is often used as a therapeutical application in the spiritual care provided in hospice and palliative care (Bruce and Davies 2005; Mcgrath 1998; Johns 2004; Lee et al. 2021). The chosen imagery of the documentary supports the mindfulness approach. Buddhist objects, such as statues of Buddha and Ganesha, a Hindu god of beginnings, and sometimes also such Christian symbols as crosses and rosaries, create the background of the interviews. The aural world of singing bowls adds to the spiritual atmosphere. The vibrating and harmonious sounds of the bowls connect to the Tibetan Buddhist canon for spiritual, medicinal and musical purposes. In the United States, in particular, the bowls have become a part of mindfulness commodities (Brown 2020). The bowls' connection to both spirituality and healing has been recognised in some medical studies (Stanhope and Weinstein 2020), and as such they serve a purpose in the documentary to further emphasise the healing aspects of spiritual knowledge that can be found and explored.

However, the use of mindfulness as part of spiritual care has also been questioned, not because of its potential to alleviate anxiety, but *how* it is used in hospice contexts. In an ethnographic study, John Eric Baugher found that when mindfulness was adopted by hospice volunteers, it guided them to pay attention to those patients that wanted to review their lives and have deep and meaningful discussions. While doing this, they tended to ignore the patients who did not or could not engage in such processes (Baugher 2008). Similar criticism is often directed towards expository documentaries that are seen to choose editing that supports the main message and leaves other interpretations in the margins. In *Solace: Wisdom of the Dying*, the benefits of the spiritual approach to end of life are supported by overwhelmingly positive tones and stories. When the narration focuses on interviews, the imagery excludes all references to physical aspects of dying. All interviewed people appear to be in a good condition, and thus, the attention is guided towards their rhetorical and discursive argumentation. Whether viewers find this positivity comforting depends on whether they accept the discursive testimony of the documentary narrator.

Existential Testimony about Death

Krämer counters discursive 'truth' with existential 'truth' in documentary narration. She draws this concept from Søren Kierkegaard's (1991, 205–7) dichotomy between 'knowing a truth' and 'being a truth', where knowing is language-based and being has a performative dimension. So, an existential approach to 'truth' becomes experienced by someone, and when shared with others, they need to believe in it (Krämer 2016, 32–3). In this process of believing, Krämer continues to draw from Kierkegaard's existential philosophy, where authority makes it possible to distinguish between truth and belief. These authorities do not speak in their own name, but in the name of what they represent, such as religion, and their embodied experience of this higher construct turns into 'being a truth' (Kierkegaard 1991, 227). While Krämer recognises that Kierkegaard's authority-based approach to knowledge can be frustrating, she argues that the same logic is often used in documentary films where trust and belief in the authorities serve to 'generate a form of *knowledge*'. She calls this a second-person model of witnessing; the trust in the message is based on interaction between the film and the viewer. The authority serves as eyewitness and takes responsibility for the message, and if the viewers accept this guarantee, they can also accept this testimony as 'truth' (Krämer 2016, 33–4). What is interesting in Krämer's argument is that whereas discursive 'truth' is always language-oriented, images can serve as existential testimonies. In other words, if the viewer trusts the authority of the image, it can offer a way to explore existential 'truth'.

Here, I turn to *Living Your Dying* (2003), because this documentary combines expert and image authority in its desire to assure the viewer of the benefits of a spiritual approach to death and dying. The documentary was directed by Robert Pennybacker and commissioned by the Mits Aoki Legacy Foundation, which honours the work of Reverend Mits Aoki and promotes and teaches a holistic approach to healing and death. Aoki was a theologian and founder of the University of Hawaii's Department of Religion. His work centred on spirituality in the transition to death, where his aim was 'conscious dying': people should be 'living their dying' (Tasaka 2014). The film builds on the experiences and viewpoints of Aoki, who becomes the documentary's main source of expertise and authority on knowledge about death.

The film starts with images of nature, instrumental background music and a voiceover that defines birth as a beginning, death as a destination and life as a sacred journey between these. Images of floating memorial lanterns on water fill the screen, when Aoki starts talking:

> This is a realm of mystery. And I tell you when I work with dying people, so many times the dying person manifests to me something of the sense of mystery. I don't see this as a problem or something to cure but something to really experience in such a way that it can enlarge a person. It can make a person more authentic, more real. (Pennybacker 2003)

The camera cuts to a close-up of Aoki who speaks directly to the camera. After this initial interview, nature images return, and the voiceover promises the viewer 'an extraordinary journey into the mystery of death'. The following section alternates between voiceover and Aoki's own voice, which together build an image of Aoki's life and interest in death and dying. This section shows that Aoki has become 'being a truth' by virtue of his dedication to study death and dying, his witnessing and helping thousands of people to die, and his encounters with death and dying in his personal life. Aoki is presented as an embodiment and personification of spiritual knowledge. After this introduction, the film moves on to show through images what Aoki's knowledge means in practice.

In what follows, Aoki describes his wife's death, and the viewer meets three terminally ill people, Mike, Fay and Ululani. In a voiceover introduction, they are each given a spiritual theme to represent in the narration: individual journey, significance of community and meaningfulness of nature. The scenes include meetings between the patients and Aoki, who helps the dying and their families to work through whatever issues they may face. Aoki encourages them to live as fully as possible until the end, emphasising the meaning of family, community and relationships until the very end. By showing glimpses of these individuals' lives, their stories turn into testimonials of Aoki's spiritual knowledge. We meet these people when they are calm and peaceful even when discussing negative experiences and emotions. The calmness of the images speaks for existential evidence in accepting death as a part of life. The spiritual message is created through Aoki's authority and testimonial imagery.

Mike serves as an example of the individual journey towards himself. He says, while playing with his grandchildren, that his cancer has made everything in his life more poignant. The colours, sounds and smiles have become more vivid, and life has more meaning. The garden where they play is awash with lush green scenery, and blue skies add to the vivid view. Fay, in turn, is an example of the importance of community and relationships. After seeing the smiling images from her daughter's graduation party, Fay shares in an interview that reaching her goal to see her daughter graduate has made her ready to die, 'because I've done what I wanted to do, and that's enough'. Aoki confirms this experience by assuring Fay that her ability to accept death has made her more open to her dying. In the last example, Ululani testifies for a transition towards the sacred. Aoki helps this native Hawaiian to draw support both from Christianity and the Hula tradition, a Hawaiian dance with religious meanings. Aoki enables Ululani to use visualisations and meditation to be comforted by sacred and spiritual aspects of nature. Beautiful and vivid images of nature and the Hula traditions enhance Aoki's words that if Ululani learns to draw power from these spiritual experiences, healing can take place.

Spirituality supports the dying people, but instead of framing their experiences as merely peaceful journeys, the film does not shy away from the fears and negative emotions that these people have. Aoki does not deny these emotions, but uses meditation and religion to alleviate them. The film also portrays the physical transition of the dying people into growing frailty. The viewer is invited to their deathbeds, even if the exact moment of death is excluded from the scenes. The deathbed scenes serve as final evidence of Aoki's message that life is a journey to a transformative horizon, a journey that one does not need to be afraid of. The dying are surrounded by their loved ones, who are leaving their goodbyes, and by Aoki who encourages the dying to go on in their journey. The scenes are peaceful and comforting, and as such, these images become performed testimonials of existential knowledge.

Whereas *Solace: Wisdom of the Dying* trusted a (third-person) talking-heads approach without death-related imagery, *Living Your Dying* combines Reverend Aoki's authority with testimonial use of images of the dying people. By inviting the viewer to witness Aoki in action – providing spiritual care for the terminally ill – the film embodies spiritual testimony. In Krämer's terms, Aoki performs second-person knowledge for the viewer, and the image testimonials invite the viewer to trust Aoki's expertise. In turn, this existential approach to knowing about death assures the viewer that death should be understood as the ultimate transformation. Death can thus give meaning to life long before the actual dying process.

Transcendental Testimony about Death

The last documentary discussed in this chapter is *Die Weisse Arche* (2016), a Swiss documentary directed by Edwin Beeler, who has adopted a spiritual approach to searching for the meaning and values of life. Similar to other documentaries in this chapter, these questions are explored together with individuals dealing with death and dying in their professional and personal lives. The film introduces a hospice nurse, Monika, whose near-death experience has removed her fear of death, the mystic Sam who banishes ghosts from people's homes, cattle herder Alfons (a former Carthusian), who has a strong connection with nature and earth, and a group of Benedictine and Capuchin monks. Beeler says that he 'was interested in how different people live spirituality in their own lives personally and how they deal with death and the certainty that like everyone else they have to die' (Biasio 2017, translated from German). This quote reveals the main difference from the earlier films; while the documentary shows that the filmed subjects have special knowledge and expertise, these are framed through subjective experience instead of a universally applied 'truth'.

In this documentary, too, the experts talk to the camera, and occasionally we see them in sit-down interviews. However, most often the interview material is used as voiceovers while the camera films the subjects in their daily activities. While travelling through the Alps by train, Monika talks about her own near-death experience after getting caught in an avalanche. The monastery gardener, filmed arranging funeral wreaths, talks about helping to organise funerals, while the monastery painter, filmed painting angels on canvas, shares with the viewer his experiences of working with dying people. Combined, the spoken words and the images of the interviewees' activities diminish a sense of lecturing. The documentary brings together observatory aspects and the expository elements of searching for knowledge about death.

The use of everyday activities connects these subjects' knowledge to their lived experience instead of producing a universal 'truth'. In addition, the observatory aspects of narration invite the viewer to witness first-person argumentation instead of third- or second-person perspectives. In this process, the viewer's attention shifts from evaluating the spoken truth claims to witnessing whether these people follow through their values and attitudes. This is what happens, for example, when Monika confesses that she used to be afraid of death and was uncomfortable to be with dying people. However, her own positive experience of dying, where she experienced that her consciousness continued to exist, has made death her friend, which has enabled her to comfort the dying and their families. In the images, the viewer sees her taking care of patients with compassion. Monika's actions embody her spiritual knowledge and assures the viewer that death acceptance has become a lived experience for Monika. The viewer no longer experiences the testimonies through an authority, instead the viewer is expected to be the first-hand witness. This witnessing offers the viewer the potential to experience the realities of the other and to embody this experience.

Knudsen argues that when dealing with transcendental topics, documentary expressions should not be limited to rational or rhetoric argumentation.

To process the holistic view of life and death, one should search for emotions and feelings that both prompt the documentary-making and result from the viewing of the documentary. He claims that to widen our understanding of realities, documentaries need to find ways to 'move the viewer in such a way as to also address their spiritual and transcendental reality'. Knudsen claims that we are less dominated by our intellect than by our embodied emotions, and thus, the transcendental in documentaries should be searched through emotional stimuli (Knudsen 2008, 8–12, quote from 10). This argumentation shows the potential of first-person approach, where the viewer is invited to be the first-person whose first task is to experience the argumentation, not to evaluate its factual validity.

The reception of *Die Weisse Arche* recognises the transcendental potential of the film. According to Rolf Breiner, a film critic, Beeler combines human experience and knowledge about death with sublime images of mountains and monastic life. These images grant the documentary grandeur and represent dying as a transition to another dimension (Breiner 2016). Breiner's words translate the viewing into a transcendental experience. The viewer is encouraged to experience the sense of awe and spirituality that the filmed subjects are living with, whereby spiritual argumentation transforms into a spiritual experience that can become subjective knowledge for the viewer as well.

Knudsen finds that 'transcendental realism' in documentaries involves inaction and stillness (instead of dramatic events), which encourage the viewers to internalise the themes and engage with their inner thoughts and emotions. The transcendental is further created by reducing rational reasoning and scientific explanation while giving mystical experiences a central role. The documentaries should therefore try to reach beyond the material world to immaterial or existential questions, and by doing so, 'transcend attachment to the physical world' (Knudsen 2008, 13–22). The documentaries could thus distance themselves from trying to make sense of the world, and pay attention to what moves the viewer, as the focus on emotions and the mystical allows transcendental ways of knowing.

Die Weisse Arche utilises many of these expressive options. The daily activities do not build on any dramatic turn of events but rather on quiet moments of walking in nature, being present for the dying people, participating in religious rituals, and, for example, baking an apple pie. These scenes are edited to intertwine with images of nature, particularly the spectacular images of the Alps, or snow falling quietly on a monastery. Anna Elsner argues that the documentary's natural and grand landscapes support the film's spiritual argumentation that death is beyond any scientific understanding. In addition, the aesthetic use of landscape and the accompanying sounds of instrumental music and chanting familiar from the Catholic tradition gain a spiritual role in themselves, because they construct a transcendental experience for the viewer and 'reinforce the sense of indomitability' (Elsner 2020, 3–5, quote from 5).

A shot with Alfons the cattle herder emphasises the transcendental testimony of nature imagery. Previously, Alfons has told he left his Carthusian community, because he found that his inner voice and divine nature connection resonated better with his illness. What follows is sixty-eight seconds of a long-shot. The shot starts with tranquillity and focuses on a majestic wintery scene, where Alfons wades slowly through the snow (Figure 4.1).

Alfons appears a small figure amid the mountains. Quiet instrumental music adds a few chords to the shot before Alfons's calm and soft voiceover describes:

> For me, there is no spirituality without the relationship with earth. And there's no bread of life without earth. And of course, there is no earth, and no growth on earth without heaven, without everything surrounding this earth, surrounding this table. The earth as a table. For me, earth is a table. (Beeler 2016)

Alfons's voice fades away, and by the end of the shot, he has waded through the image. This single shot from the documentary emphasises the transcendental connection that Alfons experiences between earth and heaven, and between life and death. The aesthetics of the image creates the same sense of connection with nature, and a sense of the majesty of nature for the viewer. In her analysis of the film, Elsner connects *Die Weisse Arche*'s sense of transcendence as an alternative to the disillusionment produced by secularisation and modernisation. While disillusionment, or disenchantment, can lead to a sense

Figure 4.1 A wintery landscape and Alfons in *Die Weisse Arche* (Beeler 2016).

of alienation from the natural world and its mysteries, the transcendental images enable the revival of enchantment (Elsner 2020, 3). *Die Weisse Arche* does not lecture about spirituality, but invites the viewer to experience spirituality and form first-person testimony about it. In other words, while the film is a testimony to spiritual knowledge and the filmed subjects testify to the meaningfulness of death awareness, the viewer can embody spiritual testimony through affective witnessing.

As part of her argument, Elsner refers to Jane Bennett's discussion on enchantment. Bennett (2001, 4) defines this experience as '[t]o be enchanted is to be struck and shaken by the extraordinary that lives amid the familiar and the everyday'. Enchantment appears as another way to describe a transcendental experience, but Bennett's argument gains significance through its connection to ethical thinking. For Bennett, a sense of enchantment is crucial to ethical experiences. She emphasises that ethics should not be seen as an obligation to do something, but as affective aspirations, as a capability to be moved, surprised and challenged through experience (Bennett 2001, 3–4). This view resonates with the phenomenological discussions within cinema studies about ethical experience, which reaches beyond rational evaluation towards utilising the viewer's affective and embodied reactions to filmed materials. Jane Stadler (2008, 2), for example, argues that at best, films have an afterlife, or in other words, 'influence what remains with us when we are affected by the sensory impacts of the films, captivated by story, character, and conflict, and left wondering about the issues they raise'. When the viewer is left wondering, transformations in thinking and experiencing may emerge. Thus, embodied and affective cinematic experiences can create ethical space to encounter new ideas, to search for potential realities and to understand others' experiences. These can nurture care, compassion and responsibility towards others (Raviv 2021, 2, 7; Stadler 2008, 6, 38). Thus, the transcendental way of knowing in documentary films have similarities with ethical experiences.

The way in which *Die Weisse Arche* creates enchantment through sublime aesthetics together with the filmed subject's embodied spiritual knowledge also creates potential for a transcendental and ethical experience. Here, the viewer can construct first-person knowledge about spiritual aspects of death and dying. Instead of suggesting a universal or an objective 'truth', the film suggests that there are empowering aspects in subjective knowledge. The documentary questions the exact limits between life and death. These people, the nurse with a near-death experience, the healer/mystic who banishes ghosts, and the Catholic monks, are united in their conviction that there is an afterlife, a continuation of consciousness. According to their transcendental testimony, there is no need to fear death as an end.

Conclusion

Spiritual end-of-life documentaries argue that death is a more complex question than scientific understanding allows room for. Death is also a source for existential and transcendental questions and experiences. These films highlight death acceptance narratives, and they do so by providing teachable interviews and moments for the viewer. In their desire to expose or reveal the benefits of spirituality, these documentaries portray death as a meaningful part of life, and by acknowledging this, one can focus on living and experience less death anxiety. These documentaries do not discuss how death should (or should not) be approached from a medical perspective or how dying should be cared for, but they focus on how making death meaningful could add quality to everyone's lives.

Spiritual end-of-life documentaries tend to explore their topic with the help of people who deal with death and dying in their professional lives. These films prioritise expertise and institutional views on spiritual aspects of death and dying. However, the ways in which this knowledge is built vary. To build a more factual validation of the benefits of spiritual care, some documentaries, such as *Solace: Wisdom of the Dying*, *Lessons for the Living* and *For One More Moment* use the discursive knowledge of experts teaching and transforming their knowledge for the viewer. Other films, such as *Living Your Dying*, use expert knowledge and testimonial images to build a second-person aspect where truth can become existentially known. And *Die Weisse Arche* invites the viewer to build first-person testimony by providing transcendental experiences.

In all these approaches, we can recognise different epistemological paths to how we can know about the world. Both third- and second-person approaches want to validate spiritual knowledge by presenting it educationally through discursive testimonial evidence. Their approach conforms with the traditions of early modern western philosophy. These philosophical discussions have framed subjective knowledge as a secondary, and potentially a misleading, way of knowing. Empirical knowledge is the primary way of knowing because it can be detected in the physical and empirical world (Bolton 2022). Thus, when spiritual knowledge is represented as part of something that professionals have empirically gained and observed, this knowledge gains cultural and societal validation. It should therefore be given a position equal to that of medical knowledge in western countries' understanding about death. And consequently, the subjective way of knowing would limit spirituality to the sphere of belief.

However, when these goals of emphasising the spiritual aspects of death are brought to documentary-making, the roles of both subjective and empirical ways of knowing turn around. The subjective approach of *Die Weisse Arche* invites the viewer to experience the argumentation in first-person. In this process, the viewers become witnesses of others' experiences and can create their own empirical views on the topic. In comparison, universal argumentation about spirituality makes the viewer dependent on the experts' views, and the viewers need to evaluate whether their knowledge appears as trustworthy or too subjective and conditional. As such, in the documentary context, the transcendental testimonies can offer subjective and affective, yet empirical, ways of knowing, and this internalised mode can provide an ethical space to explore the mysteries of death and life.

References

Adair, Camille. 2008. *Solace: Wisdom of the Dying*. Documentary. Point of Light Productions.

———/Sacredigm Alliances, Llc. n.d. 'About | Meet Camille'. Camille Adair. https://camilleadair.com/camille/. Last accessed 4 January 2022.

Baker, Robert. 1994. 'If Looks Could Kill and Words Could Heal'. *Skeptical Inquirer, A Skeptic's Notebook*, 4 (3). https://skepticalinquirer.org/newsletter/if-looks-could-kill-and-words-could-heal/. Last accessed 27 June 2023.

Baugher, John Eric. 2008. 'Facing Death: Buddhist and Western Hospice Approaches'. *Symbolic Interaction* 31 (3): 259–84. https://doi.org/10.1525/si.2008.31.3.259.

Beeler, Edwin. 2016. *Die Weisse Arche*. Documentary. Calypso Film AG.

Bennett, Jane. 2001. *The Enchantment of Modern Life: Attachments, Crossings, and Ethics*. Princeton, NJ: Princeton University Press.

Biasio, Fabian. 2017. 'Die Weisse Arche: Interview Mit Filmemacher Edwin Beeler'. Letzte Reise. 17 January 2017. https://geschichten.letztereise.ch/beitraege/2017/die-weisse-arche/index.html. Last accessed 12 December 2022.

Bolton, Martha. 2022. 'Primary and Secondary Qualities in Early Modern Philosophy'. In *The Stanford Encyclopedia of Philosophy*, edited by Edward N. Zalta and Uri Nodelman. Stanford, CA: Metaphysics Research Lab, Stanford University. https://plato.stanford.edu/archives/fall2022/entries/qualities-prim-sec/.

Bovero, A., P. Leombruni, M. Miniotti, G. Rocca, and R. Torta. 2016. 'Spirituality, Quality of Life, Psychological Adjustment in Terminal Cancer Patients in Hospice'. *European Journal of Cancer Care* 25 (6): 961–9. https://doi.org/10.1111/ecc.12360.

Braga, Joseph L., and Laurie D. Braga. 1975. 'Foreword'. In *Death: The Final Stage of Growth*, edited by Elisabeth Kübler-Ross, i–xiii. New York: Touchstone.

Breiner, Rolf. 2016. 'Dem Tode ganz nah'. Cineman. 2 July 2016. https://www.cineman.ch/movie/2016/DieWeisseArche/review.html. Last accessed 12 December 2022.

Brown, Candy Gunther. 2020. 'Tibetan Singing Bowls – Los Cuencos Cantores Tibetanos'. *American Religion* 1 (2): 52–73. https://doi.org/10.2979/amerreli.1.2.03.

Bruce, Anne, and Betty Davies. 2005. 'Mindfulness in Hospice Care: Practicing Meditation-in-Action'. *Qualitative Health Research* 15 (10): 1329–44. https://doi.org/10.1177/1049732305281657.

Brylla, Catalin, and Mette Kramer. 2018. 'A Pragmatic Framework for the Cognitive Study of Documentary'. *Projections* 12 (2): 159–80. https://doi.org/10.3167/proj.2018.120216.

Dossey, Larry. 1993. *Healing Words: The Power of Prayer and the Practice of Medicine*. San Francisco, CA: HarperSanFrancisco.

Elsner, Anna Magdalena. 2020. 'Landscapes of Care and the Enchantment of Dying in Edwin Beeler's *Die Weisse Arche* (2016)'. *Studies in Documentary Film* 14 (2): 147–60. https://doi.org/10.1080/17503280.2020.1725994.

Ferrell, Betty R. 2017. 'Spiritual Care in Hospice and Palliative Care'. *The Korean Journal of Hospice and Palliative Care* 20 (4): 215–20. https://doi.org/10.14475/kjhpc.2017.20.4.215.

Grierson, John. 1966. *Grierson on Documentary*, edited by Forsyth Hardy. Berkeley; Los Angeles: University of California Press.

Halifax, Joan. 2009. *Being with Dying: Cultivating Compassion and Fearlessness in the Presence of Death*. Boston, MA: Shambhala Publications, Inc.

Henderson, Lily. 2010. *Lessons for the Living*. Documentary. ThinPlace Pictures.

———. 2019. Personal interview by Outi Hakola.

Johns, Christopher. 2004. *Being Mindful, Easing Suffering: Reflections on Palliative Care*. London; New York: J. Kingsley Publishers.

Kates, Jeannette. 2020. 'Self-Reported Fears by Hospice Patients at the End of Life'. *Innovation in Aging* 4 (Suppl. 1): 246–7. https://doi.org/10.1093/geroni/igaa057.795.

Kierkegaard, Søren Aabye. 1991. *Practice in Christianity: Kierkegaard's Writings, Vol. 20*. First published 1850. Princeton, NJ: Princeton University Press.

Knudsen, Erik. 2008. 'Transcendental Realism in Documentary'. In *Rethinking the Documentary: New Perspectives, New Practices*, edited by W. De Jong and T. R. Austin, 108–20. Berkshire; New York: Open University Press. https://eprints.bourne mouth.ac.uk/21857/.

Krämer, Sybille. 2016. 'Truth in Testimony: Or Can a Documentary Film "Bear Witness"? Some Reflections on the Difference between Discursive and Existential Truth'. In *In the Beginning Was the Image: The Omnipresence of Pictures*, edited by András Benedek and Ágnes Veszelszki, 29–40. Frankfurt am Main: Peter Lang AG. https://www.jstor.org/stable/j.ctv2t4cns.5.

Kübler-Ross, Elisabeth. 1975. *Death: The Final Stage of Growth*. New York: Touchstone.

———. 2009. *On Death and Dying: What the Dying Have to Teach Doctors, Nurses, Clergy and Their Own Families*. London: Routledge.

Kuusela, Matti. 2017. '23-vuotias Jenny Timonen esitti vaikean kysymyksen äitinsä kuolinvuoteen äärellä – Hoitajan rohkea vastaus sai hänet tarttumaan vaikeaan aiheeseen'. *Aamulehti*, 12 October 2017. https://www.aamulehti.fi/kulttuuri/art-2000007276575.html. Last accessed 8 December 2022.

Lee, Jihyun, Kwan Hoon Kim, Craig S. Webster, and Marcus A. Henning. 2021. 'The Evolution of Mindfulness from 1916 to 2019'. *Mindfulness* 12 (8): 1849–59. https://doi.org/10.1007/s12671-021-01603-x.

McCabe, Marilyn. 2003. *The Paradox of Loss: Toward a Relational Theory of Grief*. Westport, CT: Praeger.

Mcgrath, Pam. 1998. 'Buddhist Spirituality—a Compassionate Perspective on Hospice Care'. *Mortality* 3 (3): 251–63. https://doi.org/10.1080/713685956.

Martin-Stone, Karen. 2013. 'The Ethics of Television Archaeology.' In *World Archaeological Congress (WAC7)*. Jordan.

Merriam-Webster. n.d. 'Knowledge'. In *Merriam-Webster.com Dictionary*. https://www.merriam-webster.com/dictionary/knowledge. Last accessed 27 June 2023.

———. n.d. 'Testimony'. In *Merriam-Webster.com Dictionary*. https://www.merriam-webster.com/dictionary/testimony. Last accessed 27 June 2023.

Nichols, Bill. 2016. *Speaking Truths with Film: Evidence, Ethics, Politics in Documentary*. Oakland: University of California Press. https://www.jstor.org/stable/10.1525/j.ctv1wxtcp.

———. 2017. *Introduction to Documentary, Third Edition*. Bloomington: Indiana University Press.

Pennybacker, Robert. 2003. *Living Your Dying*. Documentary. Lotus Film Productions.

Raviv, Orna. 2021. *Ethics of Cinematic Experience: Screens of Alterity*. New York: Routledge.

Roberts, John. 1995. 'Healing Words: The Power of Prayer and the Practice of Medicine'. *BMJ* 311 (7013): 1174. https://doi.org/10.1136/bmj.311.7013.1174.

Savola, Pauliina. 2019. 'Vielä pienen hetken vierelläsi, arvostelu'. Film-O-Holic.com. 8 February 2019. http://www.film-o-holic.com/dvd-arvostelut/viela-pienen-hetken-vierellasi/. Last accessed 8 December 2022.

Sitar, Dana. 2012. 'What Is the SOLACE Project? – An Interview with Camille Adair'. *SevenPonds* (blog). 4 August 2012. https://blog.sevenponds.com/professional-advice/an-interview-with-camille-adair. Last accessed 11 January 2022.

Stadler, Jane. 2008. *Pulling Focus: Intersubjective Experience, Narrative Film, and Ethics*. New York: Continuum.

Stanhope, Jessica, and Philip Weinstein. 2020. 'The Human Health Effects of Singing Bowls: A Systematic Review'. *Complementary Therapies in Medicine* 51 (June): 102412. https://doi.org/10.1016/j.ctim.2020.102412.

Stephenson, Pamela L., Claire B. Draucker, and Donna S. Martsolf. 2003. 'The Experience of Spirituality in the Lives of Hospice Patients'. *Journal of Hospice & Palliative Nursing* 5 (1): 51–8.

Tasaka, David. 2014. '"Light, Love and Wisdom" Live On'. Mits Aoki Legacy Foundation. 6 December 2014. https://mitsaoki.com/. Last accessed 13 January 2022.

Timonen, Jenny. 2017. *For One More Moment* (*Vielä Pienen Hetken Vierelläsi*). Documentary, Short. Elokuvapalvelu J. Suomalainen.

Wells, Justin. 2018. *How to Film Truth: The Story of Documentary Film as a Spiritual Journey*. Eugene: Cascade Books.

5. ADVOCACY DOCUMENTARIES
Investigating the Legalisation of Assisted Dying

End Credits (Decommere 2013), a Belgian documentary on assisted dying, opens with a scene from Frans Buyens's autobiographical film *Less Dead than the Others* (1992). The featured scene portrays Irma before her assisted death. She smiles sweetly, declares that her time has come and thanks the man holding her hands. In *End Credits*, twenty years later, Frank Buyens's life partner recalls how the film influenced the debates on assisted dying in Belgium, and how Buyens, similarly to this scene, mumbled his own thank you at the moment of his assisted death. In *Fatal Flaws: Legalising Assisted Death* (2018), another documentary on assisted dying, a Dutch journalist complains to Canadian filmmaker Kevin Dunn that several new documentaries portray euthanasia in a favourable light. Dunn asks another journalist if this is propaganda, and gets a decidedly affirmative answer. Both documentaries recognise and acknowledge the influence that cinematic narratives have on public debates about assisted dying.

Consequently, many assisted dying documentaries follow advocacy practices. Advocacy documentaries play a role in civil society by using strategic communication to engage the viewer in civic participation, to promote a certain perspective and to mobilise action (Aufderheide 2008). Advocacy films openly embrace their drive for social change and push the boundaries of social issue documentaries. Diana Barrett and Sheila Leddy categorise the potential impact of advocacy documentaries and recognise that films can aim for (1) individual responses to the film, (2) public awareness on issue, (3) public engagement

91

that mobilises audiences, (4) social movement that mobilises groups of people to commit to campaigning, and (5) social change that provides long-term change, such as policy or legislative changes (Barrett and Leddy 2008, 16–19). Documentaries on assisted dying tend to aim higher than raising awareness. Often they openly desire to influence legislative issues related to end of life. Documentaries provide accessible narratives on the issues, and as Nina Zeldis (2005, 131–3) argues, they take assisted dying debates outside courtrooms by adding the appeal of personal stories to legal debates.

Documentaries about assisted dying have been popular in the twenty-first century when the legal aspects of assisted dying have been in flux in western countries. While most western countries allow some form of passive euthanasia (refusal or withdrawal of treatment and life support), active euthanasia remains illegal in most places. These laws, however, are under debate, and an increasing number of countries and areas have legalised some form of assisted dying over the past twenty to twenty-five years. Switzerland does not criminalise supplying means for suicide, and non-profit organisations have since the 1980s helped those wanting to end their lives. Oregon, a state in the north-west of the United States, started assisted dying practices in 1997, and other states have slowly started to follow its lead: Washington (2008), Montana (2009), Vermont (2013), California (2016), Colorado (2016), District of Columbia (2017), New Jersey (2019), Hawaii (2019), Maine (2020) and New Mexico (2021). In Europe, assisted dying is legal in the Netherlands (2001), Belgium (2002), Luxembourg (2009) and Spain (2021). Canada legalised assisted dying in 2016, Australian states and territories passed legislation between 2017 and 2022, and New Zealand changed its laws in 2021. Several documentary films have been dedicated to the debates related to these changes in attitudes and legislation.

Jan Grue (2022, 2) argues that documentaries on assisted dying participate in creating these changes. He explains the processes with the Foucauldian concept of biopolitics. Biopolitics describes the processes where a state's power intersects with body management, such as reproductive practices and health management (Foucault 1990, 133–59). In the context of death, biopolitics often functions in a negative context. For example, the term necropolitics coined by Achille Mbembe (2019) refers to the state's authoritative use of power in causing death through war and capital punishments or by exploiting natural resources. Grue argues that a state's politics could also approach death in a positive, productive and collaborative manner. In the positive 'thanatopolitics', a term borrowed from S. J. Murray (2018, 718–19), the state could aim to ensure a good or meaningful death for its citizens (Grue 2022, 4–6). The biopolitics of death, indeed, revolves around society's understanding of a 'good death'. For some, it refers to the so-called natural death supported by comfort care. For others, 'good death' refers to the ability to control the manner and time of one's own death. In the documentaries, this tension transforms into a debate over the ethics of the state's normative death-related biopolitics. The documentaries often serve assisted dying as a moral dilemma that needs to be investigated. Daniel Shaw (2012, 2) argues that the cinema tends to explore ethical concepts, exemplify ethical theories and thought experiments or discuss various perspectives on moral issues, such as assisted dying. In documentary films, similarly, the filmmakers investigate this controversial topic, and the viewer is given the position of a critical evaluator, and consequently, the role of an active agent in the processes of social change.

In this chapter, I analyse the ways in which the documentary films participate in the biopolitics of death. I will start by briefly reviewing the expository approach of the documentaries on assisted dying, and will then move on to study three independent documentary films. I analyse the above-mentioned Belgian documentary *End Credits* (Decommere 2013), which takes an evaluative stance on existing practices of assisted death. I will then discuss the other film mentioned above, the Canadian documentary *Fatal Flaws: Legalising Assisted Death* (Dunn 2018), where the filmmaker Kevin Dunn visits the Netherlands, Belgium, the United States and Canada to discuss the problematic aspects of legalising assisted dying, and an Australian documentary, *Fade to Black* (Ervine 2017), which supports the right-to-die campaign in Victoria, Australia. My analysis shows that these documentaries have different understandings of the relationship between the state and the individual. The films that are critical on the issue advocate the state's responsibility to protect (vulnerable) citizens, whereas documentaries favouring the legalisation emphasise the individual's right to choose. These two perspectives relate to different ethical principles about right and wrong. Supporting human rights and avoidance of causing harm are both considered ethical acts (Velasquez et al. 2010), but in the documentaries about assisted dying, they are often contradicted. The opponents of assisted dying consider death assistance to be an unethical practice because it harms human lives, whereas advocates for the legalisation frame assisted dying as an ethical issue of human rights.

Investigative and Evaluative Approaches

Media stories on assisted dying, in general, use social, cultural and political power in generating and guiding the public discussions (Winnington 2021, 177; Grue 2022, 2, 6–7; Booth and Blake 2022, 107; Johnstone 2013). Several studies show that media coverage on assisted dying has been unbalanced and has favoured the legalisation arguments in the twenty-first century (Johnstone 2013; Kis-Rigo et al. 2021; Booth and Blake 2022, 110–12). In the case of documentary films, Peter Saunders (2022, 11) explains the bias with the media tendency to prioritise 'new' topics and social change stories. He accuses the BBC of failing as a public broadcaster to represent a proper cross-examination of assisted dying and for focusing on documentaries that portray assisted dying in a positive light (Saunders 2011, 244–50). These kinds of positive portrayals, Megan-Jane Johnstone (2013) argues, normalise assisted dying and, consequently, shift the public opinion.

Television documentaries, particularly, explore the topic through the international legalisation context. Film crews travel to countries where assisted dying is legal to investigate their practices. For example, in *Live and Let Die* (SBS Australia 2002), the film crew heads to the Netherlands to find out 'why the Dutch tolerate euthanasia', while in *Choosing Death* (Fellows 2018), an episode in the BBC documentary series *Altered States*, Louis Theroux travels to the United States to meet with people preparing for assisted dying. One of the most popular destinations is Switzerland, where a non-citizen can receive death assistance; Frontline documentary *The Suicide Tourist* (Zaritsky 2010) follows a Chicago native to clinic in Switzerland. Swiss assisted death practitioners are interviewed in several documentaries. For example, Dr Erika Preisig, president of Lifecircle, an organisation for assisted suicide, appears in such documentaries as *Terry Pratchett: Choosing to Die* (C. Russell 2011), *Final Exit* (2014) and *The Good Death* (Krupa 2018). Travelling allows the documentary makers to research the practices of assisted dying, including the acceptance process, use of lethal drugs, and the environments where deaths take place. For example, the French documentary *Dignitas – la mort sur ordonnance* (Menoud 2010) and the (Swedish-language) Finnish documentary series *Med rätt att dö* (Svarvar and Holmberg 2020) explore how assisted dying works as a practice and as an industry. The documentary crews talk with physicians, representatives of advocacy groups, lawyers, politicians and researchers. Such institutional and authoritative perspectives turn the focus towards rational argumentation related to both critical and positive aspects of assisted dying.

It is difficult unequivocally to define whether assisted dying is treated negatively or positively in the television documentaries, although the latter appears to be more common. The inclusion of personal stories of those seeking assisted dying creates understanding towards their decisions, and many of these protagonists want to act as examples and contribute to the legalisation of assisted dying in their home countries. For example, the Australian television documentary *My Own Choice* (Jackson 2013) introduces 35-year-old Jay who is severely, but not terminally, ill. He campaigns publicly, not only to change Australian laws, but to raise funds to travel to Switzerland for assisted dying. Similarly, in *Allow Me to Die* (Mason and Weitenberg 2015), an Australian journalist explores how assisted dying functions in Belgium, and alongside with physicians and politicians, two patients, Peter and Simona have an important role. These patients represent the individual need and desire for assisted dying, while the authorities voice both negative and positive aspects of death assistance. Once again, embodied personal stories place a strong emphasis on feelings and seem to add emotive persuasion to what is otherwise presented as rational argumentation for and against assisted dying.

The investigative approach encourages the viewer to cognitively evaluate the credibility and reliability of the claims that these documentaries create. The theories of reception of documentary film emphasise that the viewers have responsibility to use their earlier knowledge to evaluate whether a documentary's content seems reliable. Yet, how the issues are represented and argued for the viewers influences their evaluation and interpretation (Eitzen 2007, 185; Austin 2012; Nichols 2017, 33; Brylla and Kramer 2018). Carl Plantinga (2013, 44–5), for example, argues that the viewers trust the content if they can assume that the filmmakers are handling the topic with respect. This respect, however, does not translate into objectivity or a neutral perspective; instead the creative non-fiction storytelling provides viewpoints that can help the viewer to understand life and people (Borum Chattoo 2020, 15). Thus, the viewing experience is influenced by the need to evaluate both the reliability of the content and the ethical practices related to its representation.

The Belgian film *End Credits* (Decommere 2013) engages the viewer to evaluate the moral complexity of assisted dying. The film, released ten years after the legalisation of assisted dying in Belgium, aims to study those aspects of the law that have remained questioned. To do this, the film director Alexander Decommere introduces two ethically challenging cases. First, the filmmaker follows 83-year-old Adelin's life in a care facility. Adelin has dementia and years ago, before he became ill, filed for assisted dying in case he would no longer be himself. In the care facility, Adelin tells the nurses that it is difficult to find meaning in life, and he occasionally repeats his plea for help to die. However, when discussing this request with his physician, Adelin gets angry and offended and accuses the doctor of wanting to get rid of him. One of the nurses admits to the camera that Adelin's changing moods are disturbing. While the staff want to support Adelin's choice, his memory problems make it difficult to know whether his choice is still the same as it was when he was healthy.

The second case introduces Eva and her physician. In an interview, Eva faces the camera calmly and explains that she suffers from psychiatric issues and that nothing has helped her suffering. Thus, she seeks assisted dying as a young person. Eva wishes to donate her organs, because helping others would give meaning to her otherwise miserable life. The physician supports her wishes, and after evaluation, Eva's request is accepted. Yet, Eva's own hospital cannot benefit from her death, and they need to seek approval from another hospital to receive Eva's organ donation. The receiving hospital's ethical committee, however, rejects Eva's request for assisted dying and suggests further treatment options.

These two introductory sequences pose dementia and mental health as morally problematic cases of assisted dying. Both stories view death assistance as a situational and a societal question. According to C. H. Whiteley (2022, 21–5), 'moral' as a concept has two sides: a sociological aspect that refers to communal moral beliefs and a psychological side that refers to the inner morality of person. In advocacy documentaries, the two aspects intertwine. The shared moral values guide what kind of choices are available for the individual, and individual cases require society and its institutions to evaluate their normative practices. In *End Credits* the viewer is invited to participate in the evaluation of these practices, along with various professionals. After introducing these cases, the filmmaker adds another evaluative level to the narration. He shows the filmed material, for example, to professors of ethical medicine and medical law, psychiatrists and members of ethical committees. The specialists are shown to watch the same footage that viewer has just seen on Decommere's laptop before offering their evaluation of the cases.

In Eva's case, most professionals argue that she conveys her desires clearly and she should be granted permission for assisted dying. They argue that the new committee should not intervene with the decision made by another committee. One enraged expert blames the other hospital for undermining Eva's autonomy. Few question Eva's young age, and only one professional claims that if even one ethical committee sees problems in this case, 'we as a society should accept' their decision. Here, the majority defend individual choice, and the minority vote for society's responsibility to protect its citizens. In Adelin's case, most experts hesitate to follow through with an assisted death. The debate focuses on whether Adelin is the same person as before, and whether we should honour his earlier wishes or respect the person he has become and, thus, refrain from hastening death. The memory problems suggest that Adelin's autonomous subjectivity and capability to make choices are compromised. Whereas the views vary on his current capability to make rational choices, most of the professionals would follow the guideline of 'when in doubt, we should do nothing'.

These varied professional viewpoints serve to emphasise the complexity of evaluation of ethical principles related to assisted dying. The viewers have been able to first evaluate the cases based on their values about what is right and wrong, and then, experts provide additional ethical argumentation into the mix. Finally, the filmmaker reveals how Adelin's and Eva's cases are resolved. Eva opts out of organ donation in favour of keeping her date for assisted dying. The filmmaker witnesses Eva's final moments, when she settles on the couch and the physician administers the medication. The doctor watches over Eva when she turns sleepy, starts to breathe heavily and finally stops breathing.

Her death is quick, peaceful and takes place in the comfort of her own home. In Adelin's case, the physician decides on comfort care instead of assisted death. Adelin quickly becomes fragile and his breathing turns laboured. The care facility invites people to join Adelin during his last moments, and while his death takes long and is physically demanding, he is surrounded by those who love and support him.

According to Jennifer Malkowski, both these cinematic deaths could come under the modern category of a 'good death', because the representations offer customised and unique deaths which continue their lifestyles and life stories. Consequently, a good death also becomes a personal responsibility that is constructed through action, such as making an active choice about end of life. At the same time, individualism allows distance between the dying person and the viewer because uniqueness promises that your death will be different. Therefore you do not need to care so deeply (Malkowski 2017, 73–86, 104). Grue, similarly, argues that documentary portrayals of assisted death frame death as someone else's rational choice, and as such, the death of others escapes identification and invites evaluative practices (Grue 2022, 17–18). As such, while *End Credits* offers two death scenes, these scenes become part of an investigative approach where the viewer can evaluate the consequences of Eva's and Adelin's choices.

Neither of the cases offers an absolute answer to when assisted dying should be permitted. Instead, both cases encourage the viewer to participate in ethical evaluation of whether the vulnerable person should be protected or whether they have agency to make an informed choice. These debates have often been seen as relating to neoliberalism. Neoliberalism is a controversial and incoherent term, which often refers to extending the use of competitive market logic in all areas of life, including subject making (Springer, Birch, and MacLeavy 2016, 1–3). Liz Bondi (2005, 499), for example, argues that a neoliberal subject is 'an autonomous, individualized, self-directing, decision-making agent at the heart of policy-making'. Grue contends that neoliberalism also explains recent changes in end-of-life biopolitics. In neoliberal states, death becomes freely chosen, an individual's rational decision allowed by the state (Grue 2022, 4–5, 8). Consequently, public debates on assisted dying revolve around such themes as individual autonomy, choice and rights, which are contrasted to society's duty to protect vulnerable people and the sanctity of human life (Inthorn 2017, 159–64; Rawlings et al. 2023, 8–13; van Wijngaarden and Sanders 2022; Burlone 2020; Booth and Blake 2022, 110–15). Thus, the debate over the morality of assisted dying is also a debate over modern subjectivity and responsibility.

Amanda Booth and Denise Blake (2022), for example, argue that in the New Zealand media stories on assisted dying, the subject could take a position of 'my choice', or they could recognise the vulnerability of disabled and elderly people. In the first case, the (neoliberal) subject is loaded with positive terms, such as autonomy and individuality. In the second case, neoliberalism is seen as a dangerous choice for society because it makes it difficult to protect vulnerable people. These discourses, according to Booth and Blake, also create different stories of protection. In the first case, the focus is on protecting the human rights of an autonomous individual, while in the second case, society or individuals with a moral sense protect those who cannot protect themselves (Booth and Blake 2022, 110–15). *End Credits* repeats both these narratives where Eva is seen as autonomous decision-maker and Adelin is a vulnerable person needing protection. From these two positions, the film asks the viewer to evaluate how far we can take being respectful of individual choices while also being responsible for the decisions to administer lethal drugs.

PROTECTING THE VULNERABLE

The Canadian film *Fatal Flaws*, unlike *End Credits*, openly celebrates its advocacy function, while still using a similar evaluative and investigative style. It is produced in association with the North American advocate organisation The Euthanasia Prevention Coalition that aims 'to preserve and enforce legal prohibitions and ethical guidelines prohibiting "mercy killing"' (Euthanasia Prevention Coalition n.d.). In Canada, assisted suicide was legalised for terminally ill adults in 2016. The film was released in 2018, when the discussions to extend the law were underway. In 2021, Canadian legislation was amended to allow assisted dying in more varied situations. *Fatal Flaws* appears as a counter-argument to such demands, and the context explains the documentary's focus on the dangers of the 'slippery slope', the theory that argues that if assisted dying is accepted in any form, it inevitably leads to killing the citizens who have become a burden on society. On the film's website, director Kevin Dunn writes that 'it's impossible to ignore the cultural shift in attitude towards euthanasia and assisted suicide. What was once considered murder under the law is now being accepted as medical "treatment" in many countries' (Dunn 2017). To investigate these dangers, the filmmaker visits the Netherlands, Belgium and the United States to study the undesirable consequences of legalisation processes.

The documentary is a collection of interviews framed by Dunn's voiceover and questions. He interviews people on both sides of the argument, yet his style creates a narrative of 'us' versus 'them'. For example, his voiceover opens the film:

> They call it with a lot of different things. Death with Dignity, Doctor Assisted Death, medical aid in dying. Those are all pretty turns of the phrase. [...] The ugly truth is we are talking about giving doctors the legal right to kill their patients. (Dunn 2018)

Here, Dunn positions those supporting assisted dying as 'them', whereas 'we' are the critical voices who have a moral duty to oppose assisted dying.

Repeatedly, Dunn declares a need to protect the vulnerable, particularly those who are elderly, who have memory issues, who are depressed, disabled or young. These are the people, he argues, that will be collateral damage in the slippery-slope practices of assisted dying. Dunn accompanies the slippery-slope argument with strong emotional reactions that add a sense of threat to the narration. In these contexts, Dunn uses the first-person 'I' narration. For example, when discussing the expansion in the Netherlands to include those suffering from psychiatric and existential suffering to assisted dying practices, Dunn responds with a personal statement that it scares him.

Personal testimonials also have their expository role in the narration. These are stories of vulnerable people, such as disabled and elderly people, to whom assisted dying was offered as a humane treatment option. In almost all these cases, a family member speaks for the vulnerable person needing protection from ill-advised healthcare personnel. A mother talks about being asked to consider assisted suicide for her disabled daughter who was given no hope of recovery. The mother, sitting next to her daughter, is offended by the suggestion, and the recollection makes both of them cry. In another case, a daughter shares her story of having had to fight to get medical care for her elderly mother when the care staff were ready to give up. And a physician recalls convincing one of his cancer patients that there is something worth waiting for after the aggressive and invasive treatments. Years later, the patient thanked him for saving her life. These testimonials expose problems with healthcare and argue repeatedly that with proper care and protection, assisted dying is an unnecessary alternative.

While testimonials add emotional persuasion to the narration, the interviews with authorities and professionals take the main stage. By focusing on rhetorical arguments, *Fatal Flaws* takes cues from expository documentary mode, where argumentation builds with expert interviews, but from a certain perspective, including propagandist approach (Grierson 1966; Nichols 2017, 107–8). Particularly, Dunn makes use of evidentiary editing, where continuity is built not on the continuous use of time or place, but on the cohesion of argumentation or perspective (Nichols 2017, 121–3). For example, when Dunn asks a journalist whether this is propaganda, the viewer assumes that the question is related to the previous comment on documentary films' influence. Yet, the interviewees change between the shots making it unclear whether the person responds to the same claim or not. This type of presentation has raised ethical concerns. Kate Nash (2011, 227), for example, argues that due to their rhetorical structure, expository documents tend to speak 'on behalf of others, placing them within the documentary's argumentative structure'. As such, individual views may become secondary to the narrator's argument. Nichols goes as far as labelling expository films as using a 'Voice of God' commentary, where the film's narrator decides how the argumentation is presented (Nichols 2016, 75–6; 2017, 121–3).

Dunn uses the interviews as conveying a seemingly balanced debate. In the early scenes of the film, for example, he uses a split-screen scene where different authorities appear on-screen one after another. Each interview was filmed separately, but on the split-screen they appear to be talking at once and in relation to each other. Even when their voices are muted, the authorities' hand movements add a debating feel to the scenes. Dunn's voiceover explains the meaning of the split-screen: 'Proponents argue that people should have the right to choose the way they die. Critics say that choice is an illusion, and a recipe for elder abuse and coercion when people are at their most vulnerable' (Dunn 2018).

After setting the tone for debate, the documentary focuses on tearing down arguments that are often used in support of legalisation of assisted dying. Dunn introduces five main claims in title cards along the film. In all these, the viewer first sees the original argument before the text transforms into a counter-argument:

1. 'It's about choice' vs. 'It's *not* about choice'
2. 'It is about terminal illness' vs. 'It is *not* about terminal illness'
3. 'It's about suffering and pain' vs. 'It's *not* about suffering and pain'
4. 'It isn't suicide' vs. 'It *is* suicide'
5. 'This is caring' vs. 'This is *killing, not* caring' (Dunn 2018)

One of the key questions in *Fatal Flaws* is the potential abuse of assisted dying in healthcare. With the help of personal testimonials, Dunn raises fears that

Figure 5.1 Split-screen image of interviewed authorities in *Fatal Flaws* (Dunn 2018).

ADVOCACY DOCUMENTARIES

healthcare professionals will pressure vulnerable people who are a (financial) burden on society to agree to kill themselves. William, a paralysed professor, blames healthcare professionals for pressuring him to refuse treatment which is expensive and uncertain. These requests to consider alternatives for treatments undermine his value and make him feel that he is not treated with similar seriousness as other patients due to his disabilities. Similar concerns are voiced by advocacy groups that oppose assisted dying. They argue that politicians put pressure on doctors to learn how to kill their patients, instead of how to care for them. Dunn also meets with physicians who argue that they do not want to be put in a position where they are expected to harm their patients. These doctors see themselves as protectors of the vulnerable, as the last line of defence – and suspect that their profession in general will not be able to live up to these high moral standards.

Dunn uses this framing to censure the arguments of the advocacy group Death with Dignity. He has a long conversation with the group representative, who assures Dunn that the organisation wants assisted dying to take place in a legal and supervised context. The representative places responsibility on the physicians because their role involves ethical standards and professional integrity. If doctors are the ones to prescribe medication for assisted dying, it is better that they should consider their responsibilities in the evaluation of each individual case. The representative of Death and Dignity aims this argument to be reassuring – one cannot just ask for assisted dying and expect to be able to die tomorrow – but the doubts that Dunn presents on the ethical integrity of the profession eat away at this assertion.

When an individual might not be able to sustain their moral and ethical integrity, Dunn demands that the state's biopolitics should provide protective guidelines. A member of the Dutch parliament, for example, argues that the state has a responsibility to protect its citizens, including those who are medically or socially vulnerable. According to a researcher interviewed by Dunn, people who want to die because they are tired of life have given up hope of a better life and feel like a burden. From this, Dunn concludes that society fails those who need support, and with better support there would be no need for assisted dying. During his journey, the filmmaker meets Aurelia, a young woman with psychiatric problems who fights for her right to die. In his interview with Aurelia, Dunn argues that she seems happy enough, and finds it difficult to understand that she wants to die. After the interview, Dunn talks to the camera in the corner of the lobby. He looks directly at the camera and the viewer, and emotions fill his voice when he asks who has let her down. He blames society and the healthcare system for failing to take good care of the citizens.

Dunn also attacks the argument that assisted dying aims to relieve suffering. He argues that there are competent ways to eliminate pain and suffering, and even more importantly, according to a survey in Oregon, current pain and suffering are not decisive factors among those requesting assisted dying, which renders the premises for assisted dying false. The rational argumentation, supported by scientific evidence adds authority to Dunn's on-camera presence: he faces the camera, holds the viewer's gaze and explains things clearly and convincingly. Dunn also introduces further survey results which show that the biggest concerns for those opting for assisted death are loss of dignity, quality of life, ability to take care of oneself and controlling the circumstances of death. He therefore argues that people are afraid of potential future suffering, which could be avoided. However, Dunn omits to mention the rest of the survey results. According to these, a lack of social, financial and emotional support was not among the significant factors for requesting assisted dying (Ganzini, Goy, and Dobscha 2008). Fears about losing control over one's life might not be solved with a better support system.

Throughout the film, Dunn makes clear arguments that assisted dying can take advantage of those in a vulnerable position. They need to be protected, and the best protection is to refuse any form of assisted dying that can be misused to get rid of those who are not considered worthy of living. Dunn also places a heavy responsibility on society to take better care of its citizens, because better care and compassion could erase the need for assisted dying. At the end of the film, Dunn returns to Aurelia's story. In a video call, Aurelia is excited to introduce the drugs she was prescribed for assisted dying. During a walk in nature, which is a thinly veiled reference to the preference of natural death, Dunn describes begging Aurelia to choose differently – to no avail. While he does not know what Aurelia has gone through, he is convinced that there is always hope for a better tomorrow. He revisits his other testimonial stories to uphold the narrative of hope, support and protection. The mother is able to take care of her disabled, yet happy daughter at home. The grandmother lived for another year and met the newborn baby of the family. Dunn's own father survived cancer. There is always hope, Dunn maintains, and while life may seem difficult, it is not a reason to give up. Dunn finishes the story by demanding that is up to each of us to enable each other's lives in a way that we maintain hope and do not fear of being a burden.

Fatal Flaws, thus, considers that the fierce protecting of the vulnerable carries ethical practices. In this approach, the people are divided in three categories: the vulnerable who are victims and who cannot act on their own behalf, but need protection; the opponents, who are ill-advised in their attempts to relieve potential future suffering, or who immorally attempt to save resources; and the protectors who morally defend the vulnerable. The protectors, here, are often moral individuals, but preferably, the state should assume this role and create biopolitics that protects the lives of the citizens instead of judging which lives are worthy of living.

ADVOCACY DOCUMENTARIES

PROTECTING INDIVIDUAL RIGHTS

In comparison to *Fatal Flaws*, *Fade to Black* builds an alternative narrative of heroes and protectors. This documentary, directed by Jeremy Ervine, introduces Peter Short, a CEO, who after a cancer recurrence joins the campaign for legalising assisted dying in his home state of Victoria, the first Australian state to permit assisted dying. In this story, Peter gains the status of a hero for protecting and battling the right to choose one's own manner of dying. In an interview for the podcast *Euthanasia: Pro and Con*, Ervine argues that he wanted to represent both sides of the argument. Yet, the film started when Peter was looking for someone to help him spread the advocacy message. After meeting Peter, Ervine suggested that a documentary about his life and campaign would be more effective and interesting than any advertisement (J. N. Russell 2016). Through Peter, the documentary embraces an advocacy role, recognised by the organisation of Dying with Dignity. On their website, the advocacy organisation celebrates that the documentary 'sends a strong message to politicians that Australians care passionately about choice at end of life. With law reform now on the national agenda, the time is right for *Fade to Black* to be a powerful force for change' (Dying with Dignity 2017).

The documentary includes scenes of Peter's life, home and family as they struggle to cope with his terminal diagnosis. Some years earlier, Peter had been diagnosed with cancer, but the treatment had worked, and he went into remission. Peter says it felt amazing to get his life back. When the cancer returned, the prognosis was not as optimistic, and Peter got scared about pain and suffering that would follow. At first, he searched the web for effective ways to kill himself. However, after consideration, he decided to deal with the situation and joined a campaign that advocated for legalising assisted dying. While the personal aspects and family reactions give rhythm to the documentary, the main content focuses on the campaign. Ervine portrays Peter giving speeches at public events, talking to media outlets and reaching out to politicians. In the campaign, Peter embodies those terminally ill people whose lives would be affected by the bill. He gives voice to fears of suffering and pain and to the desire to die in a manner and time of his own choosing. He becomes an example of what Grue (2022, 10, 16) calls a cultural narrative of celebratory rhetoric, where death-seeking characters become the protagonists the viewer is expected to root for.

Ervine, however, introduces plenty of other voices from this campaign and from its counter-campaign, such as representatives of advocacy groups, physicians and Australian politicians. Both sides of the argument are thus represented, but Ervine's representation is the result of similar evidentiary editing that was used in *Fatal Flaws*. Selective use of scenes is emphasised in two longer sequences of political debate. First, Peter is invited to Canberra to

103

talk to select members from the House of Representatives at the Parliament House. Second, he is invited to a hearing with the senators. On both occasions, Ervine edits together scenes from the hearings and the expert interviews. The scenes from both hearings focus on the arguments of proposed legislation, as well as how the politicians challenge these views. The interview scenes deepen these perspectives, but also situate and comment on the arguments. Here, evidentiary editing favours the right-to-die campaign.

For example, as a part of these hearing sequences, the filmmaker introduces Margaret Tighe, a representative for Right to Life Australia. Tighe opposes the bill and often uses religious reasoning to support her arguments. Her main argument, however, is that palliative care proves that there are viable care options to assisted dying. The editing focuses on undermining Tighe's arguments, in a manner rather similar to the editing decisions of *Fatal Flaws*. Ervine cuts from Tighe's argumentation to an interview with Dr Richard Di Natale, senator and leader of the Australian Greens party, who campaign alongside Peter for the Right to Die Bill. Di Natale warns the viewer that counter-campaigns use scare techniques to turn people against assisted dying, for example by deliberately calling assisted dying 'killing people'. Then, Ervine cuts back to Tighe's interview just in time for the viewer to hear Tighe claiming that society should not 'legislate to kill people'. A similar warning of scare techniques is used with the slippery-slope argument, and this way, the viewer is prompted to be critical of the claims made by the counter-campaign.

Fade to Black also engages with rationalisation, another familiar technique from *Fatal Flaws*. The campaign for assisted dying uses Peter's story as empirical evidence, supported by rational arguments and scientific research that show that assisted dying laws could provide more control and less suffering for the terminally ill and prevent suicides, which are traumatic for family members. The opposing voices are framed as irrational and based on outdated values and conservative religious beliefs. For example, Peter reacts to religious arguments with passion and addresses the camera in the corridors of the Parliament House, annoyed that some people have lived so long in their 'bullshit' that they have not familiarised themselves with the reality. Di Natale, in a calm manner, explains that while there is a right to religious beliefs, the state and the church are separate for a reason and religious values should not define the values of all members of society. In these arguments, religious values and the realities that people live are seen to contradict each other. In addition, the counter-campaign is repeatedly asked to provide empirical support for their arguments, such as that assisted dying would encourage unnecessary killing and suicides. The camera captures any hesitation as proof of missing evidence, and celebrates a moment in the senator hearing, when one of the senators dismisses opposing arguments as personal views. In other words, the right to die is represented as a rational choice based on the lived realities of the citizens.

Thematically, Peter and his fellow campaigners systematically argue that everybody should have choice at the end of life. In addition, Dr Rodney Syme, who represents Dying with Dignity Victoria, paints assisted death as a dignified, peaceful and beautiful way of dying, which enables the person to leave goodbyes. He also argues that palliative care is not an answer for everyone, and the proposed bill targets those who suffer severe symptoms and will encounter difficult deaths regardless of comfort care. In these discussions, an option to end one's life becomes a human right, a right to choose for oneself.

The latter part of the documentary witnesses Peter's weakening condition. Peter and the family are devastated and discuss their options with Dr Syme, who talks to Peter about lethal medication as an alternative to palliative care. He also walks the family through the process of assisted death, stressing that it will create a positive memory that helps with the grief. The wife admits to the camera that having a choice is a comforting gift, but Peter is the one who makes the decision. In the end, Peter decides on palliative care, but points out that his whole motivation for campaigning was about having alternatives and being able to feel in control by choosing for oneself. The filmmaker follows Peter's declining health, his hospitalisation and eventually his death, his funeral and scattering of the ashes. In these last moments, the focus is on the family and their loving goodbyes to each other. In the end, Peter dies peacefully surrounded by his loved ones.

After Peter's death, the wife writes the final entry in Peter's blog. She tells about his passing and thanks everyone for their support. The message ends with a sentence, 'As a family we will continue to strive to achieve Peter's dream of seeing Senator Richard Di Natale's Dying with Dignity Bill become law.' The film closes with updates on the campaign. Di Natale promises that if the bill is passed, it will memorialise Peter. The very last screen has been added to the film after its initial release. This addition states that 'Victoria became the first Australian State to legalise assisted dying'. The positive result of Peter's campaign adds value to his efforts and to his story. It encourages the interpretation that Peter is a hero who successfully fought for individual autonomy and choice.

Conclusion

Western countries have increasingly debated the legalisation of assisted dying during the twenty-first century. In these debates of end-of-life biopolitics, political and ethical questions intertwine. Several documentary films take part in these debates, and while many filmmakers argue that they take both sides of the argument into consideration, the narrative decisions, particularly evidentiary editing, reveals the advocacy nature of these films. Most of these documentaries, similarly to other media representations, tend to come out in favour of assisted dying, partly due to the novelty aspects of potential social change and partly due to compelling personal stories and engaging cultural discourses of individual choice, autonomy and agency. However, this does not mean that only one narrative is present in the documentary field. There are in fact two competing narratives, which openly address and oppose each other as in the case of *Fatal Flaws* and *Fade to Black*. Not only do these documentaries build their own perspective, they also commit to dismantling the counter-arguments of the competing narrative.

The two narratives emerge from a different understanding of the roles of the individual and the state or society. First, those against assisted dying subscribe to a state-led society where the state assumes responsibility for the citizens, ideally providing good care and support but at the very least protecting the lives of its citizens. Here, death becomes the ultimate threat, something to be feared and avoided. If the state fails in its role, morally strong citizens need to step up and recognise and protect the value of vulnerable people. Here, the protector of the vulnerable is the ethical hero of the narrative, and life in any form is the celebrated prize.

Second, those fighting for legalisation of assisted dying prioritise the individual over the state or society. Individuals have the right (and responsibility) to make their own informed decisions, and it is this human right that the state needs to protect and enable at the end of life too. In these stories, the human rights and individual autonomy are championed by those fighting for assisted dying. In particular, the people who fight for their own right to choose the manner of death are celebrated as warriors of the cause. In this narrative, death is not something to be feared, but there is concern over the manner of death, and potential pain, suffering or loss of dignity and personal autonomy. The coveted prize of this narrative is the good quality of life, followed by a controlled death.

Both narratives draw support from rational argumentation which is under-pinned by empirical evidence (testimonials and personal life stories). Both sides also argue that the other side falls into emotional and purposeful argumentation that does not stand up to (scientific) scrutiny. In these debates, which take place both between and within the films, the filmmaker, who investigates and explores the topic also organises the arguments together and offers them as truth claims for the viewer. While the documentary viewer is always expected to evaluate the truth claims and reliability of the documentary content, the importance of evaluation is further highlighted in the case of advocacy films that openly take part in building the civic society. The discourses of such advocacy documentaries admit that there is no singular truth on the issue, which is why the viewer needs to consider the ethics related to the storytelling, but also the ethics related to the debated issue. The documentaries serve assisted dying as a moral and ethical dilemma that must be explored. While the filmmakers have done their part of the investigation, the viewer is asked to do the same. This position implies that film is expected to do more than raise awareness, it is hoped to invite the viewer to be an active participant in society's biopolitics of death.

REFERENCES

Aufderheide, Patricia. 2008. *Documentary Film: A Very Short Introduction*. Oxford: Oxford University Press.

Austin, Thomas. 2012. *Watching the World: Screen Documentary and Audiences*. Manchester: Manchester University Press.

Barrett, Diana, and Sheila Leddy. 2008. 'Assessing Creative Media's Social Impact'. The Fledgling Fund. 2008. https://mediaimpact.issuelab.org/resource/assessing-crea tive-media-s-social-impact.html. Last accessed 4 January 2022.

Bondi, Liz. 2005. 'Working the Spaces of Neoliberal Subjectivity: Psychotherapeutic Technologies, Professionalisation and Counselling'. *Antipode* 37 (3): 497–514. https://doi.org/10.1111/j.0066-4812.2005.00508.x.

Booth, Amanda, and Denise Blake. 2022. 'Assisted Dying in the Aotearoa New Zealand Media: A Critical Discourse Analysis'. *Mortality* 27 (1): 107–23. https://doi.org/10.1 080/13576275.2020.1823355.

Borum Chattoo, Caty. 2020. *Story Movements: How Documentaries Empower People and Inspire Social Change*. New York: Oxford University Press. https://doi. org/10.1093/oso/9780190943417.001.0001.

Brylla, Catalin, and Mette Kramer. 2018. 'A Pragmatic Framework for the Cognitive Study of Documentary'. *Projections* 12 (2): 159–80. https://doi.org/10.3167/ proj.2018.120216.

Burlone, Nathalie. 2020. 'Value-Based Issues and Policy Change: Medical Assistance in Dying in Four Narratives'. *Social Policy & Administration* 54 (7): 1096–109. https:// doi.org/10.1111/spol.12587.

Buyens, Frans. 1992. *Less Dead than Others (Minder Dood Dan de Anderen)*. Film. Films Lyda.

Decommere, Alexander. 2013. *End Credits*. Documentary. Recht op Waardig Sterven vzw.

Dunn, Kevin. 2017. 'From the Director'. Fatal Flaws - Film. 15 October 2017. https:// fatalflawsfilm.com/2017/10/15/from-the-director/. Last accessed 13 February 2023.

———. 2018. *Fatal Flaws: Legalising Assisted Death*. Documentary. Sideways Film.

Dying with Dignity. 2017. 'Peter Short's Story Told in Fade to Black Film'. Dying with Dignity: New South Wales. 2017. https://dwdnsw.org.au/fade-to-black-film-peter-shorts-legacy/. Last accessed 14 February 2023.

Eitzen, Dick. 2007. 'Documentary's Peculiar Appeals'. In *Moving Image Theory: Ecological Considerations*, edited by Barbara Fisher Anderson and Joseph Anderson, 183–99. Carbondale: Southern Illinois University Press.

Ervine, Jeremy. 2017. *Fade to Black*. Documentary. Torrential Pictures.

Euthanasia Prevention Coalition. n.d. 'About'. Euthanasia Prevention Coalition. https:// epcc.ca/about/. Last accessed 13 February 2023.

Fellows, Arron. 2018. 'Choosing Death'. *Louis Theroux's Altered States*. British Broadcasting Company (BBC).

Final Exit (Notausgang). 2014. Documentary. Medienproject Wuppertal.

Foucault, Michel. 1990. *The History of Sexuality. Vol. 1: An Introduction*. Translated by Michael Hurley. First published 1976. New York: Vintage.

Ganzini, Linda, Elizabeth R. Goy, and Steven K. Dobscha. 2008. 'Why Oregon Patients Request Assisted Death: Family Members' Views'. *Journal of General Internal Medicine* 23 (2): 154–7. https://doi.org/10.1007/s11606-007-0476-x.

Grierson, John. 1966. *Grierson on Documentary*, edited by Forsyth Hardy. Berkeley; Los Angeles: University of California Press.

Grue, Jan. 2022. 'The Death of Others. On the Narrative Rhetoric of Neoliberal Thanatopolitics'. *Disability Studies Quarterly* 42 (1). https://doi.org/10.18061/dsq. v42i1.7799.

Inthorn, Sanna. 2017. 'Audience Responses to Representations of Family-Assisted Suicide on British Television'. *Participations* 14 (2): 153–74.

Jackson, Liz. 2013. *My Own Choice*. Documentary. ABC Australia.

Johnstone, Megan-Jane. 2013. *Alzheimer's Disease, Media Representations, and the Politics of Euthanasia: Constructing Risk and Selling Death in an Ageing Society*. London; New York: Routledge.

Kis-Rigo, Andrew, Anna Collins, Stacey Panozzo, and Jennifer Philip. 2021. 'Negative Media Portrayal of Palliative Care: A Content Analysis of Print Media Prior to the Passage of Voluntary Assisted Dying Legislation in Victoria'. *Internal Medicine Journal* 51 (8): 1336–9. https://doi.org/10.1111/imj.15458.

Krupa, Tomáš. 2018. *The Good Death*. Documentary. ARTE; Czech Television; Golden Girls Filmproduktion.

Malkowski, Jennifer. 2017. *Dying in Full Detail: Mortality and Digital Documentary*. Durham, NC; London: Duke University Press. https://doi.org/10.1215/97808223 73414.

Mason, Brett, and Calliste Weitenberg. 2015. 'Allow Me to Die'. *Dateline*. Special Broadcasting Service (SBS).

Mbembe, Achille. 2019. *Necropolitics*. Translated by Steve Corcoran. First published 2016. Durham, NC: Duke University Press.

Menoud, Jean-Bernard. 2010. *Dignitas – la mort sur ordonnance*. Documentary. RTS.

Murray, S. J. 2018. 'Thanatopolitics'. In *Bloomsbury Handbook to Literary and Cultural Theory*, edited by J. R. Di Leo, 718–19. London: Bloomsbury.

Nash, Kate. 2011. 'Documentary-for-the-Other: Relationships, Ethics and (Observational) Documentary'. *Journal of Mass Media Ethics* 26 (3): 224–39. https://doi.org/10.1080/08900523.2011.581971.

Nichols, Bill. 2016. *Speaking Truths with Film: Evidence, Ethics, Politics in Documentary*. Oakland: University of California Press.

———. 2017. *Introduction to Documentary, Third Edition*. Bloomington: Indiana University Press.

Plantinga, Carl. 2013. '"I'll Believe It When I Trust the Source": Documentary Images and Visual Evidence'. In *The Documentary Film Book*, edited by Brian Winston, 40–7. London: British Film Institute.

Rawlings, Deb, Megan Winsall, Lauren Miller-Lewis, and Jennifer Tieman. 2023. 'Natural Death Versus Known Date-Of-Death: A Qualitative Study of Views on Voluntary Assisted Dying in an Online Course About Death'. *OMEGA – Journal of Death and Dying* 86 (4): 1272–90. https://doi.org/10.1177/00302228211008771.

Russell, Charlie. 2011. *Terry Pratchett: Choosing to Die*. Documentary. BBC Two.

Russell, James N. 2016. 'Jeremy Ervine – Doc Filmmaker – Fade to Black'. *Euthanasia: Pro and Con* (podcast). Listen Notes. 20 October 2016. https://www.listennotes.com/podcasts/euthanasia-pro-and/jeremy-ervine-doc-filmmaker-sR0MwHXn4ui/. Last accessed 2 January 2023.

Saunders, Peter. 2011. 'The Role of the Media in Shaping the UK Debate on "Assisted Dying"'. *Medical Law International* 11 (3): 239–56. https://doi.org/10.1177/0968 53321101100307.

SBS Australia. 2002. *Live and Let Die*. Documentary, Short. Journeyman Pictures.
Shaw, Daniel. 2012. *Morality and the Movies: Reading Ethics through Film*. New York: Continuum.
Springer, Simon, Kean Birch, and Julie MacLeavy, eds. 2016. 'An Introduction to Neoliberalism'. In *The Handbook of Neoliberalism*, 1–14. New York: Routledge, Taylor & Francis Group.
Svarvar, Jan-Olof, and Maria Holmberg. 2020. *Oikeus kuolla (Med rätt att dö)*. Documentary. Yleisradio.
Velasquez, Manuel, Claire Andre, Tom Shanks, and Micheal J. Meyer. 2010. 'What Is Ethics? (Revised from an article that originally appeared in *Issues in Ethics* IIE V1 N1, Fall 1987)'. *Markkula Center for Applied Ethics at Santa Clara University* (blog). 2010. https://www.scu.edu/ethics/ethics-resources/ethical-decision-making/what-is-ethics/. Last accessed 1 January 2023.
Whiteley, C. H. 2022. 'On Defining "Moral"'. In *The Definition of Morality*, edited by G. Wallace and A. D. M. Walker. First published 1970. London; New York: Routledge.
Wijngaarden, Els van, and José Sanders. 2022. '"I Want to Die on My Own Terms": Dominant Interpretative Repertoires of "a Good Death" in Old Age in Dutch Newspapers'. *Social Science & Medicine* 311 (October): 115361. https://doi.org/10.1016/j.socscimed.2022.115361.
Winnington, Rhona. 2021. 'The Assisted Dying Movement: How Media Platforms Influence Our Response to Events That Challenge the Boundaries of Contemporary Social Control'. In *Death and Events: International Perspectives on Events Marking the End of Life*, edited by Ian R. Lamond and Lisa Dowson, 177–93. London; New York: Routledge.
Zaritsky, John. 2010. 'The Suicide Tourist'. *Frontline*. Public Broadcasting Service (PBS).
Zeldis, Nina. 2005. 'To Be or Not to Be: Terminal Illness in Film and in Life'. *Nursing Forum* 40 (4): 129–33. https://doi.org/10.1111/j.1744-6198.2005.00025.x.

SECTION II
THE VOICES OF THE DYING PEOPLE

6. PERFORMATIVE DOCUMENTARIES

Life-Affirming Stories about Mortality

In the recesses of La Monnaie, the national opera house in Brussels, an old man peeks into a storage room. From behind a wall of plants, a dancer dressed in a skeleton suit steps into the frame. A chase ensues, the skeleton running away from the old man. Finally, the man drags the skeleton out in the open by its feet. The old man gently caresses the skeleton's face and removes the hood (Figure 6.1). The skeleton returns the touch, and they join hands, eyes fixed on one another. Slowly, the old man takes off his jacket and hangs it on a dummy. One piece after another, they remove their clothing and redress the old man to be a skeleton. They touch each other until the metamorphosis is complete, and the old man walks out of the frame as a skeleton, inviting the dancer to follow.

This scene is from Jorge León's film *Before We Go* (2014), where three terminally ill people meet with choreographers, actors and musicians to co-create artistic expressions about mortality. León describes the film as an artistic process. Patients from a hospice in Brussels and local artists were committed to the project and became as much creators as the filmmaker. While the filming at the opera house took two weeks, the work had started much earlier through workshops, researching the topic of death together, and planning and rehearsing the scenes up until saturation point. This skeleton scene, León says, was carefully outlined and prepared, but proved difficult to capture and took plenty of takes (León 2020). The atmospheric, lyrical and symbolic result suggests that acknowledging death allows an intimate, even a loving relationship with it. The scene also displays quiet humour: small smiles play on the old

FILMING DEATH

Figure 6.1 Noël faces a skeleton in *Before We Go* (León 2014).

man's face when he chases the skeleton, and the skeleton costume imitates popular Mexican Day of the Dead outfits. These elements further reduce death anxiety, for they appear as Bakhtian carnivalesque (Bakhtin 1984), subverting and turning upside down the assumed social norms (death as an anxious and sombre event) through humour. Consequently, in this intimate encounter, death becomes an approachable and a non-threatening character.

Before We Go, with its rehearsed scenes with real people, is a performative end-of-life documentary. Performative documentaries use stylistic and unconventional practices where the subjects and filmmakers not only acknowledge the presence of the camera, but act out for the viewer (Nichols 2017, 151; Bruzzi 2010, 185). According to Stella Bruzzi (2010, 185, 187), performative documentaries feature the subjects' stylised performances or the filmmaker's emphasised presence. I will discuss the filmmaker's role and the performative first-person narratives in Chapter 10, while in this chapter, my focus is on documentaries which narrate the experiences of dying people through creative art. In addition to *Before We Go*, I will discuss the Swiss documentary *Bouton* (Balzli 2011) of a terminally ill ventriloquist giving voice to her emotions with the help of a puppet, and a Scottish documentary, *Seven Songs for a Long Life* (Hardie 2015), where six hospice patients choose and perform their 'final songs' to describe their feelings about their lived lives and their approaching deaths. These documentaries employ planned performances to tell unique and arresting narratives, mixing rehearsed moments with more typical documentary events, such as spontaneous attempts to show the way out to a pigeon that accidentally enters the workshop room at the opera house.

In end-of-life documentaries, act-out performances are more than alternative documentary modes: creating art is a widely recognised form of therapy in hospice and palliative care, aimed to alleviate anxiety and existential fears at the end of life (Pratt and Wood 2015; Safrai 2013). Art therapy practices play a supportive role in performative documentaries as well. León (2020) acknowledges that the starting point for the workshops between the patients and the artists lay in the long traditions in art therapy at the hospice in Brussels. Amy Hardie (2016, 257–9), director of *Seven Songs for a Long Life*, was an artist in residence at a Scottish hospice where she helped the patients to create short films about their lives, and slowly these encounters turned into a full documentary. However, rather than being representations of art therapy as a practice, the art-based performances in performative documentaries are public explorations of the dying subjects' inner emotions. León (2020), for example, emphasises that *Before We Go* is not a story about art therapy, but an experience – for the subjects and for the viewer. Performative end-of-life documentaries thus foreground the experiences and voices of the dying. In this chapter, I analyse the ethical aspects that performativity adds to the documentary experience.

Performativity and Ethical Experience

In performative documentaries, the filmed subjects become actors. They consciously create the content and roles or characters, much like in *Before We Go*. Jorge León (2020) argues that the dying people, who the viewer can recognise as actual persons as opposed to being hired actors, build their characters for staged moments. It is this combination that erases boundaries between documentary and fiction. Documentary films' history of observation, *cinéma vérité* and direct cinema have prioritised witnessing of the events with minimal influence on the scenes by the filmmaker. Consequently, documentary filmmaking and its emphasis on acting for the camera appears as an alternative approach.

J. L. Austin's speech act theory has provided a way to understanding what performativity has to offer for documentary filmmaking. In Austin's theory, words and sentences are not only descriptive, but various utterances, such as 'I now pronounce you husband and wife', also act in their own right, and as such they perform (Austin 1975). Edward Lamberti (2019, 19) adds that similarly to words, images and film have performative power, particularly when words fail to communicate the experiences. Often, our relationship with mortality can be more an embodied feeling than a conceptualised understanding. Following the embodied and affective experiences of others might therefore show us a way of reflecting our own attitudes and feelings about end of life.

Rehearsed and performed elements blurring the boundaries of documentary expression have also raised ethical questions of inauthenticity and trustworthiness. For example, according to Bill Nichols (2017, 149–50), performative moments that turn the viewer's attention to style and (emotional) experiences distance the filmmaker and the viewer from realist representation and the film's attempt to say something authentic about the topic. From another perspective, Calvin Pryluck (2005, 200) argues that staged performances may be more ethical than actuality filming because they are signs of self-expression instead of the filmmaker's interpretations of events. I agree with Bruzzi's (2010) argument that no documentary can live up to the intention of representation of 'real', because both 'reality' and 'authenticity' are constructed in the filmmaking. Because performative documentaries include their subjects in creative processes of storytelling and openly admit that their representations are fluidly produced through filmmaking, the purposefully created scenes can thus become a source of, not a threat to, the documentary's ethical potential (Bruzzi 2010, 6–8; Hongisto 2018). Rehearsed scenes create transparency to filmmaking, while the acknowledged presence of the camera (and the viewer) demonstrates the filmed subjects' consent to being filmed.

Rehearsed performances do not invalidate documentary representations, so the question is how we understand authenticity. At its best, says Nichols (2017, 149–50), authenticity translates into spontaneous events that take place in front of the camera. However, based on Gilles Deleuze's application of Austin's speech act theory, Ilona Hongisto notes that when filmed subjects act for the camera, they are making fiction, yet they are not fictional. This turns filming into a 'creative story-telling act that has an immediate impact on the lives of the filmed subject' (Hongisto 2018, 192). These impacts are authentic and lived experiences. León saw this process take place in the filming of *Before We Go*. He realised that he was creating realities and encounters that the terminally ill would not otherwise meet in their daily lives. The staged encounters nevertheless produced experiences that had presence and meaning (León 2020). Staging turned to co-creating experiences that affected the lives of the participants – and also the viewer. Performances such as the old man's encounter with the skeleton dancer communicate unarticulated emotions related to facing death, and make claims about various, even alternative, ways of encountering it. Similarly to Bruzzi (2010, 185), who claims that performativity offers an opening for the viewer to experience what is represented, I argue that it does not erase authenticity but offers another understanding of authenticity, one where performativity emphasises the authenticity of experiences.

In other words, performative films do not seek authenticity or trustworthiness in spontaneity of events or factual knowledge, but in the desire to understand emotional, embodied and personal experiences that often lie beyond linguistic expressions or conceptualisation. León calls this 'experiential knowledge'. He argues that a terminally ill person's understanding of life and death differs from that of a healthy person. *Before We Go* was his window to the 'very material realization that life is short, and you might die soon. This sense of limited time transforms a person, and everyone deals with it differently.' While León thinks experiential knowledge cannot be taught or explained, art can provide an outlet to exploring these experiences in an embodied manner (León 2020).

Nichols (2017, 150) also recognises that performativity can provide documentaries affective and embodied dimensions to explore experiences outside the sphere of language and conceptualisations. *Before We Go* offers no grand narrative, but it is constructed of fragmented scenes of various art workshops. In addition to the skeleton scene, we see, for example, interpretive dance scenes; a rendition of 'The Mercy Seat', performed in a service lift, where the singer proclaims to not be afraid of death; and an HIV patient with a history of drug use creating geometric shapes on coloured paper and looking out of the window through these shapes lit up by daylight – reminding him of the drug-induced hallucinations of his youth. In these scenes, embodied and artistic performances allow the viewer access to comforting scenes to experience mortality. The creative style's ability to act, to perform, was also noted in the film's reception. *The Hollywood Reporter*'s film critic Neil Young writes:

> While inescapably and unapologetically an artificial construct from the start, *Before We Go* provides ample rewards to those willing to suspend disbelief and go with its gnomic flow. The film operates at the extremities of life and emotion, places where anything goes and there's nothing to lose but pain and inhibition. (Young 2014)

This comment, similarly, acknowledges the performative power of embodied expressions where death anxiety is turned into productive and contemplative performances.

The ability to perform experiences shows that the filming process is not the sole source of ethical potential – this can also be found in the style and aesthetics. Edward Lamberti (2019, 19–22) argues that the viewer's ethical experience in performative documentaries is associated with the style, not only because it draws attention to the constructed nature of films, but also because it has the power to approach experiences where words fail us and still create expressions that resonate. The non-linguistic potential of cinema, which taps into the visceral aspects of human action, extends to showing ambiguous, disruptive and messy experiences. This rawness, according to Robert Sinnerbrink (2016, 3), evokes the viewer's philosophical and existential thinking, which in turn invites ethical experiences about being in the world.

In *Before We Go*, performances enable the subjects to portray what it is to live the acute understanding of impending death. The encounters become embodied and affective stories about living with a sense of loss. At the beginning of the film, a few scenes take place outside the opera house. In one of them, Lidia wakes up at home and tries to get up. Her movements are tiny and slow and cause her pain. She sighs deeply when she tries to reach for her shoes. Next, she is having a bath, singing while washing herself. She emerges from the bathroom and holds onto the wall for support. The intimate scene exposes and embodies her fragility, limited mobility and living with pain. On arrival at the opera house, Lidia flings herself into an interpretive dance, where a professional dancer's fluid movements and loving caresses invite her to participate and express joy at being able to communicate through movement, no matter how minimal this movement may be. The dance scene grows to be an affective experience, because we have just witnessed how Lidia feels being limited by her body, and now, movement provides pleasure, not pain. León explains that this introductory scene to Lidia's life was based on their preparation workshops, where he had asked the participants to write about a typical day. Lidia dedicated three pages to describe waking up in the morning. The intimate scenes in the bedroom and bathroom force the viewer to pay attention to 'pain without identity, it is pain that you can't identify with, because you do not know the person who is suffering' (León 2020). The performance of pain turns into an experience of fragile mortality, as the film director's comment shows, an experience that can be co-shared by the subject and the viewer.

In *Before We Go*, the intellectual, cognitive or conceptual understanding of end of life is less important than the embodied and symbolic understanding of end-of-life experience. This decision forefronts the experiences of dying subjects, and there is no room for institutional or expert voices to explain their experiences for the viewer. Instead, the dying people are actively and knowingly creating and performing documentary content. The chosen mise-en-scène, La Monnaie, adds symbolic depth to the performances. The opera house is a place to perform, and was for the filmmaker a conscious choice of location. Not only is opera a stage, León (2020) argues, but it is also entwined with traditions of tragedy: people die and take their time dying on the opera stage. As such, the location adds symbolic elements to the staging of events, and to the embodied fantasies of mortality that were created together with filmmakers and co-creators. The artistic performances challenge the viewer to think and feel together with the images, with the performances. The performativity invites the viewer to see the end of life from someone else's unique perspective, and to recognise diversity in these experiences. By doing so, performative documentary builds a particular kind of avenue to ethical imagination, one where the viewer sees both the filmmaker's chosen perspective to the issue and also witnesses a film that has been actively co-created by the dying subjects. The experience of witnessing emphasises affective connection with the other.

Performativity and Affective Connection

While *Before We Go* paints fragmented scenes to emphasise how art can try to create a connection for the viewer to understand the experiences of the dying persons, Res Balzli's documentary film *Bouton* (2011) tells the story of one person, Johana, who has terminal breast cancer. Johana is a young actress who performs with an eponymous ventriloquist doll, Bouton. In his film review, Sven Zaugg (2011) describes *Bouton* as Johana's last leading role and creation. While I missed out on an opportunity to interview Balzli about the filming process (he died in 2019), Zaugg quotes the director's words: 'Precisely because she was an actress, we had the chance to create something with her, to even be able to repeat certain scenes' (Zaugg 2011, translated from German). In the film, performances are built in various ways: Johana performs on stage with Bouton, but she also performs her experiences for the viewer through the puppet and the imaginary conversations with three fairies – the past, the present and the future. *Bouton* uses performativity and theatricality to offer a unique and emotional story about death and dying, and provides profound insights into how performative documentaries can create a personal connection between the dying subject and the viewer.

First, Bouton the puppet gives access to Johana's thoughts and emotions. Bouton becomes an outlet for her to manage her fears and sense of losing the opportunities to live a full life. At the beginning of the film, Johana confides in Bouton (and in the viewer at the same time) that she is sick. The scene opens with Johana and Bouton sitting on a sofa. Johana is dialling her phone. Bouton hears static noise while Johana moves the phone above her breasts. Bouton follows the movement with vivid interest. After the call ends, Bouton asks who that was. In order to share, yet keep her secrets, Johana draws a blanket to cover them both. The viewer is left outside, but can hear a heartfelt discussion going on underneath the blanket. Johana explains that the phone sent her healing tones, which Bouton considers nonsense. While Bouton represents the other side of Johana, the argument shows both the doubt and the hope that alternative healing offers for Johana. She goes on to tell Bouton about her illness. The puppet had been aware that something was not right, confirming the intimate link between the two. To sympathise, Bouton claims to be feeling a bit under the weather as well. Johana is forced to admit that her illness is slightly more serious, a terminal cancer. Johana declares that she needs to fight. Bouton emerges from beneath the blanket and proclaims: 'You must not fight. You must rest. You are a princess.' Johana removes the blanket from her face and snuggles with Bouton: 'You are right. I would also like to rest.' This dialogue allows the viewer to follow Johana's conflicting inner thoughts and emotions – the desire to find a cure, being tired of fighting and longing to rest. 'Everything is magical with Bouton, nothing seems real,' Johana says, but it is

FILMING DEATH

with Bouton that she gets most real. It is Bouton that gets to hear her deepest fears, regrets, hopes and desires. In this scene, Bouton also manages to coax Johana to uncover her illness – literally. From hiding her illness beneath layers (of blanket), Johana brings her secret fears of a shortened lifespan out in the open.

Bouton, in many ways, becomes an aid for Johana to perform her struggles with terminal illness, but at the same time, Bouton also provides the viewer access to Johana's inner thoughts. Brenda Werth argues that when an intimate testimony turns into a public performance, through film, for example, the viewer's focus shifts from questioning the authenticity of experiences to the affective elements of these experiences. The intimacy of self-expression encourages attachment, and in turn, the viewer's attachment transforms into a shared experience that reaches beyond the space of performance. For Werth, the created affective attachment can transcend 'boundaries between individual and collective subjectivities' (Werth 2013, quote from 94). In *Bouton*, while the viewer witnesses Johana going through cancer treatments, therapy and everyday moments, her performed experiences through Bouton the puppet encourage affective engagement.

Engagement with characters functions as a source of films' rhetorical power. Engagement is constructed by developing 'round', complex characters, giving them time and space in narration, providing subjective access to their thoughts and emotion, and presenting them in a morally favourable light (Smith 2022; Plantinga 2018b, 193–210). In *Bouton*, similar strategies invite the viewer to connect with Johana, the centre of the narration, while the performance enables the puppet to find a way to her inner world. The better the viewer gets to know her, the more unfair her situation feels. The viewer can feel compassion for her feeling of dying too young, in her early thirties, and not being able to experience what life has to offer, such as having children. Johana's dreams, wanting to become a mother and to entertain children with theatre, are both personally and socioculturally likable goals. In their experimental study on the reception of fictional characters, Elly Konijn and Johan Hoorn (2005) found that morally good, realistic and beautiful characters were most likely to encourage the viewer's positive engagement. Similarly, being a likeable, young and beautiful woman adds to the affectivity of tragedy in Johana's story.

Carl Plantinga argues that while encouraged closeness could be interpreted as a manipulative immersion into the story, the viewers' emotional connection with the characters should not be condemned but studied in context. The more complex the characters are, the more varied experiences the viewer is offered; the film's emotional appeal and power can lead to significant thought processes and discussion (Plantinga 2018b, 250). In documentary films, particularly, the use of complex characters creates both affective connections with the viewer and builds an ethical connection where the viewers can co-share

PERFORMATIVE DOCUMENTARIES

their experiences (Canet 2016; Plantinga 2018a). The construction of complex characters serves as an ethical act in giving the subjects a voice of their own. Neither the filmmaker nor anyone else speaks for the filmed subject, but the subject's own voice carves an opening for the viewer to understand the complexity of human experiences, such as what they might go through themselves if they were faced with an unexpected terminal diagnosis. And, as Johana's deep inner dialogues through Bouton show, moments of stylised and emphasised performances can be used to increase the complexity of the character in performative documentaries and thus add both to the authenticity and affectivity of the experience.

In *Bouton*, the magical meetings with three fairies enhance the sense of performativity and affectivity. Whereas Bouton the puppet stands by Johana through her everyday struggles, the fairies represent Johana's understanding of what death is and what might be beyond it. In these scenes, three themes emerge – time, journey and death – which are introduced in the opening image of the film. The three fairies are singing by the roadside memorial for a child. The road represents a journey, the fairies serve as the mystical elements of life and death, and the child's toys symbolise time, which is limited. In voiceover, Johana's and Bouton's dialogue is woven into the fairies' chanting when Johana explains to Bouton that even young people, such as children, can die. Johana, too, becomes an embodied example of having to let go of life too early.

These themes are developed further in a sequence halfway through the film. The sequence opens with winter scenery. Johana steps out on the snowy terrace and sits herself down in a lounge chair, holding on to a blanket and Bouton. Johana presses the puppet to her chest while resting, giving an impression of falling asleep. Shortly after, we hear Johana's voiceover: she is hurting, and this experience has taught her to understand those whose pain is so overbearing that they want to die. She stands up, as if she were sleepwalking, and asks what is left if you cannot enjoy the good things about life, good food and wine, laughter, making love. The scene cuts to three 'fairies', wearing white and sitting in a snowbank under a tree. They are chanting while Johana walks through the snow towards them, the puppet's suitcase with her. When Johana reaches them, they introduce themselves as past, present and future. The future fairy is holding a baby, a dream of Johana's that is now escaping her. Johana takes the fairies' place under the tree, when they disappear down the hill, chanting and dancing. The lyrical and poetic dream sequence rehearses the alliance of time, death and journey, but unlike the mournful atmosphere of the opening, this meeting with smiling and approachable fairies gives a promise of another realm that might be waiting for Johana after her pain and suffering ends. The fairies are not taking Johana with them yet, but their magical existence serves as a comforting pledge.

The last time the viewer meets the fairies is after Johana's death. Instead of a deathbed scene, where the viewer would witness dying, the film pictures Johana's death as a journey to another dimension, or as she describes it in the film, to 'another planet'. The metaphor of a journey is highlighted in two ways when Johana dies. First, her death is implied: her partner Lukas is performing to children at a hospital, where, after the happy clown performance, he withdraws to a dressing room, crying and singing a song to Johana, the love of his life. We then see Lukas sitting on a train, eating a sandwich on his way back from the performance. Mournful, he gazes out of the window at the grey scenery. He sits backwards, as if gazing into the past, into memories, while the train moves on, life continues, and future exists.

From this, the film cuts to the closing scene of the three fairies in a rowing boat. The fairy of the future leads the way, the present rows the boat and the past has a place at the rear, holding a beautiful umbrella. They row up the river, chanting. The image distances itself from them, and in an establishment shot, the viewer can see the boat towing a floating casket (Figure 6.2). In a staged performance, Johana is portrayed on her way towards a mystical journey beyond death, to another dimension. This ending symbolises the mysticism of death implied throughout the narrative. Here, the viewer is cut off from Johana, but is left with imagination and hope for her story to continue, leaving a positive, albeit melancholic, feeling. The ending becomes Johana's last performance – planned, stylised and affective.

Figure 6.2 Johana's last performance, a journey towards the unknown in *Bouton* (Balzli 2011).

PERFORMATIVE DOCUMENTARIES

FILMED SUBJECTS AND PERFORMING AGENCY

Amy Hardie's documentary *Seven Songs for a Long Life* similarly engages with performativity in documentary-making by creating musical performances with hospice patients at Strathcarron Hospice in Scotland. Six patients get to perform for the camera the 'final songs' that fit their feelings, lives and personalities. The songs are made meaningful by the life stories of each participant, which bears a resemblance to *Bouton*'s way of building affective connection with the viewer through access to the dying subjects' personal experiences. In getting to know the performing patients, the viewer can also understand their song choices, which Hardie (2018) says are 'a way to people's inner worlds'. In this film as well, the performances and the supportive material offer an insight into the dying person's emotions, thinking and experiences.

Musical performances also make argumentative claims of the realities faced by dying people, and as such, the personal experiences turn into political notions about the sociocultural attitudes towards the end of life. In terms of Austin's speech act theory, all documentaries come into being through performance when they make some claim about the represented topic. However, Bruzzi (2010, 185–6) argues that performative documentaries add a layer to this act of 'performing claim', because they intentionally guide the viewer's attention towards acting for the camera, to the form and style of the documentary. These are purposefully used to advertise films' active agency in creating claims, or 'performing the actions they name'.

Seven Songs for a Long Life is introduced by Tosh, one of the six hospice patients. He performs three songs during the film, each one of them a Frank Sinatra standard. Tosh opens the documentary with his rendition of Sinatra's 'I Left My Heart in San Francisco' (Cory and Cross 1953). An impeccably dressed gentleman, he sits in a chair, slightly turned away from other patients, who are participating in an arts and crafts session. Facing the camera, occasionally even looking straight at the camera and acknowledging the viewer by returning the gaze, Tosh sings about the past glory of cities, being lonely and abandoned, and going home (Figure 6.3). The scene sets the stage for what follows, welcoming the viewer to the world of the hospice where the patients are prepared to perform, willing to be heard and seen as active, living persons. The stage-like setting and reciprocal gazing highlight the subjects' willing participation in the creative and ethical process of filming, and access to a unique embodied and affective experience that invites ethical connection. Furthermore, through performative scenes with music and singing, the documentary 'performs' a claim about life's end as a meaningful phase of life.

Music has a contested role in the documentary field. The influential *cinéma vérité* style favours sounds of fuzziness, background noise and talking to give an impression of authenticity and non-produced documentary films (Paget and

Figure 6.3 Opening of *Seven Songs for a Long Life* where Tosh sings during an arts and crafts session (Hardie 2015).

Roscoe 2006; Corner 2002). Yet, similarly to fiction films, music can drive the narrative, link different scenes together and provide emotional texture to the film by intensifying the viewer's engagement with the images (Corner 2002; Nichols 2016, 92). In documentary musicals such as *Seven Songs for a Long Life*, songs refuse to remain in the background. Instead, they become an integral part of the documentary musical, adding to its mediated experiences, as Derek Paget and Jane Roscoe argue. They continue that while the active and performative use of songs has an impact on the experience and mediated information (as does a soundtrack in general), it also gives the film a sense of theatricality (Paget and Roscoe 2006).

Theatricality is recognisable in another song by Tosh, where he asks a fellow patient to duet 'Strangers in the Night' (Kaempfert, Singleton, and Snyder 1966). Together, they flirt for the camera and put on a show. The images of them having a laugh are edited together with scenes of Tosh having a haircut at the hospice salon, as if getting ready for a night of romance and dating. The montage-like section confirms that even though the two are singing for those in the hospice common room, the film viewer remains the primary audience. The viewer is allowed to witness the preparations and is invited to step into the spaces of theatricality. Theatricality is also present in saying goodbye to Tosh, who died during the filming. The viewer can hear his interpretation of 'The Good Life' (Distel and Reardon 1962), but instead of seeing Tosh, the camera is back at the salon, where a lonely seat mediates the sudden departure that leaves emptiness in its wake. The song touches upon all the experiences that life has to offer, and the loneliness and longing that goes along with the journey (Distel and Reardon 1962). The lyrics of discovering the unknown and bidding the good life farewell embrace the bittersweet reluctance to let go of life.

Tosh's musical moments, similarly to *Before We Go*, are carefully planned, rehearsed and filmed. Yet, these moments have an indexical relationship with Tosh's lived experiences. Amy Hardie, the filmmaker, reminisces that the idea of the documentary took form when she met Tosh the storyteller:

> He came from such a tough background. He had been working since he was thirteen. His father had died when he was two. He had had so little money. And he said, the only thing I got, the only thing when anyone paid attention to me was when I started singing when I was thirteen. (Hardie 2018)

Hardie had asked Tosh to sing for her. The film idea grew from these small encounters, from stories such as Tosh's dreams, 'his longing for a bigger world to be part of, the world of Frank Sinatra' (Hardie 2018). In the documentary, Tosh's longing shifts beyond performing personally meaningful songs to become an act of empowerment. Performativity gives him visibility. The film is his last stage to being validated and acknowledged by local, national and even global audiences.

Tosh is not alone with his feeling of invisibility. Iain, who has multiple sclerosis (MS), talks about his loneliness in a voiceover while walking the corridors of the hospice:

> When you get MS you get disconnected from everybody because all your friends disappear. A lot of them don't get back to you anymore, they just don't communicate anymore. A lot of them don't even understand what MS is and half of them think they can get it. (Hardie 2015)

These experiences speak to the social marginalisation that many severely ill people encounter. The marginalisation of terminally ill people is conceptualised through 'social death', a concept familiar from social history, at its most striking in slavery and genocide, where a person's social influence and vitality have ended, even if they are still physically alive (Card 2003; Mulkay 1993; Patterson 1982). 'Social death' has been extended to describe the institutionalised old, ill and dying people whose interaction with other people and ability to make decisions about their daily lives become limited. They are forced into the liminal state of social death, which ends at physiological death (Brennan 2019; Sweeting and Gilhooly 1992). At the end of life, it is not only the institutions that can produce the social death of their patients, but marginalisation can extend to social relationships as Iain's and Tosh's concerns disclose.

There is frustration in the situation where they still have plenty to give, but others, perhaps out of fear, refuse to understand this. Their musical performances are both emotional self-expressions and acts of (re)claiming their place as members of the public.

Rather than being a mere colourful addition to the documentary about end-of-life experiences, the performances become the means of validating the film's claim about the agency of the terminally ill. Hardie recalls how the filming process turned into a co-creation with the filmed subjects, who were managing their self-expression by performances and were simultaneously inspired by the possibility of the film contributing to the world. The filming allowed them to recognise themselves as people who can 'create and contribute pleasure and value' (Hardie 2016, 260). Their ability to co-create musical performances gave them an active role in public discussions about end of life.

That the terminally ill have agency is a response to some public discussions in the early twenty-first century, when documentary and reality television representations of end of life began to take hold. The debate was commonly framed by concerns over exploiting vulnerable persons' privacy (Gibson 2011; Hakola 2013). For example, Kevin David Kendrick and John Costello argued that the BBC's reality series *Nurse* exploited the ill and infirm, potentially endangering their capability to make conscious choices. Moral compassion should be more important than the viewers' option to witness intimate moments in the name of public access, education or demystifying anxiety related to illness and death (Kendrick and Costello 2000, 16–20). These claims have been met with counter-arguments, where the participation of dying people is seen as an empowering and a meaningful social engagement (Horne 2013; Fox 2011; Haraldsdottir 2017; West 2018). The theatrical performances in *Seven Songs for a Long Life* make clear that the dying are conscious of the presence of the camera, the filmmaker and, consequently, the viewer. Tosh and Iain, for example, urge the viewer not to understand their vulnerable positions as lack of agency. In a way, they hold up a mirror to the viewer: you claim to protect our privacy, but are you just avoiding being reminded of your own mortality and temporary nature of life?

These notions for the need to validate the agency of the dying are supported by Erna Haraldsdottir's observational study of Hardie's filming of *Seven Songs for a Long Life*. Haraldsdottir found that the hospice patients did not want to dwell on death and dying. Instead, they wanted to tell their life stories, share their dreams and give people insight into their daily lives. As Haraldsdottir contends, these notions also reproduce the ideology of the hospice movement about empowering the dying, openness about death and the healing impact of engagement. It is here that art projects can offer ways of coping with difficult emotions (Haraldsdottir 2017). Naomi Richards (2013, 199, 201), who has ethnographically studied film art projects at other British hospices, similarly emphasises that performative stories give dying subjects an opportunity to leave an empowered testimony of themselves by creating something positive and meaningful. Performativity can thus give voice and agency to the dying subjects, resist social marginalisation and, at the same time, invite the viewer to be part of the engaging and empowering experience through witnessing the other in their own terms.

Positive empowerment also makes an emphatic point about being alive. According to Richards (2013, 193), hospice-based film projects connect with the hospice movement's desire to help patients to 'live until they die'. This the hospices do by providing activities, empowerment and person-centred care. For Amy Hardie, the attitude of 'living until you die' was a conscious and goal-oriented choice in the filmmaking. She argues that life, not death, is what defines us (Hardie 2018). In one particular scene, hospice nurse Mandy Malcomson discusses this ideology in a voiceover: 'Even when people come to us and they're told they're dying, to me they're still living.' She explains this through her own experience. She used to work in intensive care, but the longer she worked there, the more she wanted to connect with the person in bed, behind all the technology. The hospice environment enables her to do this, to connect, for example, with music, which is one of the last things that the brain remembers. In this documentary, then, singing also becomes a performance about life. While the documentary also includes intimate moments of the subjects reflecting on their uncertain futures or experiencing pain and suffering, the subjects are determined to keep making memories. Participation in a documentary musical becomes a way of embracing life.

Life-Affirming Viewing Experience

The life-affirming performances also exist for the sake of the viewer. If the viewers are willing to engage with the subjects, to open up for their experiences and to validate their agency, the subjects give a comforting promise in return that the end of life is not a meaningless phase of life and waiting to die, but it can also be fun, engaging and worthy of memories. Based on fiction films, Diana Rieger and Matthias Hofer (2017) contend that 'meaningful films' dealing with existential questions, such as death, have the potential to manage death anxiety. In their experimental study, films that emphasise life instead of death efficiently prove coping mechanisms: the survival of characters in life-threatening situations confirms the meaning of life for the viewers and reduces their death anxiety (Rieger and Hofer 2017). In end-of-life documentaries, life-threatening illnesses are neither cured nor solved, yet performative documentaries offer life-affirming experiences in their own ways. First, to be able to perform, the filmed subjects are in good physical condition and active. There are not too many physical reminders of mortality. Second, the subjects' deaths are not shown to the viewer. In *Seven Songs for a Long Life*, for example, death is communicated through absence, as in the case of Tosh, or in the final credits listing the dates of death. The on-screen subjects remain full of life. Thus, in a roundabout way the documentary engages the viewer with the topic of mortality, while the life-affirming tone provides a safe and comforting distance from the topic.

Both Naomi Richards (2013, 202) and Jennifer Malkowski (2017, 107) argue that life-affirming representations enable the viewer's cathartic release. Dying can be witnessed at a safe distance from the frail dying bodies, and this distance makes the films watchable and approachable. For Amy Hardie, the positive narrative tone is both welcomed and needed. Audiences might be anxious about death and would thus avoid a documentary about the topic, says Hardie, but the positive tone of the musical performances suggest that there is potential for connection:

> I wanted the film to allow the audience to get in that place in their own heads where they could bear that confrontation. And I realised music was one way to let me do that. Because singing is so pleasurable that it lets you get over the discomfort when thinking about death. (Hardie 2018)

The audience appears to accept this choice and demonstrated it in their positive responses (Haraldsdottir 2017, 271; Hardie 2016, 261–3). Even a quick look at the reviews of Hardie's documentary supports these notions. The reviews recognise the difficulty of the topic – facing death – but praise the documentary as 'incredibly moving' thanks to its 'honesty, dignity and affection' (Felperin 2015). They also see the documentary as 'heart-warming, life-affirming' (Carson 2017), 'heart-affecting', 'magical', 'mesmerising' (Brussat and Brussat 2017) and 'charming, soulful and bittersweet' (Bär 2015). It is a film that 'intimately' explores 'the vitality of life' (Bär 2015). Even these few examples show that the reviewers are positively surprised by the positive emotions that the dying people are represented with.

Hardie (2016) argues that the combination of positivity and performativity gives her documentary its transformative power which can help people to deal with death anxiety. She sees this transformation take place both on-screen and off-screen. In the course of the filming, she found that the functions given to singing by the participants changed during the process. At first,

> [t]he songs were used as a distraction from illness, from the experience of being a patient. The performances were a way of proving to themselves and those around them that they were more than 'patients'; that they were still people with dreams and desires. They used the songs to distract themselves and the hospice audience from the possibility of death. (Hardie 2016, 259)

The participants used their chosen songs for self-expression and agency, but the very choosing of the songs turned to self-exploration of their mortality: 'In the last year of filming the patients began to use song to reflect on their fears and hopes around end of life' (Hardie 2016, 260). In the film's reception, evaluated in an audience questionnaire after the screenings, Hardie recognises a similar transformation from escaping mortality to engaging with it. At first, the songs give the audience an easy entrance to the story, but they also help the audience members to discuss death with others, to feel more confident to think about their mortality and to feel less anxious about the hospice and death. Most of all, Hardie claims, the film gave the audience members a sense of hope that the end of life can be a meaningful phase of living (Hardie 2016, 262–4). The seemingly 'escapist' or 'distancing' use of songs can discreetly entice the viewers to encounter their own mortality. It may also alleviate anxiety (if not about death, perhaps about hospice care).

Such transformations in attitudes and beliefs, whether permanent or temporary, are often desired outcomes of documentary films and the performative claims about their topics. In addition, these transformations are at the very core of the documentaries' ethical aspects. At its best, as Hongisto argues, documentary ethics means more than ethical procedures of filming; it is the ways in which these films imagine, 'fabulate' and create affection. The documentaries can propose meanings and create potential for realities that are to come (Hongisto 2015, 135–7). In the case of end-of-life documentaries, these films can propose a society which is open to engaging with death and mortality and which acknowledges the dying persons as valid members of society and social relationships.

CONCLUSION

Seven Songs for a Long Life, Before We Go and *Bouton* all make the life-affirming claim of a meaningful end of life through highlighted performativity. Artistic performances can enchant the viewer, but they can also serve as comments on social issues. According to Paget and Roscoe (2006), the performative documentary can break free from the history of seriousness and step into the realm of melodrama, yet it is not a diversion from the 'real' story, but the very core of the text. The use of joyous musical scenes, interpretative dances or magical fairies as life-affirming performances enables performative documentaries to make claims of dying persons' agency and end of life as a meaningful phase of life. On-screen, Tosh, Iain, Lidia, Johana and others become rounded and complex personalities who promise the viewer that the end of life is not only about waiting to die, but about life. These personalities should not be marginalised and excluded from social interaction. They should rather be included, acknowledged and appreciated. The performative scenes which are supported by anecdotes of the subjects' lives give these claims discretion; the viewers are not preached to or lectured. Instead, they are allowed to create a personal connection with their experiences, and these connections, then, can turn into ethical imagination and transformed attitudes.

In performative documentaries, the terminally ill people are active and in good enough physical condition to participate in filming, which is not always the case with patients in palliative care. The decision to film active people is related to the ethics of filming – the active participation already suggests that the subjects have consented to being filmed – and to the life-affirming goals of these documentaries. The filming of dying people who are well enough follows contemporary cultural practices, where, for example, memorial photographs represent lively and often young persons. In this way, the person can live forever through images, and the preserved moments push any reminders of mortality, death, dying or dead bodies to the margins (Walter 2015, 225; Aceti 2015, 319–27; Bennett and Huberman 2015). In film theory, André Bazin calls this process a 'mummification effect', which refers to the camera not only recording change but having the power to replay and repeat that change in photographic images. Cinema can eternally kill characters and then bring them back to life by replaying the scenes. This is how the cinema can mummify change and 'embalm time' (Bazin 1960). Every time the viewer restarts the film, Johana and Tosh, for example, are back to their active selves, death only as a forever anticipated outcome. Thus, even if *Bouton*, for example, is a story about end of life, it becomes a performance about life.

This kind of life-affirming approach has had a mixed response. Richards, for example, recognises that the positive tones of these kinds of films can support the hospice movement's desire to focus on living, not on the life-limiting aspects of dying, and that these projects can empower the dying persons and support their well-being. Still, the life-affirming documentaries also freeze a person's representation (and their physical decline) in time, as the footage conveys a sense that everything is happening now (Richards 2013, 193, 197–8). The life-affirming tone of performances crops physical frailty out of the picture, instead focusing on the scenes where the subjects remain active. We are therefore back to ethical questions of authenticity raised at the beginning of this chapter. The question is whether performative documentaries give a realistic representation of dying or whether it idealises these processes and builds unrealistic expectations. And certainly, in one way, the life-affirming documentaries offer a limited vantage point on the dying process, yet this view is not any less authentic in its claims. It merely creates one perspective to the topic of end of life, and this perspective performs an argument that the dying persons have plenty to give while they are alive and that living does not end with a terminal diagnosis. Thus, while it might not be a full image – how would we even define a 'full image'? – it does constitute a positively framed invitation to think about mortality in a world where fear and anxiety commonly lead to our avoiding the topic. Thus, for many, these films can be the start of a meaningful conversation, not the only representation they ever encounter about dying.

References

Aceti, Lanfranco. 2015. 'Eternally Present and Eternally Absent: The Cultural Politics of a Thanatophobic Internet and Its Visual Representations of Artificial Existences'. *Mortality* 20 (4): 319–33. https://doi.org/10.1080/13576275.2015.1085297.

Austin, J. L. 1975. *How to Do Things with Words*, edited by Marina Sbisà and J. O. Urmson. First published 1962. Oxford: Clarendon.

Bakhtin, M. M. 1984. *Rabelais and His World*. First published 1965. Bloomington: Indiana University Press.

Balzli, Res. 2011. *Bouton*. Documentary. First Hand Films.

Bär, Daryl. 2015. 'Review: Seven Songs For A Long Life'. *Film Reviews, Interviews, Features | BRWC* (blog). 19 October 2015. https://battleroyalewithcheese.com/2015/10/review-seven-songs-for-a-long-life/. Last accessed 12 April 2022.

Bazin, André. 1960. 'The Ontology of the Photographic Image'. Translated by Hugh Gray. *Film Quarterly* 13 (4): 4–9. https://doi.org/10.2307/1210183.

Bennett, Jeffrey, and Jenny Huberman. 2015. 'From Monuments to Megapixels: Death, Memory, and Symbolic Immortality in the Contemporary United States'. *Anthropological Theory* 15 (3): 338–57. https://doi.org/10.1177/1463499615575943.

Brennan, Michael. 2019. 'Social Death'. In *Non-Death Loss and Grief*, edited by Darcy L. Harris, 36–49. New York; London: Routledge.

Brussat, Mary Ann, and Frederic Brussat. 2017. 'Seven Songs for a Long Life, Film Review'. Spirituality & Practice. 2017. https://www.spiritualityandpractice.com/films/reviews/view/28362/seven-songs-for-a-long-life. Last accessed 12 April 2022.

Bruzzi, Stella. 2010. *New Documentary*. First published 2000. London; New York: Routledge.

Canet, Fernando. 2016. 'The Filmmaker's Engagement with the Subject in Contemporary Documentary: *Foreign Parts* as a Case Study'. *Studies in European Cinema* 13 (2): 149–62. https://doi.org/10.1080/17411548.2016.1213582.

Card, Claudia. 2003. 'Genocide and Social Death'. *Hypatia* 18 (1): 63–79. https://doi.org/10.1111/j.1527-2001.2003.tb00779.x.

Carson, Diane. 2017. '"Seven Songs for a Long Life" Affirms Life'. KDHX. 1 April 2017. https://kdhx.org/articles/film-reviews/439-seven-songs-for-a-long-life-affirms-life. Last accessed 12 April 2022.

Cave, Nick, and Mick Harvey. 1988. *The Mercy Seat*. Music album.

Corner, John. 2002. 'Sounds Real: Music and Documentary'. *Popular Music* 21 (3): 357–66.

Cory, George, and Douglass Cross. 1953. 'I Left My Heart in San Francisco'. Song.

Distel, Sacha, and Jack Reardon. 1962. 'The Good Life'. Song.

Felperin, Leslie. 2015. 'Seven Songs for a Long Life Review – Going down Singing'. *The Guardian*, 1 October 2015. https://www.theguardian.com/film/2015/oct/01/seven-songs-long-life-review-honesty-documentary-hospice-dying. Last accessed 12 April 2022.

Fox, Broderick. 2011. 'The Final Cut: End-of-Life Empowerment through Video Documentary'. In *Exploring Issues of Care, Dying and the End of Life*, edited by Sue Steele and Glenys Caswell, 55–62. Leiden: Brill. https://doi.org/10.1163/9781848880580.

Gibson, Margaret. 2011. 'Real-Life Death: Between Public and Private, Interior and Exterior, the Real and the Fictional'. *South Atlantic Quarterly* 110 (4): 917–32. https://doi.org/10.1215/00382876-1382321.

Hakola, Outi. 2013. 'Normal Death on Television: Balancing Privacy and Voyeurism'. *Thanatos* 2 (2): 32.

Haraldsdottir, Erna. 2017. 'Enhancing Openness around Death and Dying through Documentary Film-Making in a Hospice'. *European Journal of Palliative Care* 24 (6): 268–71.

Hardie, Amy. 2015. *Seven Songs for a Long Life*. Documentary. SDI Productions.

———. 2016. 'Movie-Making as Palliative Care'. In *On the Feminist Philosophy of Gillian Howie: Materialism and Mortality*, edited by V. Browne and D. Whistler, 247–65. London: Bloomsbury Academic.

———. 2018. Personal interview by Outi Hakola.

Hongisto, Ilona. 2015. *Soul of the Documentary*. Amsterdam: Amsterdam University Press. https://doi.org/10.5117/9789089647559.

———. 2018. 'Realities in the Making: The Ethics of Fabulation in Observational Documentary Cinema'. In *Storytelling and Ethics*, edited by Hanna Meretoja and Colin Davis, 190–9. New York: Routledge.

Horne, John. 2013. 'Unsettling Structures of Otherness: Visualising the Dying Individual and End of Life Care Reform'. In *Envisaging Death: Visual Culture and Dying*, edited by Michele Aaron, 224–42. Newcastle upon Tyne: Cambridge Scholars Publishers.

Kaempfert, Bert, Charles Singleton, and Eddie Snyder. 1966. 'Strangers in the Night'. Song.

Kendrick, Kevin David, and John Costello. 2000. '"Healthy Viewing?": Experiencing Life and Death through a Voyeuristic Gaze'. *Nursing Ethics* 7 (1): 15–22. https://doi.org/10.1177/096973300000700104.

Konijn, Elly A., and Johan F. Hoorn. 2005. 'Some Like It Bad: Testing a Model for Perceiving and Experiencing Fictional Characters'. *Media Psychology* 7 (2): 107–44. https://doi.org/10.1207/S1532785XMEP0702_1.

Lamberti, Edward. 2019. *Performing Ethics through Film Style: Levinas with the Dardenne Brothers, Barbet Schroeder and Paul Schrader*. Edinburgh: Edinburgh University Press.

León, Jorge. 2014. *Before We Go*. Documentary. Films de Force Majeure.

———. 2020. Personal interview by Outi Hakola.

Malkowski, Jennifer. 2017. *Dying in Full Detail: Mortality and Digital Documentary*. Durham, NC; London: Duke University Press.

Mulkay, Michael. 1993. 'Social Death in Britain.' In *The Sociology of Death*, edited by David Clark, 31–49. Oxford; Cambridge: Blackwell Publishers.

Nichols, Bill. 2016. *Speaking Truths with Film: Evidence, Ethics, Politics in Documentary*. Oakland: University of California Press. https://www.jstor.org/stable/10.1525/j.ctv1wxtcp.

———. 2017. *Introduction to Documentary, Third Edition*. Bloomington: Indiana University Press.

Paget, Derek, and Jane Roscoe. 2006. 'Giving Voice: Performance and Authenticity in the Documentary Musical'. *Jump Cut: A Review of Contemporary Media*, no. 48. https://www.ejumpcut.org/archive/jc48.2006/MusicalDocy/index.html. Last accessed 11 April 2022.

Patterson, Orlando. 1982. *Slavery and Social Death: A Comparative Study*. Cambridge, MA: Harvard University Press.

Plantinga, Carl. 2018a. 'Characterization and Character Engagement in the Documentary'. In *Cognitive Theory and Documentary Film*, edited by Catalin Brylla and Mette Kramer, 115–34. Cham: Springer International Publishing. https://doi. org/10.1007/978-3-319-90332-3_7.

———. 2018b. *Screen Stories*. Oxford: Oxford University Press. https://doi.org/10.1093/ oso/9780190867133.001.0001.

Pratt, Mandy, and Michele Wood, eds. 2015. *Art Therapy in Palliative Care*. First published 1998. London: Routledge. https://doi.org/10.4324/9781315788012.

Pryluck, Calvin. 2005. 'Ultimately We Are All Outsiders: The Ethics of Documentary Filming'. In *New Challenges for Documentary*, edited by Alan Rosenthal and John Corner, second edition, 194–208. Manchester; New York: Manchester University Press.

Richards, Naomi. 2013. 'Rosetta Life: Using Film to Create "Bearable Fictions" of People's Experiences of Life-Limiting Illness'. In *Envisaging Death: Visual Culture and Dying*, edited by Michele Aaron, 190–205. Newcastle upon Tyne: Cambridge Scholars Publishing.

Rieger, Diana, and Matthias Hofer. 2017. 'How Movies Can Ease the Fear of Death: The Survival or Death of the Protagonists in Meaningful Movies'. *Mass Communication and Society* 20 (5): 710–33. https://doi.org/10.1080/15205436.2017.1300666.

Safrai, Mary B. 2013. 'Art Therapy in Hospice: A Catalyst for Insight and Healing'. *Art Therapy* 30 (3): 122–9. https://doi.org/10.1080/07421656.2013.819283.

Sinnerbrink, Robert. 2016. *Cinematic Ethics: Exploring Ethical Experience through Film*. London; New York: Routledge.

Smith, Murray. 2022. *Engaging Characters: Fiction, Emotion, and the Cinema*. First published 1995. New York: Oxford University Press.

Sweeting, Helen N., and Mary L. M. Gilhooly. 1992. 'Doctor, Am I Dead? A Review of Social Death in Modern Societies'. *OMEGA – Journal of Death and Dying* 24 (4): 251–69. https://doi.org/10.2190/L0N6-P489-NR8N-JQ6K.

Walter, Tony. 2015. 'Communication Media and the Dead: From the Stone Age to Facebook'. *Mortality* 20 (3): 215–32. https://doi.org/10.1080/13576275.2014.993 598.

Werth, Brenda. 2013. 'A Malvinas Veteran Onstage: From Intimate Testimony to Public Memorialization'. *South Central Review* 30 (3): 83–100.

West, Emily. 2018. 'Invitation to Witness: The Role of Subjects in Documentary Representations of the End of Life'. *International Journal of Communication* 12: 1481–500.

Young, Neil. 2014. '"Before We Go": Marseille Review'. *The Hollywood Reporter* (blog). 9 July 2014. https://www.hollywoodreporter.com/movies/movie-reviews/be fore-we-go-marseille-review-717379/. Last accessed 22 September 2022.

Zaugg, Sven. 2011. 'Das Sterben hat keine Logik'. St. Galler Tagblatt. 16 April 2011. https://www.tagblatt.ch/kultur/film/das-sterben-hat-keine-logik-ld.2054104. Last accessed 16 September 2022.

7. LEGACY DOCUMENTARIES

Reaching beyond Death

Helen's Story (Davidson and Gibb 2016), a New Zealand documentary, is the story of a young mother with terminal cancer. Devastated by the limited time she has left, Helen wants to leave her children a special memory. She asks filmmakers Paul Davidson and Barbara Gibb to record her last months. During these months, the filmmakers let Helen make her voice heard, to have control over her life and death, and, as Gibb says, to 'enable her legacy' (Davidson and Gibb 2020). By giving meaning to Helen's life story and by building a legacy that reaches beyond death, this end-of-life documentary helps to make death bearable.

Legacy translates into how and for what a person will be remembered. As such, it engages with the meaning-making of one's life at its end (Boles and Jones 2021; Breitbart 2016; Hunter 2008). Legacy has been conceptualised in contexts of continuing social bonds. The legacies of those who came before us (parents, ancestors, society) influence our values, norms, traditions, and spiritual and cultural knowledge, while our legacies influence those who come after us (Breitbart 2016; Hunter 2008). Legacies which are passed on beyond death, are part of an evolving continuum. Documentary projects give personal legacies a wider audience, and turn something personal into something public; they leave a mark on historical and social communities.

Creating a legacy through documentary film is an act that reaches beyond death, towards symbolic immortality. The term originates from Robert Jay Lifton and Eric Olson (1974), referring to the desire to be publicly remembered by the following generations. This memorialisation is attempted through public artefacts, such as monuments and statues, or by having one's name written in history books or by creating lasting art, such as films (Longfellow 2013; Werth 2013). Being the protagonist of a documentary film about oneself becomes a recognition of existence, which is evident in Paul Davidson's perspective: 'I think we enabled Helen to live on in a film. Helen can be alive in that way as long as she likes' (Davidson and Gibb 2020). Symbolic immortality, thus, gives comfort that some part of us lives on, and death is not the end of a person's social influence. Jeffrey Bennett and Jenny Huberman argue that the promise of symbolic immortality can alleviate death anxiety, particularly a form of death anxiety that stems from forced disconnection from others and the world through bodily failure. While the biological aspects of death remain a reality, people have searched for ways to cross the limits between life and death and to continue to be connected to those left behind (Bennett and Huberman 2015, 340–1). Any form of memorialisation ensures continuing social bonds, yet a publicly built symbolic immortalisation creates an open legacy for a person's life, actions, values and beliefs.

Because legacies are built in historical and sociocultural contexts, they are connected to social norms, values, attitudes and practices. Elizabeth Hunter observes that legacies can be positive, negative or something in-between. Also, some persons are more conscious of their potential legacies, and they plan what belongings, actions or values they would like to share and pass along (Hunter 2008, 325). This self-reflective practice can aim for idealised versions of ourselves, a polished image of how we want to be viewed by future generations (Bennett and Huberman 2015; Carter 2007). The documentary films can provide a medium for these practices where the subjects self-memorialise and self-moralise their actions, and where these representations are evaluated by the viewers. Catalin Brylla and Mette Kramer (2018), for example, argue that because documentary films invite the viewer to engage with the filmed subjects, this practice includes the viewer's evaluation of whether the filmed subject is a morally and socially acceptable character. A moral evaluation is needed for the viewer to engage and to create an allegiance, a deep connection, with any character. The evaluation emphasises the character's behaviour in relation to moral norms and social expectations (Smith 2022, 187–93). In an ethical perspective on cinema, the characters do not need to be morally valued to encourage ethical thinking in the viewer, because both morally questionable and morally celebrated actions inspire emotional, embodied and cognitive evaluation of social norms and expectations. Similarly, both positive and negative legacies – or those which are something in-between – can turn into morally and ethically engaging stories for the documentary viewer.

In this chapter, I analyse end-of-life documentary films where legacy-building underpins the filmmaking and viewing. These films typically memorialise one person at a time to highlight their unique experiences and legacy. In addition to *Helen's Story* (Davidson and Gibb 2016), a New Zealand documentary about a half-white and half-Māori woman, the analysis draws from the American documentary *Prison Terminal: The Last Days of Private Jack Hall* (Barens 2013), which portrays Jack's death at a prison hospice; and a Finnish documentary *Marika's Passing* (Wallenius 2021a), where terminally ill Marika is preparing for death.

I interpret these documentaries both as 'belongings' and 'actions', based on Hunter's (2008, 318) argument that legacies can be transmitted through materiality, such as memorials and monuments, and through actions and their consequences. In the case of end-of-life documentaries, the materiality of the film, including the arguments it performs, represents 'belongings'. These include, on the one hand, the personal legacy-building of the filmed subject, and, on the other hand, the general legacy of the documentary, or in other words, its claim for end of life. In terms of actions, three actors participate in the legacy-building. First, the filmed subjects create their legacies by active participation in filming. Second, filmmakers enable these personal processes and use them to create an argument – a legacy – for the film. And third, through witnessing and evaluation, the viewer either actualises or disowns the suggested legacies. Thus, the belongings and activities related to constructing and mediating legacies through documentary films are complex, and each aspect brings different ethical or moral questions into play.

Filmed Subject and Morality of Legacy-Building

In hospice and palliative care contexts, organising legacy-oriented activities is part of the therapeutical care practices where patients can give meanings to lived lives. Legacy-building activities, such as writing journals, encouraging storytelling, creating scrapbooks and filming life stories increase the patients' well-being and reduce the symptoms of depression (Boles and Jones 2021). The legacy activities come under the umbrella of 'narrative therapy', which emphasises reviewing one's life at such moments as being diagnosed with an illness, when the need for self-reflection and reconstructing one's life story arises (de Muijnck 2019, 63; Fioretti et al. 2016). Besides legacy, 'autobiographical work' and 'narrative identity' are used to describe the ongoing processes where we tell stories about ourselves, our lives and our values to ourselves and others. Autobiographies are consciously made reflections of self that often assume an audience, thus mixing private and public spheres (van Dijck 2004), while narrative identity refers to both conscious and unconscious processes where we construct our identities through storytelling. This involves facticity and fabulation as well as continuity and change (Ricœur 1980; Rimmon-Kenan 2002; Ricœur 1992; McAdams 2011; Hunter 2008). All these forms of life narratives can deepen our understanding of ourselves and our experiences, where we come from, where we are going and who we are.

Despite the similarities, or sometimes interchangeable uses of 'legacy', 'autobiography' and 'narrative identity', these concepts vary in their assumptions of an audience and temporality. Legacies are created with others in mind, because others validate what we consider worth remembering about ourselves. Mediated autobiographies are statements of self that assume, but do not require, someone witnessing (van Dijck 2004). And narrative identity constructs our sense of self primarily to ourselves and secondarily to others. The narrative identity is an ongoing process throughout a person's life, where continuity is created between the past, the present and an anticipation of the future (McAdams 2011, 100; Rimmon-Kenan 2002, 11–12, 22–3). The need for reconstructing the identity often arises from a disruptive experience, such as a life-threatening illness, when we need to change our anticipation of the future and re-imagine what our lives will be. Autobiographies, in turn, are acts of memories and remembering (van Dijck 2004), and as such they focus on explaining the past. In contrast, legacy builds around mortality and death. While legacy is also about identity and remembrance, it anticipates a posthumous future, where others have the power to either validate or reconstruct our legacy-building.

For the dying subjects, participation in end-of-life documentaries where the narration is based on their life stories provides a venue to build their personal and public legacies. For Private Jack Hall, for example, the filming of *Prison Terminal: The Last Days of Private Jack Hall* (Barens 2013) serves as a possibility to reconcile his troubled identity and ask for social redemption in front of the public. The film opens with Jack confessing that he ended up in prison for killing a dealer whom he suspected of selling drugs to his son. His declining health has made him aware that 'I get out of here one day. In a box.' His acute sense of mortality strengthens an inner conflict when he starts reflecting on how he will be remembered. What legacy will he leave behind?

First, the documentary's claims become a part of Jack's legacy, a thought that comforts him, according to film director Edgar Barens (2019). *Prison Terminal* taps into Jack's story to shed light on incarceration practices in the US. The film illustrates the aging prison population and how, due to long prison sentences, many prisoners die within these institutions. Some prisons, such as Iowa State Penitentiary, where the film was shot, have started hospice programmes to deal with the issue. The documentary uses Jack's experiences as an example of the benefits and practices of these programmes. Barens (2019) argues that he cannot claim that his film has led to dozens of new prison hospices, but it did start at least five: 'At least I can say that I know that a lot people have died better than they would have normally died in prison, and the film is still out there doing a lot of good work.' Furthermore, Barens argues that Jack helped to create the film's legacy, its argument for prison hospices: 'He knew what the film was about, and I asked Jack, do you want to be part of this film? He said, "absolutely". I think he was leaving a legacy for other prisoners, and he felt honoured in a way' (Barens 2019). This legacy, Barens emphasises, extends to other subjects in the film, the prisoners who volunteered at the hospice when Jack died. They helped to make changes in incarceration care practices, and Barens argues that knowing this means a lot to him and the volunteers (Barens 2019). Thus, *Prison Terminal* combines arguments for enabling a dignified death for the incarcerated population together with providing opportunities for prisoners to create a meaningful legacy.

In addition to this general legacy, the documentary also enables Jack to build his personal legacy, which is a more troubled process. Jack is afraid of what happens after he dies, both regarding whether his punishment will continue in the afterlife (punishment for sins) and how he will be remembered. Jack expresses a strong desire to rewrite his legacy to include positive aspects. This process compares to Dan McAdams's argument that 'redemption' functions as a building stone for 'good life' and 'generativity script', where a person achieves positive legacy and leaves a valuable legacy. Consequently, many life narrations have built-in morality. People tend to highlight elements of their lives that society can interpret as signs for a 'good and worthy life' (McAdams 2011, 110). Deborah de Muijnck (2019, 49, 57, 64), similarly, observes that the forthcoming death can trigger a person to self-reflect on their choices and values from a moral perspective in order to experience, or at least express, a sense of personal growth, a socially worthy goal in life. For Jack, his impending death inspires legacy-building, whereby he embarks on a moral evaluation and redemption of his life choices and invites the viewer to join him on a journey of personal growth.

As the opening of *Prison Terminal* shows, Jack does not deny why he ended up in the prison; he openly admits he was sentenced for life for murder. However, Jack is worried that everyone else judges him based only on this aspect of his existence, and the filming becomes a way to emphasise the other parts of his life – being a family man, a contributing member of the prison community and a World War II veteran. These aspects of his identity are not only about what he has done, but what kind of relationships are important to Jack. Hunter argues that legacies always rely on relationships that create, transform and pass legacies on. These relationships include both interpersonal and socially interconnected relationships, such as culture and society as a whole (Hunter 2008, 318). Similarly, Jack seeks redemption in all these relationships, with his family, community and society.

The most personal level of these redemptive relationships involves his family. Jack sees himself as a family man, even if he has made troubling choices due to mental health issues (post-traumatic stress disorder following military service during World War II) and alcohol abuse. Throughout the filming, Jack proclaims how proud he is of his son and grandchildren, and the prison hospice enables him to spend time with his family. Unlike other wards, the hospice ward allows flexible visiting rights, which makes it possible for Jack to rebuild a strong and affective connection with his family. At the end, Jack's son is sitting by his deathbed. The filmmaker captures the son's caresses when Jack takes his lasts breaths (Figure 7.1). The opportunity to witness this affective connection creates a transformative experience: the viewer sees Jack through a humanising lens. Despite his mistakes, Jack is loved and worth caring for. The family's affection and ability to forgive help the viewer to support Jack's desire to redeem his morality and honour.

The second level of Jack's redemptive relationships takes place within the prison community. He has lived and worked within that community for decades, and during his last weeks the viewer sees glimpses of what personal growth has taken place during these years. First, Jack seeks comfort and atonement in Christianity. The religious rituals, particularly the holy communion, symbolise his repentance and atonement. Second, Jack is recorded in the prison infirmary, where he had been placed for twelve years after a heart attack in his early seventies, and later, in hospice, being taken care of by black volunteers. These prisoners sit by Jack's bed and share moments of laughter and sorrow. Jack's son reads this as a sign of personal growth because Jack used to be a racist and a supporter of segregation. Jack has had a change of heart and has abandoned his racial prejudices, which marks his seeking

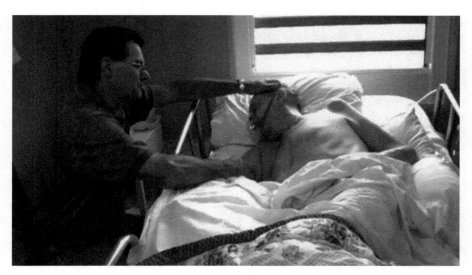

Figure 7.1 Jack on his deathbed, fragile, comforted by his family in *Prison Terminal* (Barens 2013).

redemption and also makes him more relatable in the contemporary viewer's eyes.

The third level of Jack's redemptive relationships is society and his role in it. Because of his conviction, Jack feels like an outcast, yet his past as a soldier brings him comfort. On several occasions, he returns to the memories of serving in the war and being a celebrated war hero who protected his country, its people, values and lifestyle. These memories and experiences are not tainted by his later actions, and he hopes to build his public legacy on being a veteran. He hopes to be transferred to a soldiers' home for hospice care, but when the decisions are delayed, he settles into the prison hospice and feels comforted by the thought of getting to be buried in the military section of the cemetery. The final resting place in the war veterans' section serves as his release from prison and a restoration of his role as a respected veteran and citizen in the eyes of society. The film ends with Jack's coffin being transported outside the prison walls. He is free, and he has reconciled his identity for himself, for his family, for his prison mates, but also for the wider public, who can now evaluate how he will be remembered.

For Jack, participation in the documentary project is an attempt to create a redeeming legacy. While he cannot determine how others will define his legacy, he can attempt to shape it. William Breitbart (2016) calls this process the 'legacy that one lives', witnessing oneself, observing and appraising potential legacies and searching for significance. In this process, knowledge of forthcoming death gives meaning and context to the search of significance and evaluating which values one wants to transfer to those witnessing and to the following generations. Similarly, Naomi Richards (2013, 197) argues that the experience of witnessing such storytelling processes becomes meaningful because both the subject and the viewer know that the subject is going to die, which guides attention to the passage of time. Legacy documentaries do not seek to freeze their subjects in the moments when they are alive and active, because the final evaluation of the meaningfulness of their lives can only be actualised after their death. Consequently, legacy documentaries include physical aspects of the dying process in on-screen images, they dedicate space and time to increasing bodily fragility, and sometimes, as in the case of Jack, these films invite the viewer to the deathbed to witness the death of the subject. Jack's death serves as a point of reference, where the viewer has all the information about his actions, morals and values to decide whether they want to align themselves with Jack's desired mode of remembering.

Jack's death in incarceration can appear as an ultimate punishment for his crimes, but his death also adds a humanising element to his legacy. Film director Edgar Barens (2019) recognised that the prisoners had hurt other people, but he wanted to show that at the end of the day, prisoners are just people, and death carries emotional affects to humanise the prison population:

> The biggest common denominator for everybody is to see somebody to die. And I know it sounds kind of ruthless, but I thought that if they [the viewers] see someone die, it might remind them of their father, or grandfather, who they saw pass away. It also brings it all down to the same level. And also I was able to show the prisoner's family who loves this person despite their flaws, show the path to a grieving process as the person dies. That can be so powerful. (Barens 2019)

As this quote illustrates, Barens builds a story where the viewer can learn to understand, if not necessarily accept, Jack's experiences, and to recognise his desire and need for redemption of his soul, but also his legacy. Scott Combs's (2006, 281) argument that 'cinema wants to solve the basic problem of the loneliness of death, to mediate the event of someone's death so that it communicates to the outside world' adds an interesting perspective to Jack's story. The film project ensures that Jack is not dying alone, but his death is witnessed by his family, the prison community and the public. Consequently, being by his deathbed, whether physically or through the camera, becomes both a sad and a cathartic moment. The redemptive legacy provides comfort for Jack and for the viewer because his hospice death was better than the alternative – dying alone in his cell – and because his attempts to become a man worthy of his war hero status provide a kind of happy ending for the film. Jack does not die as a murderer, but as a family man and a veteran, gaining his freedom in a publicly acceptable way. The morality of these actions allows the viewer to mourn the loss of his life.

FILMMAKER AND ETHICAL COMMITMENT TO LEGACY-BUILDING

While end-of-life documentary films enable legacy-building for the filmed subjects, these legacies are also mediated and built through filmmaking. A successfully documented legacy requires the interpretative and productive work of the filmmaker. José van Dijck argues that mediated autobiographical memories represent both personal and cultural practices. In other words, narrated memories are related to a person's manifested perceptions and experiences, but at the same time, cultural practices, such as documentary traditions, influence the forms of expression and guide what is remembered and how (van Dijck 2004). In *Helen's Story*, too, the filming process enables a young mother to leave a tangible legacy for her children, to self-reflect on her emotions, particularly the shifting moods between hope for recovery and desperation over progressing cancer, and to explore her roots for deepened self-knowledge. However, these personal legacy processes are filtered through documentary practices. Co-director Paul Davidson says that first they recorded the events as sensitively as possible, but the story was only created after all the footage had been filmed. And, while the documentary is not a scripted art form, 'it still has to have almost the classic movie structure, with the opening, the tension point, and resolution of tension, unexpected things and the viewer wondering what was going to happen' (Davidson and Gibb 2020). Consequently, the film narration includes various creative aspects, music, illustrations, interviews and moments without Helen's presence.

The film opens with a funeral scene of Helen's coffin being carried. From these images, the film cuts to family photos where Helen poses with her children, while the opening lines of the song 'The Biggest Love' play on the background, lyrics describing a beginning of a journey and life that is waiting to be lived (Davidson 1990). For Paul Davidson and Barbara Gibb (2020), the directors, the decision to open with the funeral scene and to reveal the sad ending of the story, was a difficult one. The opening removes any possibility of recovery from cancer. The certainty of death changes how the viewer engages with Helen: the viewer pays attention to how Helen deals with her mortality and what kind of legacy she leaves behind.

From this starting point, the film narration builds two legacies. The documentary portrays Helen's dealing with terminal illness and receiving help from hospice care. Helen describes the day of receiving her diagnosis as a moment when 'everything just changed, that day'. The knowledge that she might die earlier than expected launches a difficult and emotional journey. At first, Helen processes her progressing illness through a metaphor of 'fighting' the cancer, a rather typical even if a problematic cultural expression in illness stories (de Muijnck 2019, 48; Rimmon-Kenan 2002, 14). Later, however, the battle transforms into finding 'inner strength' to die a dignified death. Along the way, hospice staff, palliative treatments and activities such as art therapy help her. The film uses Helen's experiences to show the benefits of hospice care and the emotional advantages of learning to accept one's death. Thus, the film's public legacy that Helen helps to build is to claim that good end-of-life care can lead to dignified dying.

Still, the film becomes as much a story of Helen's reconnecting with her roots and creating her personal legacy based on her heritage. Helen has been adopted by a Caucasian family, but the forthcoming death prompts her to learn the whole story. She tracks down her Caucasian biological mother, and later, the Māori family from her biological father's side. The terminal illness encourages her to search for her long-lost relatives and Māori roots, and enables her to embrace Māori cultural practices. From the perspective of the filmmakers, this level of personal legacy added positive interest to the story. Davidson and Gibb (2020) argue that one person's journey towards death might not be a good story by itself, so while they did not initiate the search for lost family connections, this storyline gave added tension and structure to the narrative. The search for family roots drives the scenes, and Helen's desire to reconciliate her family backgrounds – that of her European-descended, Christian family and her aboriginal, Māori family – becomes a part of her life. To search for closure increases the story's appeal because it provides an option for a 'happy ending'. Naomi Richards, who followed the filmmakers' work with hospice patients to create films, also noted that the filmmakers typically built a redemptive narrative into the stories. In other words, they presented a problem that could be resolved during the film, and while the main character's illness or dying process could not be resolved, the viewer could be offered at least one kind of catharsis during the film (Richards 2013, 196).

For Davidson and Gibb (2020), emphasising the 'happy' elements and resolution was a conscious decision. The filmmakers wanted to balance the tragedy of Helen's story with other emotions, such as joy from successful medical interventions, the happiness that a baby brings to the family, the love for the family members and the reconciliation with the lost relatives. Gibb argues that they paced the film so that the emotional arcs encourage the viewer to stay with the film:

> If you just watch all the sad parts, you would lose your audience, because it would just be too much. So, I think, it is also about hospice journey, that despite all, you get better and you get back into your life and then you get sicker and there is this other world of death. [...] Especially visually we were aware not just keeping the mood in balance, but also physically we had some really beautiful up-moments as well which were, I think, well paced. Just to keep the whole thing uplifted. Letting people know that it is okay to have pure joy. (Davidson and Gibb 2020)

This emotional structure that eases the viewer's entry into the story is highlighted in the culmination point of the documentary, where Helen successfully reconciles the two sides of her heritage – the white, Christian culture and the indigenous culture. Helen's story started from her need to renegotiate her identity, to embrace her Māori roots and to gain knowledge of where she comes from and to whom she is linked. However, during the film this personal identity project turns to a quest for legacy, a desire to achieve something that lasts beyond her death. In other words, Helen desires to create a lasting connection between the families so that when she is gone, the connection would endure for her children, and she would become an important link in the ancestral line.

To achieve this, Helen organises a farewell party for all sides of her family. Bringing everybody together, she mends different parts of her identity, but in addition, she uses this event to build a legacy. The party is organised in a *marae*, a Māori cultural space for social gatherings. Food and other proceedings are prepared by using Māori rituals and traditions. The social gathering celebrates Helen while she is still alive, but Helen uses the event to introduce people to each other and make them a family. Helen's own assessment, 'I think I achieved it,' is supported by her brother's comments on Helen's efforts: 'She is the connection that brought us together.' Helen dies shortly after, which highlights the reconciliation story's cathartic function. The viewer is comforted that Helen managed to achieve something lasting, a legacy to reach beyond her death. This achievement makes both her life and death meaningful.

Coming back to the filmmakers' decision to open the film with the funeral scene, we can see that their structural decision anticipates death and marks the forthcoming death as something that gives meaning to the story that is about to unfold. In addition, it includes elements of both tragic and happy endings. The funeral signifies the devastating death of Helen, but it also includes images of reconciled family connections. When Helen's coffin is brought out from a Catholic church, it is welcomed by a group of people performing *haka*, an expressive cultural art by Māori. In Māori culture, *haka*, a posture dance performed together with chanted or shouted song, has various expressive functions, including farewelling and mourning the deceased family members. It can be interpreted as a ritualised sign of respect (Matthews 2004). The multicultural coexistence of Christian and Māori cultures is testimony to Helen's legacy, a healer of family connections. Thus, the opening already implies that the film is both an end-of-life story and a reconciliation story about legacy.

From the ethical perspective, Davidson and Gibb were committed to giving space to Helen's personal legacy. At the same time, they wanted to ease the viewers into the topic gently, so that they would not be shocked but could share emotionally a positive connection with Helen (Davidson and Gibb 2020). This editing process compares to Asbjørn Grønstad's reading of Michael Haneke's fiction film *Amour* (2012), where the husband takes care of his wife after her stroke. Similarly to legacy documentaries, Grønstad argues that anticipation of death gives form to the film because care and illness bring mortality into the lived life. Still, instead of focusing merely on subjective experience, the film highlights the ethics of love and responsibility. Grønstad sees the husband's role as an ethical commitment to the situation. Here, ethics is not a social practice at first glance. It negotiates a relationship, when the forthcoming death gives 'the responsibility of legacy upon the one who is left behind' (Grønstad 2016, 139–43, quote from 139). While Grønstad's interpretation is based on a relationship between two fictitious characters in a drama, it paints a picture where ethics can be seen as a social practice. Those who remain after the subject's death have responsibility to care, not only physically and emotionally but also in terms of understanding the legacy. Similar expectations can be extended to filming end-of-life stories. The filmmakers have a responsibility to care, and one form of this care is to mediate the legacy desired by the dying subject. Thus, respect for legacy-building is an ethical act of social practice, in which the filmmakers commit to telling a dying subject's story.

Viewer and Validation of Legacy

All films expect a viewer, legacy films even more so. One's legacy and symbolic immortality remains inactivated if others do not acknowledge and validate it. Thus, in end-of-life documentaries, it is the viewer's responsibility to determine how the filmed subjects are remembered. Richards (2013, 191) suggests that hospice film projects where the patients build legacies need to be recognised by the audiences, because otherwise their thoughts and words would lack the empowering aspect of leaving something behind. This recognition requires ethical engagement from the viewer. The engagement and remembering are ethical actions that validate the experiences of the dying and confirm their continuing social influence after death. In a way, the expectation and promise of the viewer's gaze comforts the dying subjects, who can be assured of a posthumous legacy.

The nature of the validation, however, is in the hands of the viewer. Instead of leaning on the theoretical viewer to study the validation of legacy, reception study deepens the understanding of how the actual audiences react to end-of-life documentaries. I organised twelve focus-group interviews with forty-eight participants recruited from universities, universities of applied sciences, and cancer and grief support groups in Finland. The participants watched a Finnish documentary, *Marika's Passing* (Wallenius 2021a), and then joined a group discussion to share their feelings (a detailed reception study results, Hakola 2022; 2023). The documentary follows a middle-aged woman's last months in hospice care. Marika has terminal cancer, but she is determined to live fully until the end while preparing for her forthcoming death. Marika displays a self-made death doll that she wants to be buried with, a nature-inspired coffin gown, and she also invites the filmmaker (and consequently, the viewer) to test her custom-made green coffin. Open discussions about death and dying, a positive attitude and individual choices for funeral rituals serve as the film's and her legacy: the documentary celebrates the opportunities and freedom to plan a unique death and funeral in Finnish culture where death rituals have been quite homogeneous. The film's director Peter Wallenius (2021b) interpreted Marika's willingness to participate in the documentary as her wanting to help others in a similar situation, living with a terminal illness. Crucially, the film also enabled Marika to build a legacy and continue to live through the film.

The group interview participants reacted positively to Marika's preparations for death. They felt that she had enough time from the diagnosis to death to process and accept the situation. She had both the time and the courage to discuss death with her family and friends. Her willingness to participate in the planning of her own funeral was mostly seen in a positive light. The unique and individual choices that differ from the 'typical' Finnish funeral rituals were welcomed as liberating and empowering. Many participants felt that Marika showed that it was possible to renew 'old' and 'dusty' traditions, and they were inspired by the promise that they would not have to follow a certain model for death rituals, either. These rituals can be customised to fit personal styles and desires. Marika's choices were, however, questioned by some participants. These resistant voices felt that the funeral and the mourning rituals are for those who are left behind, which is why they should have more say on them. For many, a traditional funeral might be more comforting than a bespoke occasion of unique choices. Despite the perspective on the topic, the viewers recognised that the filmmaker and Marika wanted to use the film to open a discussion on the changing roles of end-of-life and death rituals in Finland. The viewers thereby validated the accepting and open approach to planning one's end of life as the film's sociocultural legacy.

However, the discussion on death rituals was not the main topic that the viewers wanted to tackle. Most attention was given to Marika's relationship with her spouse. At the beginning of the film, Marika's spouse is standing by her, and they do all kinds of fun things together – enjoy a music festival and try to make the best out of the last months together. When Marika's physical and psychological condition weakens, the relationship faces challenges. The moment of their ultimate conflict is not recorded on camera, but both parties comment on it in interviews. Marika explains being hurt by the spouse's comment in an argument: 'Your death is the least of my worries at the moment.' She feels she is not getting support and care at home and therefore distances herself from the situation and seeks solace by switching from home care to in-house hospice care. The spouse regrets his ill-chosen words, maintains that Marika refuses to accept his apologies and is hurt to be shunned. This sets up a conflict, an issue that screams for reconciliation and for a 'happy ending' of the documentary.

In the same manner as in *Prison Terminal* and *Helen's Story*, Marika's personal relationships add drama and build narrative tension. Wallenius recognises that the marital rift lent the film a captivating storyline, which also served the director's interests to show what people talk about before death. The relationship conflict stressed that life, with its twists and turns, continues until the end. Relationships continue to evolve and change, and life does not freeze. Therefore, a complicated relationship allowed Wallenius to build an honest portrayal of being human until the end, with all kinds of emotions, not only smiles, good humour and positive feelings (Wallenius 2021b).

The decision to let things play out lasts until the end. Unlike in the other documentaries discussed in this chapter, there is no happy ending, no reconciliation between spouses. The film's last scenes are dedicated to Marika's death. She is lying on her hospice bed, breathing heavily and looking fragile. She is surrounded by people. Her brother, a priest, gives her the final blessing. While the camera, and the viewer, are invited to this intimate moment of goodbyes, the spouse is missing. The camera pans away from the scene, and the filmmaker cuts to an interview with the spouse. In a close-up, the spouse looks directly at the camera. He shares the unpleasant feeling of being cut off and not being able to say goodbye. The interview ends when he tells that one Monday morning the call came that Marika had died, and a lone tear rolls down his cheek revealing the raw emotion of distress. In the next images, Marika's hair is gently combed, her corpse is covered up and she is transported out of the hospice. The final scene is pre-recorded with Marika, who in her coffin gown and with her death doll strolls through a forest, peaceful, as if on another plane. These scenes implicate that while Marika is at peace, the spouse is left with the burden of unresolved issues.

The viewers had strong reactions to the representation of this course of events. Many blamed the spouse and said that he should have supported Marika; he should have kept his inconsiderate comments to himself. They found that the end of life was such a short time that one should be able to stay supportive. Others allocated some of the blame towards Marika, too. They felt that she should have been forgiving and understanding in an emotionally difficult situation. Regardless of who the viewers chose to side with, they shared their disappointment of the continued conflict. The unresolved situation became traumatic not only for the filmed subjects but also for the viewers. The viewers kept hoping for reconciliation, which would have given them closure and a 'happy' ending for a life story, a respectful legacy.

The anticipation of reconciliation originated from social expectations of a desirable relationship and death. The demand for strong and durable relationships at difficult times is comforting, because the representations of such relationships promise that the viewers are entitled to expect the same from their own relationships – unwavering support in sickness and in health. The demand to settle arguments before death would promise a 'good death'. One of the respondents argued that 'peace and harmony with everything and everyone is part of the good death experience', and continues that 'from this perspective, her [Marika's] death was not a good death. After all, this was a beloved person, and then there was this disturbing issue.' A public promise, or claim, that people can put an end to disagreements would strengthen the expectations that we can hope for the same at the end of life.

Thus, when Marika refuses to aim for reconciliation, the documentary can turn into a 'demoralising experience', as Jennifer Malkowski contends. In this experience, the narrative appears to lose its sense of purpose and goal, particularly in a culture that values individual accomplishment (Malkowski 2017, 84). Marika's refusal to adapt to the story of reconciliation is not only an individual 'failure' to create a positive legacy but also a refusal to build a safe, cathartic experience for the viewer. Some of the participants of the group interviews openly acknowledged their desire for cathartic closure, and they, interestingly, demanded that the filmmaker should assume responsibility for the narrated conflict. They were aware that the filmmaker could have chosen to edit the conflict out of the film and include only the scenes where Marika and the others were happy, accepting of death and joyfully preparing for it. This, they thought, could have been a perfect way to reduce death anxiety. Instead, they thought that the film had conflicting elements. While its accepting attitude towards death was comforting and 'rosy', the troubled marital relationship made the film 'brutally' realistic. These discussions showed that the viewers were conscious of the filmmaker's power and role in legacy-building.

These discussions unfold the normative expectations of a positive legacy, which would involve order, closure and non-conflicting emotions. However, narrative studies show that this may be an unreasonable and unrealistic expectation in a life story. This field of study has slowly grown out of the idealisation of control, coherence and continuance that would increase well-being and provide emotional closure (Frank 1993). The field has started to embrace realities where narrative identities are formulated in complex personal and social lives marked with discontinuities, chaos and fragmented experiences (McAdams 2011, 102–4; Rimmon-Kenan 2002, 21–3). A similar discussion could also benefit the field of legacy-building. In the reception of *Marika's Passing*, a small proportion of the viewers tried to convince others of the benefits of narrating a conflict story. For them, the documentary served as a public acknowledgement that the end of life does not turn into a polished version of life. A life-threatening illness raises complicated emotional reactions. The end of life can cause anxiety, distress, aggressiveness and guilt in the dying people and their relatives. These realistic experiences should be given time and space. Thus, *Marika's Passing* builds an honest and realistic approach to the topic and provides peer support and possibilities for self-reflection of their own experiences. The representation of difficult emotions can add to the trustworthiness of the documentary and the ethical practices of filmmaking.

Consequently, the study of the audience's validation of the film's claim and legacy reveals that the ethical expectations of the documentary can vary within the reception. For those who desired a comforting and positive approach to an end-of-life story, a redemptive or reconciliating narrative would have appeared as the desirable narrative mode. It would also have been an ethical choice to respect the privacy of the subjects' intimate issues, and to lessen the death anxiety of the viewer. However, for those preferring honest access to difficult emotions and a troubled relationship, the frank perspective served as an ethical choice in the filmmaking. This choice affords public space to discuss the various sides of end-of-life experiences, and as such, it could at least validate the lived experiences of many, instead of building idealistic and rosy images of end of life. And at the very least, the film encouraged its viewers to reflect on what they saw in relation to their own values and experiences, which is one potential of the ethical cinematic space.

Conclusion

In legacy documentaries, death is made meaningful by defining the unique aspects of a person's life and by imagining how their social influence continues after death. The documentaries give meaning to the subjects' end-of-life experiences as they are turned into messengers of what dying is as an experience. Also, these films create space for personal life stories that build personal legacies of the subjects' actions, values and beliefs. By creating affective relationships with the dying subjects, the documentaries portray them as worth remembering, and the viewer has an essential function as a witness of their legacy, and consequently, an authoriser of symbolic immortality. Brenda Longfellow (2013) points out that these kinds of memorialisation practices are always political: what or who is publicly memorialised and how they are memorialised are signs of what issues and what kinds of people are considered important for public discussions and the collective memory. While the prominent figures of history and celebrities have had several documentaries dedicated to them, such end-of-life documentaries as *Helen's Story*, *The Prison Terminal* and *Marika's Passing* represent a significant turn in that memorialisation and symbolic immortality have become available to 'normal' people as well. The digitalisation of culture, including filmmaking, has provided opportunities and a desire to document various lives for future generations (Aceti 2015; Walter 2015; Jacobsen 2017). The boundaries between the personal and the public have shifted to give room to various legacies.

The legacy-building practices also vary within end-of-life documentaries. *Prison Terminal* and *Helen's Story* use redemptive and reconciliation narratives to emphasise the morality of the filmed subjects, which builds a positive understanding of legacy. In these documentaries, death provides a tragic ending to personal experiences, yet the reconciliation of identity and relationships before death provides a partial happy ending to the stories. In these cases, the moments of the subjects' deaths are culmination points of their legacies. All is well in their worlds, and they can leave at peace, knowing that they left something meaningful behind. In contrast, *Marika's Passing* paints a more complex image. The viewer can recognise the beauty of Marika's open, and even accepting, approach to death, yet the troubled relationship with the spouse casts a shadow over this legacy.

These narrative endings are always constructed. With different editing choices, *Marika's Passing* could have constructed a similar positive story of legacy-building as did *Prison Terminal* and *Helen's Story*. In Helen's case, the filmmakers noticed that the family dynamics changed after her death, and reconciliation between the families was not as straightforward, easy or free from tensions as Helen imagined (Davidson and Gibb 2020). In Jack's case, the filmmaker says, the cemetery refused to let his body be buried in the war veterans' section because a new law stipulated that any capital crime leads to withholding all veteran benefits. This was devastating for Jack's family, but the filmmaker was glad that Jack did not know about this decision that refused him his honourable return to society (Barens 2019). Thus, while the legacy of the dying people kept evolving after their deaths, these two documentaries chose to portray a positive validation of their legacies.

These various choices on how to proceed on legacy-building are tied to the intentions for the film's public legacy. By giving the viewer the possibility of verifying the benefits of prison hospice programmes through building an allegiance with Jack's experiences, director Edgar Barens ensured that *Prison Terminal* could build public acceptance towards hospice projects. Similarly, by reconciliating two cultural traditions – European-descended culture and Māori culture – filmmakers Paul Davidson and Barbara Gibb showed that hospice care could benefit all citizens regardless of their background. In turn, *Marika's Passing* used complicated relationships to publicly acknowledge and allow space for the complex emotions and restraints that the approaching death can bring onto the surface, even if some viewers find these emotions difficult to encounter. Thus, the legacies of the dying people in end-of-life documentaries are always created in the triangle of their own legacy-building, the filmmakers' goals and the viewer's validation.

References

Aceti, Lanfranco. 2015. 'Eternally Present and Eternally Absent: The Cultural Politics of a Thanatophobic Internet and Its Visual Representations of Artificial Existences'. *Mortality* 20 (4): 319–33. https://doi.org/10.1080/13576275.2015.1085297.

Barens, Edgar. 2013. *Prison Terminal: The Last Days of Private Jack Hall*. Documentary. HBO.

———. 2019. Personal interview by Outi Hakola.

Bennett, Jeffrey, and Jenny Huberman. 2015. 'From Monuments to Megapixels: Death, Memory, and Symbolic Immortality in the Contemporary United States'. *Anthropological Theory* 15 (3): 338–57. https://doi.org/10.1177/1463499615575943.

Boles, Jessika C., and Maile T. Jones. 2021. 'Legacy Perceptions and Interventions for Adults and Children Receiving Palliative Care: A Systematic Review'. *Palliative Medicine* 35 (3): 529–51. https://doi.org/10.1177/0269216321989565.

Breitbart, William. 2016. 'Legacy in Palliative Care: Legacy That Is Lived'. *Palliative & Supportive Care* 14 (5): 453–4. https://doi.org/10.1017/S1478951516000705.

Brylla, Catalin, and Mette Kramer. 2018. 'A Pragmatic Framework for the Cognitive Study of Documentary'. *Projections* 12 (2): 159–80. https://doi.org/10.3167/proj.2018.120216.

Carter, Rodney G. S. 2007. 'Photography and Personal Mythology'. *Queen's Quarterly*, January. https://www.academia.edu/6726476/Photography_and_Personal_Mythology. Last accessed 11 April 2022.

Combs, Scott. 2006. 'Final Touches: Registering Death in American Cinema'. PhD dissertation, Berkeley: University of California.

Davidson, Paul. 1990. 'The Biggest Love'. Song.

Davidson, Paul, and Barbara Gibb. 2016. *Helen's Story*. Documentary. Bytesize Productions.

———. 2020. Personal interview by Outi Hakola.

Dijck, José van. 2004. 'Mediated Memories: Personal Cultural Memory as Object of Cultural Analysis'. *Continuum* 18 (2): 261–77. https://doi.org/10.1080/103043104 2000215040.

Fioretti, Chiara, Ketti Mazzocco, Silvia Riva, Serena Oliveri, Marianna Masiero, and Gabriella Pravettoni. 2016. 'Research Studies on Patients' Illness Experience Using the Narrative Medicine Approach: A Systematic Review'. *BMJ Open* 6 (7): e011220. https://doi.org/10.1136/bmjopen-2016-011220.

Frank, Arthur W. 1993. 'The Rhetoric of Self-Change: Illness Experience as Narrative'. *The Sociological Quarterly* 34 (1): 39–52.

Grønstad, Asbjørn. 2016. *Film and the Ethical Imagination*. London: Palgrave Macmillan. https://doi.org/10.1057/978-1-137-58374-1_10.

Hakola, Outi. 2021. 'Ethical Reflections on Filming Death in End-of-Life Documentaries'. *Mortality*, June, 1–16. https://doi.org/10.1080/13576275.2021.1946025.

———. 2022. 'Kuolemisen Mediatisaatio: Yleisön Odotukset Marikan Kuolema - Dokumenttielokuvalta'. *Media & Viestintä* 45 (4): 1–21. https://doi.org/10.23983/mv.125624.

———. 2023. 'Mielikuvat Suomalaisesta Saattohoidosta Marikan Kuolema - Dokumenttielokuvan Vastaanotossa'. *Lähikuva – Audiovisuaalisen Kulttuurin Tieteellinen Julkaisu* 36 (1): 25–44. https://doi.org/10.23994/lk.128785.

Haneke, Michael. 2012. *Amour*. Les Films du Losange.

Hunter, Elizabeth G. 2008. 'Beyond Death: Inheriting the Past and Giving to the Future, Transmitting the Legacy of One's Self'. *OMEGA – Journal of Death and Dying* 56 (4): 313–29. https://doi.org/10.2190/OM.56.4.a.

Jacobsen, Michael Hviid. 2017. *Postmortal Society: Towards a Sociology of Immortality*. Studies in Death, Materiality and the Origin of Time. London; New York: Routledge.

Lifton, Robert Jay, and Eric Olson. 1974. *Living and Dying*. London: Wildwood House.

Longfellow, Brenda. 2013. 'The Practice of Memory and the Politics of Memorialization: Denis Villeneuve's *Polytechnique*'. *Canadian Journal of Film Studies* 22 (1): 86–106. https://doi.org/10.3138/cjfs.22.1.86.

McAdams, Dan P. 2011. 'Narrative Identity'. In *Handbook of Identity Theory and Research*, edited by Seth J. Schwartz, Koen Luyckx, and Vivian L. Vignoles, 99–115. New York: Springer. https://doi.org/10.1007/978-1-4419-7988-9_5.

Malkowski, Jennifer. 2017. *Dying in Full Detail: Mortality and Digital Documentary*. Durham, NC; London: Duke University Press. https://doi.org/10.1215/9780822373414.

Matthews, Nathan. 2004. 'The Physicality of Māori Message Transmission – "Ko Te Tinana, He Waka Tuku Kōrero"'. *Junctures: The Journal for Thematic Dialogue*, no. 3. https://junctures.org/index.php/junctures/article/view/168. Last accessed 16 October 2022.

Muijnck, Deborah de. 2019. '"When Breath Becomes Air": Constructing Stable Narrative Identity during Terminal Illness'. *Colloquy*, December. https://search.informit.org/doi/abs/10.3316/informit.853861612257940.

Richards, Naomi. 2013. 'Rosetta Life: Using Film to Create "Bearable Fictions" of People's Experiences of Life-Limiting Illness'. In *Envisaging Death: Visual Culture and Dying*, edited by Michele Aaron, 190–205. Newcastle upon Tyne: Cambridge Scholars Publishing.

Ricœur, Paul. 1980. 'Narrative Time'. *Critical Inquiry* 7 (1): 169–90.

———. 1992. *Oneself as Another*. Chicago, IL: University of Chicago Press.

Rimmon-Kenan, Shlomith. 2002. 'The Story of "I": Illness and Narrative Identity'. *Narrative* 10 (1): 9–27.

Smith, Murray. 2022. *Engaging Characters: Fiction, Emotion, and the Cinema*. First published 1995. New York: Oxford University Press.

Wallenius, Peter. 2021a. *Marika's Passing (Marikan kuolema)*. Documentary. Yleisradio.

———. 2021b. Personal interview by Outi Hakola.

Walter, Tony. 2015. 'Communication Media and the Dead: From the Stone Age to Facebook'. *Mortality* 20 (3): 215–32. https://doi.org/10.1080/13576275.2014.993598.

Werth, Brenda. 2013. 'A Malvinas Veteran Onstage: From Intimate Testimony to Public Memorialization'. *South Central Review* 30 (3): 83–100.

8. PHYSICAL DOCUMENTARIES
Experiencing the Process of Dying

In 1976, American filmmaker Michael Roemer released *Dying*, a documentary of three terminally ill people facing their deaths. Filmed over a period of two years, the documentary creates intimate portraits of cancer patients' everyday lives. 'I have no fear of death,' says Sally, one of the three, in an opening scene framed by soothing classical music and a long, quiet gaze out of the hospital window. By repeating pacifying and understanding moments like this, the film seeks to alleviate the anguish of death. The approach mostly resonated with audiences, yet film critic Stefan Fleischer voiced concern that the film 'rings false':

> The main problem and limitation of the film *Dying* is, oddly, its sense of tact and good taste in dealing with a taboo subject. Perhaps these defects are, in a sense, obligatory: Roemer knew he had an important subject, he knew he wanted it on national television. He therefore produced a film which 'fit' the demands of the marketplace. In so doing he made a beautiful film on an ugly subject, whereas it could be that what is needed is an ugly film. (Fleischer 1978, 30)

Fleischer blames the film for making dying a mental rather than a physical process. Similar criticism can be levelled at most twenty-first-century end-of-life documentaries, where death anxiety is met with comforting views of how to manage and improve one's mental capability to deal with death (see, for example, Chapters 4 and 7). Some filmmakers have confronted the assumption head-on that avoiding the physical aspects of dying would serve to alleviate fear. Many end-of-life filmmakers fall back on metaphors and symbolism to soften the potentially upsetting nature of non-fictional death, but Steven Eastwood, director of *ISLAND* (2017), argues that this is not the only ethically acceptable approach to the topic:

> I wanted to enable the viewer to feel comfortable sharing in the event of the end of a life, without the protection of veils and metaphor. There is no sun going down. There are no polite symbols to reassure the audience that everything is going to be okay. That is what metaphor does; it suggests meaning, a purpose for everything, but moreover, that someone else is managing your experience. [...] We can trust ourselves to encounter dying directly, outside of the filters of metaphor and euphemistic language. (Eastwood 2018)

In this chapter, I analyse physical end-of-life documentaries that lay bare the increasing fragility, loss of independence and consciousness, and often, the moment of death. Filmed in the palliative care unit at Toronto Grace Health Centre, the Canadian documentary *Dying at Grace* (King 2003) witnesses the dying processes of five terminally ill patients: Carmela, Joyce, Richard, Lloyd and Eda. The Australian *Love in Our Own Time* (Murray and Hetherton 2011) compares the moments of birth and death through seven families, of whom John, Jutta, Doug and Noelene are living their last weeks at Calvary Hospital. *The Perfect Circle* (Tosi 2014) follows two hospice patients, Ivano and Meris, in the hills of Reggio Emilia, Northern Italy, and the British documentary *ISLAND* (Eastwood 2017) captures four dying people, Jamie, Mary, Alan and Roy, at Mountbatten Hospice on the Isle of Wight. All four films relate the physicality of dying to ideas of communicating to the viewer the experience of dying.

Ethics of Observational Documentaries

Dying at Grace opens to a white text on a black screen: 'This film is about the experience of dying' (King 2003). In the absence of titles, voiceover or other explanatory elements, this proclamation guides the viewing experience. In the audio commentary of the film's DVD release, director Allan King explains: instead of wanting to portray hospice care or meanings of death, the film set out to explore 'what it feels like to die, what it looks like to die' (King, Walker, and Hector 2008). Steven Eastwood (2018), similarly, wanted to 'show' people what death and dying is. These quotes highlight how physically oriented end-of-life documentaries focus on showing rather than explaining death.

The four documentaries follow the everyday lives of dying people at hospices and palliative care centres. The scenes observe mundane moments and avoid interviews or voiceovers. Also, the narration is about the here and now – and about the future, the prospect of death – instead of seeking to understand the subjects' past lives. The viewer does not hear detailed personal stories of who these people are, where they come from and what they have done before ending up in a hospice. For both Allan King (King, Walker, and Hector 2008) and Steven Eastwood (2018) this was a conscious choice: as the backstories would not have been about the present experience of dying, they would have focused the viewer's attention on information on the subjects. The choice to see present events and feelings as the most meaningful in the face of death guides the viewer's attention to the increasing loss of physical capability, a dimension of dying that can be observed without knowing the dying subjects.

Another way that physicality is given priority over the mental aspects of dying is the role of mundane conversations about weather, food, sports and so on. The subjects are not asked to tell their life stories to the camera or give meanings to impending death. These topics are referred to only if they come up in daily discussions with other characters. Claudia Tosi, the director of *The Perfect Circle*, was asked by the hospice to avoid intrusive questions, thus she chose to 'let the conversation go where it naturally goes'. She continues:

> if the filmmaker would ask them to talk about what they think about death, they probably would, but what would be the point in that? Why does this dying person need to talk about illness and death, why would that be more important than what for example Messi thinks about death? After all, he is going to die as well. (Tosi 2018)

Thus, instead of finding meanings for death and dying in the ways in which the subjects talk about the issue, the meanings come from showing their everyday experiences before death.

In their desire to show, physical documentaries follow the practices of observational documentaries, which prefer not to create a driving argument. They favour showing emotional experiences over telling or explaining them, and as such they position the viewer to witness the lived life (Nash 2011, 225, 229; Nichols 2017, 132–7). Allan King finds that the experience is the key in observational 'actuality drama': 'filming people as they experience their life and to do so in such a way that they will share their lives with the camera and the filmmakers. So that we can actually experience what they experience as they experience it' (King, Walker, and Hector 2008). Michele Aaron (2016, 206), accordingly, interprets the opening line of *Dying at Grace* as inviting the viewer to share or co-experience the experience of dying.

In turn, Madeleine Hetherton, co-director of *Love in Our Own Time*, argues that the observational mode helped them stay clear of expert voices explaining the subjects' experience and guiding the experience of the viewer. Rather, the unstable viewpoints allow viewers to project their own experiences to what they witness (Hetherton 2020). The opportunity to intimately witness the subjects' lived life without guidance and definite conclusions encourages the viewer to engage with the filmed subjects and the story in an active and critical manner (MacDougall 2018, 4, 8; Nash 2011, 225–9). Thus, the observational mode is as much about the viewer's experience as it is about the experience of the subject.

The observational traditions, where events apparently roll in their own space and rhythm, may comfort the viewer who can experience first-hand interaction with the subjects. Yet, in the context of observational documentaries, the risks in power relations between the filmmaker and the subject as well as between the subject and the viewer are at the very core of ethical discussions (Nichols 2017, 132–7; Nash 2011, 225, 228). Most end-of-life filmmakers are sensitive to issues of trust, consent and the inclusion of the subjects' viewpoints in the filming process (West 2018; Hakola 2021), so here I will focus on how the ethical portrayal of others is managed in the film style and its invitation for the viewer to witness death and dying. The prominent role of the viewer as an observer has raised ethical worries that observational documentaries might increase the distance between us and the other and diminish the affective connection needed for ethical space. Vivian Sobchack (1984, 299), for example, argues that the observational approach may give ethical consent to witness real-life deaths, but the witnessing often turns to impersonally and technically watching someone else die. Susan Sontag (2004, 34), similarly, questions whether a lack of background information might turn viewers into voyeurs and the dying people into distant others. In line with these concerns, several scholars have recognised an emotional and affective engagement with the subjects as a starting point for an ethical viewing experience (Gibson 2011, 924–5; Elsner 2020, 148–9). Physical documentaries create affective intimacy through tangible vulnerability of the dying subjects instead of using personalised stories to create engagement.

This opposes physical documentaries to the mainstream neoliberal imagery which celebrates unique personhood and customised death. The promise of individual exceptionalism in death allows the viewers to distance themselves from the dying subject – viewers can be assured that their future death will be different (Aaron 2020, 89; Malkowski 2017, 77–9). In contrast, in physical documentaries, the processes of dying have similar patterns and a lack of background stories guides towards universality. For Tom Murray (2020), the interconnectedness was the starting point in *Love in Our Own Time*, which proceeded to see death as something we all go through, 'an intrinsic part of life'. Similarly, Elsner (2020, 158) regards non-individualised deaths as ways of showing interconnectedness both between human beings and with nature. Death is a part of life in human lives, but in other life cycles as well.

Jennifer Malkowski (2017, 77–9, 105, 107) argues that non-individuality is one of the reasons why physical end-of-life films, which do not shy away from showing deathbed scenes, are so rare in the documentary field: repetitive scenes of the final stages of dying deny viewers a safe distance. Not getting to know the person too well can guide the viewer to engage with the physical process of dying as a human experience. Aaron claims that we need this kind of alternative imagery that reveals the physical vulnerability of the dying process (and the complexity of relationships, see Chapter 11) without compromises. In other words, when viewing someone else's suffering, an open and full confrontation with human vulnerability could create ethical space (Aaron 2020, 100–1). The observational approach to the physical dying process, thus, has ethical potential to use embodied engagement with the other in a way that invites the viewer to face their own mortality.

Physical Transformation, Time and Embodied Engagement

Embodied engagement in physical end-of-life documentaries is built through cinematic means other than life stories or individual dying processes. In physical and observational documentaries, it is the intimate aesthetics, embodiments and materiality that produce the transformative power of images. Observational documentaries create intimacy by using such cinematic techniques and filming practices as small, portable cameras and small film crews that allow close relationships with the subjects in intimate spaces and help to engender a trusting relationship (Nash 2011, 225–9). All the while, during the long filming processes, encounters between the filmmakers and the subjects evolve, grow deeper and are heightened, which translates into the viewer's experience as well.

End-of-life documentaries build an intimate and a material connection between the viewer and the subject through transformation. For example, *Dying at Grace* introduces Eda to the viewer in scenes where she wanders into other patients' rooms for gossip. She is active, talkative and even hopeful that there might be some good news on cancer treatments. At the end of the film, Eda is on her deathbed, unconscious, unable to communicate and breathing heavily. Throughout these documentaries, the viewer witnesses the declining health of the subjects, how they turn from social and talkative individuals to bodies quietly bound to their beds. It is these corporeal aspects that invite the viewer to affectively respond to the film and co-share the embodied transformation before death.

In ethical discussions, time and transformation have been in a key role in understanding documentary cinema's relationship to death. Vivian Sobchack argues that documentary cinema is not able to semiotically represent the existential shift from being to non-being (the moment of death). Instead, end-of-life representations are limited to representing the gradual dying processes and death's becoming 'ritually formalized as a moral consideration of the mortal conditions of the body, of the fragility of life' (Sobchack 1984, 297–9, quote from 299). This framing marks the process of dying as less interesting than the exact moment of death, yet many are afraid of the process of dying itself, physical decline, pain and symptoms, and loss of independence (Missler et al. 2011; Lehto and Stein 2009), which should make the portrayals of processes significant for end-of-life documentaries – precisely because of the agonising slowness of these processes. Perhaps documentary cinema can expose the 'processual, drawn-out quality of dying' (Elsner 2020, 9), enable the experience where 'mortality spills over into lived life' (Grønstad 2016, 141) or create 'transitional space' where the material presence of a dying person guides us to engage with mortality (E. Wilson 2012, 47–51).

To make death visible, cinematic expressions have tended to focus on violent death. Violence has the ability to lend movement, colour, sound and actors to the process of dying and visually transform a living body to a non-being abruptly and in a sudden transformation (Sobchack 1984, 289–90; Grønstad 2016, 9–10, 238–40). While violence can visualise the process of dying, other cinematic modes, such as slow processes of non-violent dying, could provide ethical engagement. Aaron (2016, 216) notes that natural and unexceptional deaths that are void of the historical and political traumas often connected to violent deaths (such as war deaths), can turn the gaze at death itself, not at other issues surrounding it. In this way, everyday deaths can become revolutionary forms of resistance in attempting to engage us with unavoidable mortality. Furthermore, Grønstad (2016, 119–25) argues that while the twenty-first century is marked by a constant flow of moving images that appear and disappear at a breathtaking pace, the slowness of images is almost a negation of mainstream cinema. Transformations which take their time demand the viewer's commitment; they create intimacy and offer an alternative to action-oriented society. As such, they create ethical potential for engagement with others.

Gradual transformations to death allow us to witness what the process of dying looks like. The slow progress also prepares us for the moment of death. Without backstories, the subjects' increasing vulnerability is turned to intimacy and engagement by the time we have spent together. Carl Plantinga (1999, 239), for example, links engagement and temporality because humane connection always occurs in time. Thus, time with the subjects strengthens the connection between the viewer and the dying person. Editor Nick Hector, for example, explains that the slow rhythm of *Dying at Grace* serves to increase intimacy. The viewer slowly gets to know the patients. At the beginning of the film, when the first subject, Carmela, dies, she is the one the viewer knows the least about. At the end of the film, the last subject to die – Eda – is the one that the viewer knows best (King, Walker, and Hector 2008). Eda's death becomes the film's culmination point on the emotional and embodied level. The viewer cares about her death. While this increased intimacy creates visual rhythm, our familiarity with the characters depends not on how well we know their personal stories, but on how we live along with them through their last months, weeks and days.

The slowness of dying is also visible in the slowness of the images. The observational camera is not in a hurry to cut away from the subjects. Instead, the viewer sees them shuffling with wheeled walkers or in wheelchairs, staring out of the windows, being quietly present in moments without action or dialogue. In *Love in Our Own Time*, for example, one of the dying characters, Noelene, is often filmed on a balcony having a smoke or staring outside. During the film, there is no significant action connected to Noelene, but she is filmed having breakfast or going to the bathroom. These moments are typical of observational cinema, which in its attempts to capture the events and moments as and when they happen prefers long takes that minimise fragmentation of images and create temporal unity (Nash 2011, 228; MacDougall 2018).

Slow and concentrated intimacy is why Grønstad argues that slow cinema has ethical potential. Indeed, when duration and presence become central cinematic content, the slow aesthetics, such as composition stillness, action unfolding in real time, dedramatisation of events, careful framing and long takes visualise the passing of time. The viewer can experience the flow of time on an embodied and material level. Grønstad notes that 'duration as a temporal mode and experiential frame' provides possibility for such ethical acts as 'recognition, reflection, imagination, and empathy' (Grønstad 2016, 75–6, 81, 103, 122, 127, quote from 121). The slowness of images that is dedicated to bodily transformations invites the viewer's engagement in ways that highlight both the subject's and the viewer's presence and awareness of loss of time and opportunities.

In *The Perfect Circle*, declining physical health is pictured through repeated scenes of Ivano, one of the main subjects, going to the bathroom. In the first of these scenes, Ivano struggles to get out of bed, and after succeeding, leans on his wheeled walker, and the camera follows Ivano as he makes his way to the bathroom door. The wife rolls her eyes at Ivano's independence and desire to show that he is still able and capable. Later, a similar scene is repeated. This time, Ivano needs help to get out of the bed and is assisted by the wife to walk to the bathroom. The last time the scene is repeated, Ivano is looking thin and fragile. He would like to go the bathroom, but the wife tells him that he is no longer capable of doing this. Disappointed, Ivano leans against the pillows. The signs of declining health are concrete and material, and Ivano's sense of loss of independence is palpable, an experience that the viewer can recognise and connect with. A scene like this reveals our common anxieties, which invites the viewer's responsibility over the material vulnerability of the filmed subject.

The transformation from a living and acting body to an inanimate corpse is often slow and agonising. For Steven Eastwood (2018), *ISLAND* 'is about time and the body, and the gradual shift from personhood into something else'; for Madeleine Hetherton (2010), deaths in *Love in Our Own Time* are slow transformations where you watch something disappear; and for Allan King (King, Walker, and Hector 2008), film editing needs to recognise dying as a process that takes time. This is where the film finds its rhythm – in the slow progress. The passing of time in fact became a theme in *Dying at Grace* because the film crew wanted to give the viewer a sense of unfolding days and what almost translated into boredom while waiting for death (King, Walker, and Hector 2008).

A similar sense of experiencing time has been recognised in studies of hospice and palliative care. Patients' lived experiences and bodily transformation make clock time less important than inner time, creating a sense of how time feels in relation to their bodily functions (Pasveer 2019; Ellingsen et al. 2013; Lindqvist et al. 2008). Time is sensed in terms of 'before and after I was able to go to the bathroom by myself', for example. This embodied time has been vividly described as 'it is not the clock that stops ticking, but the heart that stops beating, when lifetime is ended' (Ellingsen et al. 2013, 170). Thus, time and transformation are not merely a question of observing the slow progress of dying, but they offer an invitation to co-experience the embodied time of the dying person – the increasing loss of bodily functions, hanging on to the disappearing life, and anticipation of death. This also uncovers the ethical potential of slowing down both embodied and cinematic time in physical end-of-life documentaries. Slowness enables an intimate relationship between the viewer and the subject, a shared experience of temporality, and thus an increased demand for responsibility that encourages the viewer to recognise the mortality of the other person and of oneself.

Transforming with Affection-Images

In the discussion of transformation, time and intimacy, Gilles Deleuze's 'becoming', or transforming with images, manifests through movement-images. These are images of perception, images of affection and images of action, which together describe the embodied and affective transformation of the images and the viewer. The perception-image refers to shots which orient the viewer (and the subject) to the world, the location, the moment and various actors in that scene. Affection-images, which are key to ethical engagement, reveal the transformation from one state of experience to another. Affection-images show how the world and the situation affect the filmed subject (and the viewer) and reveal one's capability to react to events. Affection-images prioritise emotions, desires, hopes and needs, and are often close-ups, which engage the viewer to recognise and connect with the subjects' experiences and feelings. The action-image, then, can follow the affection-image, as the subjects' reaction helps the viewer to understand why they act the way they do (Deleuze 1986). While the viewers witness the slow transformation of dying through filmed subjects, their engagement with this transformation emerges from changing (intimate) images.

Among the opening scenes of *Dying at Grace* is a montage of healthcare staff taking care of the patients. Instead of filming the nurses, the image focuses on the dying people. Cinematographer Peter Walker says that this was a conscious, even if at times challenging, decision. It would have been cinematically typical to film the action of the nurses giving care, but it would have created distance between the viewer and the subject. Thus, it is not the camera focus on acts of care, but the patient's face that remains the focal point of these moments (King, Walker, and Hector 2008). These affection-images, or close-ups, as West (2018, 1489) reminds us, highlight corporeal intimacy and serve as 'a technique for connection and understanding'. In Carmela's case, the nurse is included in some of the shots, but the camera keeps focusing on Carmela's face, often in close-up. This asks the viewer to pay attention to Carmela's expressions, reactions and emotions. Carmela quietly follows the treatment, her expression meditative, sad, even absent.

In the Introduction (Chapter 1), I brought up Levinas's concern that we rarely see the other because we tend to explain the world through our own experiences. For Levinas, the face of the other suggests a way out of self-centredness and creates potential for an ethical encounter. The face and the facial expressions go beyond closed and linguistic meanings, making it conceivable that sameness and otherness can be recognised at the same time. The moving image, particularly, may elicit subtle movement of expressions, which encourages the viewer to react to the face before conscious and informational meaning-making adds sociocultural attitudes to the mix. Face-to-face encounters, Levinas suggests, thus create potential for ethical intimacy, to seeing the other and experiencing responsibility toward them (Levinas 2011).

For purposes of intimacy, physical end-of-life documentaries often linger on the face. Claudia Tosi, for example, emphasises the meaning of close-ups in *The Perfect Circle*. They are seen as tools to bring the subjects' expressions and reactions (affection-images) to the fore. Close-ups are there to create a strong emotional bond with and an emotional reaction from the viewer. Instead of using establishment shots (perception-images), Tosi prefers cutting straight to the emotion, to the point where 'nothing breaks the emotion' (Tosi 2018). In *The Perfect Circle*, the affective power of close-ups is visible in the scene of Meris's birthday party. Her family and friends are visiting at the hospice. There are presents, laughter and happiness (or at least, displayed happiness). In the midst of it all, the camera focuses on Meris's face and its obvious rawness and sadness (Figure 8.1).

Claudia Tosi remembers this scene for disclosing the inner and emotional conflicts of a dying person:

> If Meris would have been happy all the time at that party, it would only have been a description of the party. We don't know what she is thinking, but at that moment she was not in the room. This was not possible in every scene, but that is what I try to do, to find an element that builds the conflict – a visual or sound element in the scene as a focus point. By a close-up I can tell a story about her state of mind that compares to the happiness of everyone else. (Tosi 2018)

This affection-image gives the viewer a sense of intimacy, a recognition of raw feelings and a connection to the realisation of loss of opportunity to celebrate further birthdays. The affection-image transforms birthday celebrations into a melancholic anticipation of death.

In *Dying at Grace*, the closer we get to death, the more close-up images the narration uses. At the beginning of each of their stories, the dying subjects are filmed in their surroundings, walking the hospital corridors, going to their

Figure 8.1 Close-up of Meris at the birthday party in *The Perfect Circle* (Tosi 2014).

treatments. When their situation changes, the camera not only stays by their bedside, but opts for medium shots and medium close-ups. By the deathbed scenes, the camera is focused on their faces, often in close-ups. This spatial change increases the intimacy: the viewer is brought closer to the emotions, but also closer to the embodied loss. In these moments, Aaron (2016, 212) argues, the viewer can recognise the 'cessation of cognition', where the dying person 'ceases to be able to engage with others, when communication, awareness, agency and even subjectivity recede'. Aaron refers to Joyce from *Dying at Grace* as an example. At one point, the previously active Joyce turns quiet and starts to stare emptily into nothing. Aaron sees this as an example of 'raw life', where subjectivity has lessened, but is not missing. These moments enable the viewer to see and feel something otherwise unknown, something existentially raw which demands responsibility from the viewer. As such, these moments make the approaching death visible without dehumanising the subject or distancing the viewer (Aaron 2016, 212–13; 2014, 174–6). Indeed, together with the (slowly) transforming framings and affective images, the viewer becomes entwined with the character, highlighting the intimacy of the situation. The only affective contact points that the viewer has by this stage are fragile bodies and faces. This connection serves as the core of an ethical experience of what dying might feel like, or at least what it looks like.

Filming Moment of Death

Physical end-of-life documentaries commonly show the moment of death. Whereas many other end-of-life filmmakers prefer to keep the moment of death private (Merikanto 2018; Luostarinen 2020; Davidson and Gibb 2020; T. Wilson 2019; Wallenius 2021), Claudia Tosi was the only director of the analysed physical documentaries whose deathbed scene finishes before the moment of death. Because death's timing is unpredictable, Tosi was filming elsewhere at Ivano's final moment:

> Ivano was shot until after an hour until he died. He was asking me to be there and wanting me to be there. And I looked at the cinematographer and said, we'll just do what he wants. And this is when he was shooting me and Carla touching his hands. He really wanted to be touched, in that very moment, so we did it. It was a warm, not a cold moment. (Tosi 2018)

Ivano is lying in his bed, tired, weak and drawn. He lifts a finger, asking the people in the room to come closer. The camera also moves closer to his bedside. We can see the filmmaker and Ivano's wife holding Ivano's hand. The image cuts to look out of the window, into pouring rain. At the same time, the sound of difficult breathing continues in the background, until it stops, and only the rain goes on before quiet instrumental music begins. The scene, particularly the end of it, is a reminder of the film's opening with images of rain, sounds of breathing in the background, deep sighs and wind. The difference is that death is no longer a prospect waiting to happen, it has arrived, but throughout this journey, a sense of intimacy has increased. By the end, the viewer is close to Ivano, sees him looking fragile and thin on his deathbed, and hears his laboured breathing. While the sight of his thin arms can make the viewer flinch, the difficult breathing embodies the fragility of the situation. Compared to the vivid person in the earlier scenes, the loss of being is painfully visible and felt. Touching and caressing do add to the intimacy, but they also are about affect, not action. As such, the deathbed scenes are intensely affective.

The deathbed scenes are the emotional and narrative culmination of physical end-of-life films. Steven Eastwood (2018) describes the seven-minute take of Alan's death as one that 'made the film', and Allan King (King, Walker, and Hector 2008) sees the almost three-minute-long sequence of Eda's death, the subject whom the viewer knows best, as the crux of the whole documentary, something everyone has been waiting for. These filmmakers identify the moment of death as the most central aspect of their documentaries, whereas scholarly debate on filming these liminal moments has been rather critical.

In 1949, André Bazin wrote an essay 'Death Every Afternoon', where he argues that because death is a unique moment, the last moment of an individual's experienced time and life, cinema – as based on repetition and replay – would only violate moral and metaphysical aspects of death. Bazin compares the filming of death to missing the 'real presence', an image that is 'emptied of its psychological reality, a body without a soul'. As such, documenting the moment of death would be obscene, a perversion, as it can never relay the unique essence of that moment for the viewer (Bazin 2003).

In 1984, phenomenologist Vivian Sobchack returned to the topic with a similar argument that cinema could not reach the multiplicity of death as an experience: death 'is always original, unconventional, and shocking, its event always simultaneously representing both the process of sign production and the end of representation'. Thus, according to Sobchack, the non-being that death ultimately is remains unrepresented. Any documentary representation can be purely technical, not a lived-body experience (Sobchack 1984, 283–7, quote from 286).

In 2017, Jennifer Malkowski continued the discussion of death's assumed unrepresentability from a technological perspective. For Malkowski, cinematic technology can never 'meaningfully' represent a liminal event such as death. The camera can only pursue external signs. As death is an internal experience, documentary cinema is 'unable to show death "in full detail", as it remains beyond representation even amid image technologies that can record it more fully than ever' (Malkowski 2017, 7). These arguments, expanding from one decade to another, focus on the moment of death and the documentary camera's challenges to communicate the totality of that experience. Problematically, they also seem to expect first-person consciousness as the criterion for cinematic representation, a demand that is not used in other contexts of embodied or affective experiences. For example, could we ever experience love or pain as someone else does?

I argue that if we approach these filmed moments of death from the vantage point of their potential for ethical intimacy, even death can be seen as a co-sharable experience. Viewers are not expected, or even desired, to experience death in ways that would make this experience their own, but through embodied connection they can feel the loss related to the ultimate transformation from being to non-being. These filmed moments bring the undeniability of death into the sphere of experience, and it would be peculiar to claim that this should or could not be done due to existential concerns. Instead, the desire to reach towards non-being, to explore the fragile moments between animate and inanimate, or life and death, can make us ask existential questions and can make us aware of our mortality.

Stillness and Death

Still, as Malkowski suggests, death can be problematic to cinema that builds on movement. Corpses, by definition, are still. Thus, cinema often adds movement to dead bodies that are carried and pushed around (Malkowski 2017, 42). Physical documentaries also utilise this, as is evident in the opening of *Dying at Grace* with a scene of a corpse being taken to a morgue. However, in the deathbed scenes, the movement is minimal, thus forcing the viewer to pay special attention to it. The camera is in an enclosed space. The filmmakers use long takes. The focus is on dying people in their beds. The close-ups and medium close-ups create a sense of intimacy that leaves no escape route where the viewers could distance themselves from the image. The absence of a non-diegetic soundtrack increases the sense of presence and realism.

For example, Eda's death in *Dying at Grace* lasts almost three minutes, while a hand-held camera keeps shooting a close-up of her face. The death scene is primed with earlier shots of nurses visiting Eda's bedside to check on her condition. The final scene, however, starts without any further orientation for the viewer, without a perception-image. Instead, the camera dives straight into the affection-image, emphasising the viewer's connection to Eda. Her eyes are half-closed, every breath difficult, gasping for air with difficult swallows, almost as if it were an unwanted action. Breathing is the main audible and visible element in the scene, where it causes movement of cheeks and a slight bobbing of the head. Haptic connection to the affection-image invites viewers to become bodily aware of their own breathing, its rhythm and its automated nature. This consciousness makes the viewers pay attention to breathing's necessity for the lived experience and continuation of inner, embodied time (Hakola 2022).

During the scene, the silence-interspersed pauses between breaths increase until there is no single laborious gasp left. It allows the viewer to focus on Eda's vulnerable transformation from a state of aliveness to state of being dead. The film ends with this image, a close-up of inanimate Eda lying on her deathbed. In other words, there is no follow-up or action-image that would give the viewer an outlet or an example of how to properly react to the situation. Only reference to the continuation of universal time is the change from post-mortem silence to the beeping sounds of the medical equipment that gradually become audible. They remind us that life continues, leaving the viewer solely responsible for reacting to Eda's death. Thus, the scene does not assume that the viewer transforms with the image to the experience of being dead, but to the state of being responsible for their watching someone dying, for caring about her death.

For Sobchack, these kinds of deliberate decisions to focus on the deathbed scenes give the viewer an ethical permission to be present in the situation. The long take and carefully framed image promise that the camera is not accidentally in the room; the dying subject has given permission to the filmmaker, and by extension to the viewer, to witness. This 'humane stare', to use Sobchack's words, appeals to the viewer's responsibility and respect towards the other, and prompts an 'ethical stance toward the event of death s/he witnesses' (Sobchack 1984, 294, 297).

Regardless of the ethical permission to witness, both Sobchack and Malkowski argue that these scenes fail to create a connection with the viewer that is required for an ethical experience. For Sobchack, connection is impossible with an unintentional dying subject, much less with an inanimate corpse, which is a sign of 'dead', instead of 'death' as an event. Thus, when the dying person has lost subjectivity, the potential for embodied connection disappears. Sobchack takes the lack of reciprocity of the gaze, where the dying person is no longer able to return the viewer's gaze and demand responsibility for viewing, as a sign of lost subjectivity (Sobchack 1984, 287–90). However, while the gaze is an important aspect of cinematic connection, the ethical implications of reciprocity can be questioned. Aaron (2016, 214), for example, contends that even if the scene of Eda's death includes 'no-return' of the gaze, the director does 'not depend upon this humane looking back for his ethical approach'. Director King argues, indeed, that Eda's earlier consent provides reciprocity and that her continued blank stare should be interpreted as a gift from a courageous person, who gives the viewer her last breath (King, Walker, and Hector 2008).

PHYSICAL DOCUMENTARIES

According to Aaron, a feeling towards the other continues, even without a reciprocal gaze and even after the other is no longer present. The continued feeling creates a possibility for something mystical and unknowable to be made, at least on some level, knowable (Aaron 2016, 216). Aaron bases this interpretation on Anat Pick's (2011, 157) concept of the blank gaze, which describes moments where 'the subject looks into the camera, but the gaze bypasses us without endorsing the communicability between spectator and subject'. Whereas for Sobchack this lack of reciprocity is both an ethical and a metaphysical challenge, Pick approaches the issue from the perspective of recognition of vulnerability. When the viewer realises that the subject is unable to look back and recognise the presence of the viewer, viewers face their own responsibility over the situation. Pick proposes that ethics might even start with the blank gaze: 'For what is ethics if not my seeing without being seen – my unrequited attention?' (Pick 2011, 158–9) Aaron, in turn, connects this unrequited attention to 'raw life', which enables ethical encounter precisely because this unfamiliar connection decentres the viewer. The lack of confirmation of consent forces the viewer to be solely responsible for making sure that the engagement remains ethical (Aaron 2020, 89–90). The deathbed scenes suggest that potential feeling of discomfort can engage ethical feeling and thinking. The viewer must take responsibility for their choice to either engage in affective and embodied witnessing or detach themselves from the situation.

Malkowski approaches the challenges related to the moment of death from the realisation that cinematic technology cannot pinpoint the exact moment of death, the ultimate transformation from being to non-being. No matter whether the film rolls on time, or these images are slowed down to single photographs, the inner experience of dying cannot be made visible (Malkowski 2017, 28, 71). Further, the desire to pinpoint the exact moment is rather banal. Even in medical science, the exact moment, and even the very definition of death, are fluid and fleeting. Death can be declared only after it has happened. In end-of-life documentaries, we see healthcare staff checking the patients' breathing and pulse to ascertain the status of their being dead. Why should cinema, then, be able to capture the moment that can be fleeting to people present in the situation? Perhaps the viewer's intimate connection to the dying subject, carried through with long and intimate takes is meaningful because of the slow transformation to non-being, instead of a sharp moment of transition.

Both transformation and continued connection with the dying become visible in Alan's death scene in *ISLAND*. To capture the moment, Eastwood filmed for forty-eight hours straight after Alan lost consciousness. When Alan died, Eastwood was asleep, and the camera was the only witness of the moment. For Eastwood, this vigilantly and independently recording camera meant the filmmaker's role in (re)framing the moment was diminished, and as such, the

167

moment becomes shared between the viewer and the subject: 'You are used as a viewer to have the filmmaker as the chaperon, as a guide. When I am sleeping, it is just you and Alan, so in many ways the viewer gets to experience what I don't' (Eastwood 2018). While the placing of the camera relies on the filmmakers' intentions, it lessens their role when the scene momentarily prioritises the embodied link between the camera, the viewer and the subject (Nichols 1991, 86). In a close-up, similarly to Eda's case, the camera captures Alan inhaling and gasping, placing the viewer as an embodied witness. The affection-image serves also as a reminder of Levinas's ideas that face of the other can invite the viewer to abandon self-centredness in the situation. Through close connection, the viewer experiences how Alan frequently seems to take his last breath before gasping for more air. His moment of death can only be identified after it has already occurred since the viewer continues to vigilantly watch for the next breath. This makes Alan's embodied time fluid, and by extension the viewer's co-experience becomes fluid as well.

After Alan's last breath, when the gasps stop, only silence and non-movement remain, until a nurse enters the room and notes that Alan has died. There is no rush to cut away from the scene, the viewer's presence in the situation continues, as if having a personal wake for Alan. Indeed, because slow images contradict the cinematic preference for movement, these are powerful moments (Remes 2012, 259–61), and in deathbed scenes the slowness highlights the importance of the moment, the death of a person, and the ethical connection with that person.

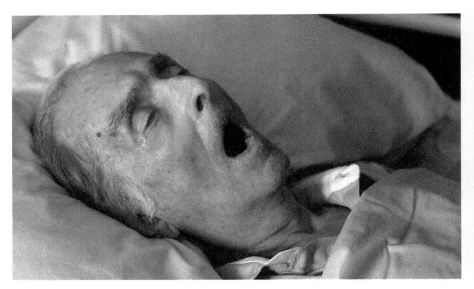

Figure 8.2 Death scene of Alan in *ISLAND* (Eastwood 2017).

PHYSICAL DOCUMENTARIES

This combination of silence and non-movement also marks a transformation in embodied time. The film does not end when both sound and movement cease. Even if nothing changes, the frames keep moving, making a spectacle out of stillness. As Justin Remes (2012, 263–7) argues, when nothing apparently happens in the image, the viewer witnesses as time goes by, and this witnessing creates a constantly evolving experience. In Alan's case, the long take by the deathbed invites embodied connection through his recognisable vulnerability, and after his death, the continued use of stasis helps the viewers to recognise the loss. When they realise that Alan has died, the viewers also recognise the continuation of life around them. Universal time moves on, the viewer's embodied time moves on, and when the nurse enters the room and action restarts, the focus readjusts to those who remain and to the viewer, who all react to Alan's death.

The differences between still and moving images have promoted philosophical discussions about images' relationship with temporality and mortality. The traditional view emphasises still and inanimate images as reminders of death and loss, whereas the movement serves as a sign of life (e.g. Bazin 1960; Sontag 2001). In Alan's scene, the continued statis breaks down this separation because the scene is not about the frozen frame but about nonaction within the moving frames, which communicates the loss, not life. From another perspective, Laura Mulvey also considers the classical division artificial. For her, the potential to freeze any moving image into a still, to break down the movement, reveals that the sense of the subject's presence is always an illusion (Mulvey 2006, 21–31). As such, any moving image carries mortality with it, only serving an illusion of aliveness.

In a way, Alan's death scene seems to fit this description of mortality – after all, this scene is directly about death and dying. However, death is not the only reference within these images. Affection-images of Alan are not merely about his experience, but in a Deleuzian manner, they become part of the viewer's experience as well. The viewer's affect happens in presence. Thus, the moment is a sign of loss and mortality, but also a lived experience of these. This recalls Emma Wilson's (2012, 5–6, quote from 6) argument that instead of communicating death, images become traces 'of embodied experience, of sensuousness, of engagement with the world, up to and beyond death'. In other words, it is the viewer's affective and embodied transformation with images that creates continuing connection. The combination of this idea of the viewer's continuing transformation and the viewer's sole responsibility without reciprocal connection in the situation reveals how the viewer may engage with the dying subjects not only up to their deaths but beyond them as well.

When the subjects die, the films do not necessarily finish. Instead, these documentaries often direct the viewer's experience of death and dying towards an experience of loss through other people, family and friends. In *Love in Our*

Own Time, Jutta's death is the culmination of the film. This documentary likens death to birth: co-director Tom Murray argues that both life and death are miraculous.

> The language that we have around these experiences speaks to the miraculousness of life seemingly coming from nothing ... and in some ways in death. We have a living human being and then when they die, they very quickly transform into something else. You can almost immediately see that their life force is gone. So, in the sense that in both birth and death there is a transition between being and non-being there seemed a kind of similarity between the two, and I wanted to deal with that. (Murray 2020)

Jutta's death heightens this connection by deviating from the typical filming practices of deathbed scenes. The scene is a montage of two women in labour and Jutta on her deathbed. The sounds of birthing women's loud breathing are edited to echo Jutta's death rattle, and from the sound of the new mothers crying with happiness, the film shifts to the sounds of desperate crying and images of Jutta's family crying around her deathbed. In the case of *Love in Our Own Time*, the comparison between the defining moments of birth and death reflects the cyclical pattern of life. References to death as a part of life and nature are a part of other physical documentaries as well, which is seen in the references to water in *The Perfect Circle*, for example. While the argument of the naturality of death is used to highlight its inevitability, it does not aim to take away the sense of loss. Instead of focusing on the joy of new families, the camera returns to Jutta's deathbed and stays there with the grieving family. When Jutta's peaceful face is in close-up, the family remains present in the image and the viewer can see a hand caressing Jutta's face. The movement centres the experience on the family and their emotional reaction to loss. For co-director Madeleine Hetherton (2020), the family's reactions were more powerful than the actual death: 'It was a very unique kind of grief that we could watch him [the husband], and grieve with him.' Thus, the viewer's engagement is directed towards embodied grief, and this connection allows the viewer to co-experience loss, to take part in a shared moment and have a permission to mourn as well.

In the lonely deathbed scenes, such as those of Alan and Eda, the viewer becomes responsible for recognition of death and loss of a person, and the inclusion of other characters invites the viewer to connect with living subjects and shares their embodied affects. Cinematographer Peter Walker, for example, describes their experience of filming Lloyd's death in *Dying at Grace*. This death differs from Eda's yet has similar elements. The camera stays by the deathbed, but this time, family members are present as well. Lloyd's difficult breathing fills the void, demanding attention while the family caresses him and gently whisper that it is okay to let go. The viewer's attention is thus divided between Lloyd's last breaths and family caresses. After death, the narrative focus re-centres on the family members' expressions of loss. The cinematographer remembers this moment as not only filming someone's death but as participating in the experience: 'I felt I was contributing, offering my support, being in the room. [...] I was doing my job, [...] allowing the audience to experience it as well' (King, Walker, and Hector 2008). Thus, the cinematographer felt that they were both co-sharing the situation with Lloyd and the family, but in addition, they mediated this potential for co-experience to the viewer as well.

Conclusion

Physical end-of-life documentaries and their deathbed scenes refuse to protect the viewer from emotionally, ethically and culturally difficult themes such as fragility of the dying and the moment of death. There is a sense of being present, which gives ethical permission to witness what the process of dying is as an experience. In addition to permission to witness, the viewer is given access to the increasing physical vulnerability of the filmed subjects, and this vulnerability calls for further responsibility – a demand to recognise the vulnerability in others and in ourselves. The responsible reaction, instead of objectification, is encouraged through cinematic means – slow aesthetics, emphasised intimacy and affection-images.

In turn, this responsible reaction to watch someone die can be seen as cinema's ethical potential: the viewers may open themselves towards the experiences of others, not by owning that experience, but by building an embodied and affective connection with the filmed subjects. This connection, I argue, reaches over the moment of death. The ambiguity in recognising the exact moment ensures fluidity for the embodied connection with the dying subject. Being present, then, sharing the fragility of the process of dying and the subtleness of transformations from being to non-being, can potentially transcend the limits of life and death. The viewer is allowed to co-experience the situation, if not death itself. In the observational documentaries that highlight the physical aspects of dying, the viewers are not asked to participate in meaning-making about death. Instead, they are expected to feel the emotions, affects and bodily experiences related to witnessing these processes. By giving the viewers access to the physical transformations of dying people, these documentaries may help the viewer to understand the process through experience and may transform the viewer as well.

References

Aaron, Michele. 2014. *Death and the Moving Image: Ideology, Iconography and I.* Edinburgh: Edinburgh University Press.

———. 2016. 'Watching Others Die: Dying at Grace (2003), Spectatorship, and the Ethics of Being Moved'. In *Malady and Mortality: Illness, Disease and Death in Literary and Visual Culture*, edited by Helen Thomas, 205–19. Newcastle upon Tyne: Cambridge Scholars Publishing.

———. 2020. 'Love's Revival: Film Practice and the Art of Dying'. *Film-Philosophy* 24 (2): 83–103. https://doi.org/10.3366/film.2020.0133.

Bazin, André. 1960. 'The Ontology of the Photographic Image'. Translated by Hugh Gray. *Film Quarterly* 13 (4): 4–9. https://doi.org/10.2307/1210183.

———. 2003. 'Death Every Afternoon'. In *Rites of Realism: Essays on Corporeal Cinema*, edited by Ivone Margulies, 27–31. New York: Duke University Press. https://doi.org/10.1515/9780822384618-003.

Davidson, Paul, and Barbara Gibb. 2020. Personal interview by Outi Hakola.

Deleuze, Gilles. 1986. *Cinema 1: The Movement-Image*. First published 1983. Minneapolis: University of Minnesota.

Eastwood, Steven. 2017. *ISLAND*. Documentary. Hakawati.

———. 2018. Personal interview by Outi Hakola.

Ellingsen, Sidsel, Åsa Roxberg, Kjell Kristoffersen, Jan Henrik Rosland, and Herdis Alvsvåg. 2013. 'Entering a World with No Future: A Phenomenological Study Describing the Embodied Experience of Time When Living with Severe Incurable Disease'. *Scandinavian Journal of Caring Sciences* 27 (1): 165–74. https://doi.org/10.1111/j.1471-6712.2012.01019.x.

Elsner, Anna Magdalena. 2020. 'Landscapes of Care and the Enchantment of Dying in Edwin Beeler's *Die Weisse Arche* (2016)'. *Studies in Documentary Film* 14 (2): 147–60. https://doi.org/10.1080/17503280.2020.1725994.

Fleischer, Stefan. 1978. 'Dying to Be on Television'. *Film Quarterly* 31 (4): 30–6. https://doi.org/10.2307/1211805.

Gibson, Margaret. 2011. 'Real-Life Death: Between Public and Private, Interior and Exterior, the Real and the Fictional'. *South Atlantic Quarterly* 110 (4): 917–32. https://doi.org/10.1215/00382876-1382321.

Grønstad, Asbjørn. 2016. *Film and the Ethical Imagination*. London: Palgrave Macmillan. https://doi.org/10.1057/978-1-137-58374-1_10.

Hakola, Outi. 2022. 'Breathing in Mortality: Demedicalization of Death in Documentary Films'. *Journal of Somaesthetics* 8 (1): 30–44.

Hetherton, Madeleine. 2020. Personal interview by Outi Hakola.

King, Allan. 2003. *Dying at Grace*. Documentary. Alan King Associates.

King, Allan, Peter Walker, and Nick Hector. 2008. *Audio Commentary. Dying at Grace*. Dir. Allan King. DVD. Alan King Associates.

Lehto, Rebecca Helen, and Karen Farchaus Stein. 2009. 'Death Anxiety: An Analysis of an Evolving Concept'. *Research and Theory for Nursing Practice* 23 (1): 23–41. https://doi.org/10.1891/1541-6577.23.1.23.

Levinas, Emmanuel. 2011. *Totality and Infinity: An Essay on Exteriority*. First published 1969. Pittsburgh, PA: Duquesne University Press.

Lindqvist, Olav, Birgit H. Rasmussen, Anders Widmark, and Lars-Christer Hydén. 2008. 'Time and Bodily Changes in Advanced Prostate Cancer: Talk About Time As Death Approaches'. *Journal of Pain and Symptom Management* 36 (6): 648–56. https://doi.org/10.1016/j.jpainsymman.2007.12.013.

Luostarinen, Kiti. 2020. Personal interview by Outi Hakola.

MacDougall, David. 2018. 'Observational Cinema'. In *The International Encyclopedia of Anthropology*, edited by Hilary Callan, 1–10. Oxford: John Wiley & Sons, Ltd. https://doi.org/10.1002/9781118924396.wbiea1535.

Malkowski, Jennifer. 2017. *Dying in Full Detail: Mortality and Digital Documentary*. Durham, NC; London: Duke University Press. https://doi.org/10.1215/9780822 373414.

Merikanto, Tiina. 2018. Personal interview by Outi Hakola.

Missler, Marjolein, Margaret Stroebe, Lilian Geurtsen, Mirjam Mastenbroek, Sara Chmoun, and Karolijne van der Houwen. 2011. 'Exploring Death Anxiety among Elderly People: A Literature Review and Empirical Investigation'. *OMEGA – Journal of Death and Dying* 64 (4): 357–79. https://doi.org/10.2190/om.64.4.e.

Mulvey, Laura. 2006. *Death 24x a Second: Stillness and the Moving Image*. Repr. London: Reaktion Books.

Murray, Tom. 2020. Personal interview by Outi Hakola.

Murray, Tom, and Madeleine Hetherton. 2011. *Love in Our Own Time*. Documentary. Tarpaulin Productions.

Nash, Kate. 2011. 'Documentary-for-the-Other: Relationships, Ethics and (Observational) Documentary'. *Journal of Mass Media Ethics* 26 (3): 224–39. https://doi.org/10.1080 /08900523.2011.581971.

Nichols, Bill. 1991. *Representing Reality: Issues and Concepts in Documentary*. Bloomington; Indianapolis: Indiana University Press.

———. 2017. *Introduction to Documentary, Third Edition*. Bloomington: Indiana University Press.

Pasveer, Bernike. 2019. 'Deadlines: Doing Times in (Dutch) Hospice'. *Mortality* 24 (3): 319–32. https://doi.org/10.1080/13576275.2018.1461817.

Pick, Anat. 2011. *Creaturely Poetics: Animality and Vulnerability in Literature and Film*. New York: Columbia University Press.

Plantinga, Carl. 1999. 'The Scene of Empathy and the Human Face in Film'. In *Passionate Views: Film, Cognition, and Emotion*, edited by Carl Plantinga and Greg M. Smith, 239–56. Baltimore, MD: Johns Hopkins University Press.

Remes, Justin. 2012. 'Motion(Less) Pictures: The Cinema of Stasis'. *The British Journal of Aesthetics* 52 (3): 257–70. https://doi.org/10.1093/aesthj/ays021.

Sobchack, Vivian. 1984. 'Inscribing Ethical Space: Ten Propositions on Death, Representation, and Documentary'. *Quarterly Review of Film Studies* 9 (4): 283–300. https://doi.org/10.1080/10509208409361220.

Sontag, Susan. 2001. *On Photography*. First published 1977. New York: Picador.

———. 2004. *Regarding the Pain of Others*. Paperback edition. First published 2003. New York: Picador.

Tosi, Claudia. 2014. *The Perfect Circle*. Documentary. Movimenta/MiaFilm/Cobos Film/Petra Pan Film Production.

———. 2018. Personal interview by Outi Hakola.

Wallenius, Peter. 2021. Personal interview by Outi Hakola.

West, Emily. 2018. 'Invitation to Witness: The Role of Subjects in Documentary Representations of the End of Life'. *International Journal of Communication* 12: 1481–500.

Wilson, Emma. 2012. *Love, Mortality and the Moving Image*. London: Palgrave Macmillan. https://doi.org/10.1057/9780230367708.

Wilson, Tim. 2019. Personal interview by Outi Hakola.

9. DIALOGICAL DOCUMENTARIES
Understanding Personal End-of-Life Choices

The Good Death (Krupa 2018a) begins with images of a garden and a house, while a woman's voice recites T. S. Eliot's poem 'A Song for Simeon'. A shot of the 72-year-old woman reading a book accompanies the last verses, which could have been written about her experience. In these verses, the poem's narrator talks about being tired with their life, and wanting to depart (Eliot 1928).

The poem sets the tone for Janette's plans to leave England for Switzerland, where non-profit organisations provide physician-assisted suicide for non-citizens like her whose own countries do not allow assisted dying. Janette has muscular dystrophy, a degenerative genetic disease her mother suffered from and which Janette has passed on to her own son. Janette recalls her mother spending thirty years just sitting in a chair, doing nothing. Janette does not want to experience a similar fate, which is hinted at in a scene of Janette struggling in an armchair. She tries different ways to pull herself up, but her movements are slow, unsure, and the progress is minimal at best. The chair symbolises the physical limitations of Janette's life, representing her struggle in everyday activities, but it is also a prison where one is forced to watch life happen to others.

In the director's statement on the film's homepage, Tomáš Krupa (2018b) commends Janette's open and intimate revelations of her physical and mental states. This, he says, makes *The Good Death* unique. Krupa continues the discussion on emotional intimacy in an interview for *Cineuropa*. He argues that emotional storytelling makes any film an instrument of change, not because the film changes society, but because it can transform the thinking of those who can change society. His ideas highlight the ethical space's capacity for transformation: an open engagement with others can result in social change. Thus, with emotionally strong films, such as *The Good Death*, Krupa seeks to make important topics 'come to life on the screen' (*Cineuropa* 2020). Similarly, while *The Good Death* is related to legalisation debates over assisted dying, the film does not openly advocate for legalisation. Instead, it provides one personal story where the viewer is invited to understand (not necessarily to accept) why Janette desires to die.

The personal stories of assisted dying continue to discuss the (neoliberal) individualism that I introduced in the context of advocacy documentaries in Chapter 5. Assisted death is once again framed as an individual choice and responsibility, but from another perspective. Where advocacy documentaries discuss rational argumentation for or against assisted dying, personal stories focus on affective experiences. The Belgian documentary *Nathan – Free as a Bird* (Nollet 2014a), *The Good Death* (Krupa 2018a), a European co-production (Slovakia, Czech Republic, Austria, France), and two documentaries from the Netherlands, *A Dignified Death* (Venrooij 2018) and *Veda's Choice* (Villerius 2019) give access to the last months, weeks, days and hours of Nathan, Janette, Eelco and Veda. These documentaries create one personal portrait at a time and focus on their protagonist's emotional and mental experiences related to dying.

These films refuse to generalise their argumentation. Juan Fariña, Irene Cambra Badii and Ailen Provenza (2016) argue that films about assisted dying provide cases to study the moral, normative and ethical aspects of end-of-life choices. Addressing a 'singular realm', which they see as 'the true ethical dimension', these films transform ethics from normative principles to lived experiences. When ethical issues are represented through singularity, the varied personal contexts can be taken into account and understood in discussions about the moral and legal aspects of assisted dying (Fariña, Cambra Badii, and Provenza 2016, 296–304, quotes from 296). This reasoning chimes with Dan McAdams's (2011, 111) argument that western life narratives prioritise self-expression, individualism and the desire for 'uniqueness of the inner self'. In this chapter, I study how the singular approach asks the viewer to understand the personal stories and decisions of those wanting an assisted death. I approach the discussion from the perspective of hermeneutic phenomenology that aims to conceptualise how processes of understanding function. I suggest that in these documentaries, the dialogical approach to narration is used to increase understanding, and later, that this dialogical narrative mode asks the viewer to listen to what the subjects have to say. Consequently, I argue that in dialogical documentaries about assisted dying, the viewer's ethical relationship with the subjects is to be found in the ethics of listening.

Processes of Understanding

The hermeneutical tradition is described as an 'art of interpretation' (Abulad 2007, 11), but also as an 'art of understanding' (Kennedy Schmidt 2016, 1–6). Particularly, scholars, including me, who draw from the early-nineteenth-century writings of Friedrich Schleiermacher (1998) and the twentieth-century philosopher Hans-Georg Gadamer (1998) consider that understanding is the aim or the result of interpretative processes. The hermeneutical process, where meanings are interpreted and understanding emerges, also relates to the phenomenology of the film-viewing process. The viewer's embodied relationship with the film moves beyond perception and reaches towards meaning-making and understanding.

Hermeneutic phenomenology gives understanding a key role in lived experiences. It discusses how events and issues are experienced and interpreted by experiencers and those witnessing these experiences, and how understanding is built from such experiential structures (Wojnar and Swanson 2007, 174; Laverty 2003, 24). This definition allows room to recognise the layered structure of cinematic experiences. The main character often becomes the focal point for understanding: the person desiring to die aims to make others understand their decision. Often the other people in the documentaries exemplify these positions of trying to understand the wishes of the main character. This process adds a dialogical aspect to the film and also provides models for the viewer to witness. The viewer's understanding is thus constructed through various relationships with the filmed material and subjects.

The layered structure of experiences emerges in *A Dignified Death*, the story of Eelco, a Dutch man whose mental suffering has led him to choose death assistance and to have it recorded. The film starts by looking back after Eelco's death. The camera records from a distance, on a rainy day, a group of people spreading ashes in the water. Gentle piano music plays in the background as they console each other with hugs. After the opening credits, the viewer hears Eelco's pre-recorded answering machine message stating calmly, 'I'm gone now. I died like you may have read or heard' (translated from Dutch). The short message confirms that death has taken place. The opening suggests that there is nothing left to do to convince Eelco to change his mind, but one can still aim to understand his decision.

However, instead of proceeding to Eelco's explanations, the narration continues from another retrospective angle when the family members – sister, mother and father – talk about their experiences. They share both happy memories and the grief that Eelco's death has brought to them. They also talk about Eelco's mental suffering, his suicide attempt and inability to live without constant support and care. All family members emphasise that despite their

DIALOGICAL DOCUMENTARIES

grief they understand Eelco's decision. In this way, the film first builds models of understanding for the viewer.

The need to create models for understanding can also be interpreted as a public recognition that assisted dying, despite its legal status in Netherlands, remains a controversial topic. The narratives of understanding add political consciousness into the film. In the director's statement, Jesse van Venrooij writes that Eelco asked him to record his last stage of dying because Eelco wanted this film to be part of his public project of tackling the stigma on mental suffering. The filmmaker agreed with Eelco's goals:

> I believe that as a society we need to be broad-minded and nuanced on euthanasia. With this work I hope to contribute to that idea. Telling a personal, but also relevant story, without judgement, is my mission. And together with Eelco's request it is my motivation for making this film: to show the other side. (Venrooij n.d.)

Thus, personal becomes political, and understanding is both personal and contextual. In hermeneutic phenomenology, Martin Heidegger's tradition emphasises the interpreting of experiences as a situated act: understanding takes place in historical and sociocultural contexts (Wojnar and Swanson 2007, 174; Laverty 2003, 24). Heidegger (1978) sees that each interpretation is influenced by a person's background and context, which makes pre-understanding and preconceptions part of the meaning-making processes. Hermeneutical phenomenology embraces ideas that the viewers do not perceive the film as an empty canvas, but their preconceptions and thoughts about assisted dying, for example, become integral to the interpretation of the viewing experiences.

A Dignified Death recognises these preconceptions by using media imagery that acknowledges the controversiality of assisted dying. It is precisely this kind of imagery that is applied, when the viewer first hears Eelco explain his experiences. His thinking is introduced through a clip from a newspaper article where Eelco talks about his choice in public, after which the film moves on to a collage of various media interviews. In one of them, Eelco claims that he has nothing to gain from life, that every night he hopes he will not wake up again and how burdensome it is when nothing makes him happy. To media audiences, Eelco talks about his autism-related disorder of PDD-NOS (a pervasive developmental disorder not otherwise specified) and says that while he has tried everything to make things better, his quality of life has not improved. He also talks about his euthanasia process, and at the end of an interview, the journalist does not know what to say, to which Eelco responds that most people wish him a great journey. When Eelco's rationalised explanation is given – again, in retrospect – in media interviews, the film recognises these as public speech acts, as participation in public discussion of what assisted dying is and in what kind of cases we are willing to accept it. These public speech acts contextualise Eelco's story by giving his background information and situating his story to be a part of public debates, thus adding one (public) part to understanding Eelco's story.

According to Heidegger (1978), the interpretative process works in circular motion: the whole and its parts are constantly compared to each other in a way that increases understanding of the topic. Similarly, supportive family members and the acknowledgement of the public context build Eelco's story by adding layers of understanding. This kind of hermeneutical circle has also been discussed by other hermeneutical phenomenologists, such as Schleiermacher (1998) and Gadamer (1998), who both consider that understanding is enhanced by ongoing movement between the parts and the whole. The hermeneutical circle, in which new material is compared to the conceptual understanding of a topic, has been mostly applied in qualitative research methodology (e.g. Suddick et al. 2020), but a similar process of understanding can also be detected in documentary film viewing.

Mareike Sera (2016, 2–3), for example, discusses the hermeneutical circle of film viewing in relation to Don Ihde's (1986) reading of Paul Ricœur's (1969) hermeneutical phenomenology. Ihde interprets the circle as two-phase transitions. First, understanding seeks to take place through a relationship between expression and experience, in a reflective meeting of prelinguistic experience and (cinematic) expression. The second transition adds an interpretation of expressions through hermeneutics (Ihde 1986, 96–101). Sera argues that in the context of film viewing, the first phase draws from the embodied perceptions of the materiality of the film, which is followed by an induced interpretation that carries cultural and contextual readings. Thus, expressions of the on-screen world are connected to the off-screen experiences and realities (Sera 2016, 3–7). The continuous and circular shifts between these phases explain why the viewer may both understand the filmed subjects' experiences and potentially criticise their decisions.

The latter half of *A Dignified Death* highlights the continuous shifts between witnessing Eelco's experience and contextual interpretation. The film jumps from the retrospective perspective to an observational mode during the last day of Eelco's life. The filmmaker captures Eelco saying his goodbyes, first to his dear friend Nicole. They have a long and intense embrace, which echoes the bittersweetness of the moment. After Nicole leaves, Eelco writes his virtual goodbyes through social media. There are no lengthy explanations in his comments, while the camera witnesses the quiet moments of preparing for the final moment. The farewells of loved ones embody the experience of grief for the viewer.

The following scene, which shows Eelco's death, emphasises haptic witnessing in a situation where desire to understand personal solutions and complex

DIALOGICAL DOCUMENTARIES

societal attitudes to assisted dying are mixed. The hand-held camera is constantly moving, as if the filmmaker is not sure where it should be located. It remains out of the way and hovers behind the physicians involved in the situation, showing glimpses of their chins or hands while they explain the process and confirm that Eelco stands behind his decision. The image shifts and moves, constantly returning to Eelco in either mid-shots or close-ups. Eelco's presence, and thus, his experience, is the centre of the camera's navigational pull. Compared to the camera, Eelco remains stoic and becomes the source of composure in the scene. The restlessness of the camera adds contextual debates on whether this kind of death can be embraced, but Eelco's personal experience of calmness invites an interpretation that he is convinced of the acceptability of his decision.

After preparations, Eelco settles in a chair, the cannula is administered, and the valve is opened. Eelco's mother stands by his side, holding his hand. Visually, her presence reassures that the family respects, supports and understands Eelco's choice. While everything else grows quiet and still, the restless camera movements increase. It is the camera that brings rawness and emotional upheaval to the experience, which shows the complexity of witnessing an assisted death, and also, sets it aside from the inanimate death scenes of physical documentaries (Chapter 8). Should one intervene in the name of saving a life or respect the personal plan? Eelco's experience appears to calm the situation; he mutters, 'This is exactly how I wanted it to be,' before dozing off. From here on, the camera slightly calms down, even if its movement continues to remind us of the hand-held filming mode. In his last words, Eelco appreciates all the people who love him. He also starts saying that he has doubts, after which he takes a longer break. The hiatus is almost heartbreaking, letting the mind run wild. The moment is enough to raise every kind of public doubt about assisted dying, adding a further layer to the cinematic expression. However, Eelco reveals that he is not sure whether he wants his last words to be 'Hodor' or 'So long and thanks for all the fish', both being well-known popular culture references. The scene shows that both Eelco and his mother are convinced that this is the best possible solution for him, and this certainness aims to help the viewer to understand why someone might want to die as young as Eelco.

In *A Dignified Death*, access to Eelco's personal experiences increases throughout the film. In the first section, his own voice is almost missing. In its stead, the viewer is offered a model of understanding by other people, as well as contextual struggles related to understanding. Later, when the camera starts to observe Eelco's last day, the viewer is allowed access to his experience, which brings a new layer to the 'circle of understanding', as Heidegger (1978, 32: 153) observes. This hermeneutical circle, indeed, is intended to increase understanding of assisted dying on multiple levels. Susann Laverty (2003, 25) sees hermeneutical phenomenology as an interaction between the viewer's expectations and the text's meanings. She draws from Gadamer (1998, 295), who finds that interpretation starts when 'a person seeking to understand something has a bond to the subject matter'. Understanding moves beyond re-creating someone else's meaning, Laverty argues. It 'opens up possibilities of meaning', whereby understanding does not force someone's perspective on another, but is about one being transformed through a dialectic relationship (Laverty 2003, 25). Similarly, in Eelco's case, the film seeks to build models of understanding, but it does not demand that the viewers abandon their preconceptions, only that they be open to understanding other people's various realities.

After Eelco's death, the film focuses on how his family and friends move on. The mother takes over the media interviews for Eelco and continues to tell his story. The best friend gets a tattoo that reminds her of Eelco, and the sister tries to manage her emotions of loss by keeping a diary. She writes a letter to Eelco, saying that while she agrees with Eelco's choice, and even feels somewhat relieved, she finds it all to be difficult. Thus, understanding and support remain, yet it does not mean that difficult emotions do not arise nor that there is no grief. Eelco's blog is published posthumously. The family members and friends read these posts aloud for the camera, as a final glimpse into the inner world of Eelco, where he writes about his struggles to engage with other people and the world. In an entry that closes the film, Eelco writes:

> For me, life is an unbearable suffering and hopeless. It's a combination of factors, of course, physically and mentally. But let me be clear. It's mainly the mental aspect that made me come to this difficult decision. I can't and don't want to go on like this. The great paradox of my life is that I'm very scared that I'll impulsively commit suicide in a weak moment. I wouldn't wish that on myself or the people around me. But in all honesty, it's just a matter of time. I want to die, but in a dignified and decent manner. I deserve that. The people around me deserve that. (Venrooij 2018)

During this blog reading, final credits roll, and Eelco's friend Nicole wipes tears from her eyes. It is thus at the very end that the film affords Eelco's own explanation the most time, after providing a model of understanding and acceptance, perhaps in the hope that the viewer is now able to listen and to understand.

DIALOGICAL 'TRUTH'

Gadamer (1998) gives special importance to dialogue in the processes of understanding. Michael Peters and Tina Besley point out that '[f]or Gadamer,

DIALOGICAL DOCUMENTARIES

dialogue is an encounter with the Other in the process of understanding which can be seen as reaching an agreement where reaching an agreement means establishing a common framework or "horizon" and understanding is the "fusion of horizons"' (Peters and Besley 2021, 672). This process compares to Bill Nichols's term 'dialogical truth' in the documentary field. According to Nichols, films that emphasise emotional and personal interaction between the filmmaker and the filmed subjects construct dialogical truth through situated interaction. The dialogical relationship makes the filmmaker a 'collaborator and confidant' and allows the viewer to listen to the filmed subject. The dialogical approach to a social issue, Nichols argues, has a complex relationship with the real. These films do not expect to reveal a certain or generalisable truth, but to enable an open-ended understanding of verifiable experiences (Nichols 2016, 82–4). In other words, dialogical documentary films construct 'truth' in their singular contexts and situations.

The dialogical pattern is visible in Jessica Villerius's documentary *Veda's Choice*, where the filmmaker's presence is a powerful narrative and visual element. Rather than hiding behind the camera, the filmmaker has on-screen dialogues with Veda, a 19-year-old who seeks assisted dying due to mental suffering. The film presents the filmmaker as a confidant seeking to understand why Veda wants to end her life. In a media interview, Villerius says that she was inspired by Veda's letter and request to be filmed:

> This letter, from an 18-year-old on a mission, radiated so much urgency that I had to do something with it. It resulted in a long journey with a lot of sadness and despair but I would do it again tomorrow. The group of young people with a psychiatric background and a death wish deserves a voice. (2Doc.nl 2019, translated from Dutch)

The film starts with Veda crying in a selfie video with a mobile phone camera that she has had enough and wants it to stop. Veda offers no rational explanations why she wants to die. Rather, she provides an embodied sense anguish and suffering. Later, her affective claims are explored through intense conversations between Veda and Villerius. The first time, they sit on a bench while Veda talks about her feelings. The filmmaker nods her head, immersed in Veda's words. Here, the filmmaker stands in for the viewer, who is invited to understand Veda's misery. The camera focuses on Veda's face and her expressions, while the filmmaker is seen in a side profile with her gaze trained on Veda. The attentive arrangement prompts the viewer to prioritise Veda's part of the dialogue.

Similar scenes repeat throughout the film. Veda explains and the filmmaker listens and asks clarifying questions. Veda shares her life with the filmmaker: she was bullied at school, there were troubles at home, she was sexually abused

181

by a family friend and she was not able to talk to anyone about her experiences. In some discussions, the filmmaker also challenges Veda. For example, after being told by Veda's grandmother that Veda has used a wheelchair since her teens due to a body integrity identity disorder where she feels that her legs do not belong to her, the filmmaker asks Veda if she is physically able to walk. Veda confirms that she can walk, but her inability to move is psychological, which is difficult for some people to understand. The filmmaker again appears in a side profile, and the camera focuses on Veda who sits in a wheelchair by a creek. The filmmaker continues the dialogue by asking what would help her to understand Veda. Gazing slightly downwards, Veda voices her thoughts: she hopes that people would understand that this is not her choice. If she could choose, she would choose to be normal. In this scene, the dialogue form is literally used to increase understanding over Veda's situation.

In addition to the explicit dialogue scenes with the filmmaker, *Veda's Choice* uses other ways to build dialogism. First, the filmmaker interviews people in Veda's life, and the perspectives of her grandmother, a friend and a psychiatrist add various voices that construct a dialogical way of building the circle of understanding. In documentary films, interviews typically add different perspectives and voices into the story (Nichols 2017, 145–6). Mikhail Bakhtin (2011) construes the plurality and polyphony of voices as 'dialogism', where multiplicity enables negotiation of meanings through ideological struggles. In the documentary films, similarly, various voices are brought together to discuss, define, explain and experience end of life. These voices react to events happening to them, to other voices, providing the viewer with various perspectives for meaning-making. For example, Veda's grandmother and friend add supportive voices by arguing that they understand Veda's choice, although they also hope that Veda would still change her mind.

The ideological struggle identified by Bakhtin has a role in Veda's story. Veda's experiences are contrasted with the voice of a psychiatrist working with young people intent on assisted dying. The psychiatrist, who is not against assisted dying, emphasises that young people are obliged to participate in intensive therapy before they can receive a referral for assisted dying. Not only does this interview add contextual information, it is also visually brought into dialogue with Veda's experiences. The psychiatrist says that Veda is not happy about the therapy requirement, which she sees as delaying the inevitable. This is edited together with shots of Veda sitting on her bed, looking sad and inconsolable with the filmmaker by her side. The psychiatrist's professional argumentation for the benefits of therapy as well as the understanding of Veda's frustration and experiences create a narrative dialogue that inserts sociocultural context into Veda's story.

Towards the end of the film, the dialogues between the filmmaker and Veda intensify. The filmmaker increasingly challenges Veda. For example, she

DIALOGICAL DOCUMENTARIES

promptly asks 'why don't you just kill yourself', before softening the question by adding 'someone might ask'. Veda argues that suicide would be traumatic for her and for her family and friends, whereas assisted dying would socially acknowledge her emotions. Yet, a few days later, Veda tries to kill herself. The filmmaker picks her up from a psychiatric ward and takes her home, where Veda heads to the bathroom to wash her dirty clothes. The filmmaker sits with her in the bathroom and the intimacy of the space adds intimacy to the dialogue where Veda tells what happened. First, she thought that she could throw herself in front of a car. The filmmaker asks why she stopped. So far, Veda has been facing away from the camera, but now she raises her gaze towards it: 'The way I would die. The driver ... And being alone. The fear that it would fail.' In the last sentence, she lowers her gaze again, as if ashamed of considering deviating from her original plan.

The narration jumps to Veda's last therapy meeting, after which she meets the filmmaker on the street. Veda admits that she has learned to manage her emotions better and that her take on life is more positive than it used to be. But she still wants to die. The filmmaker challenges this outcome, which Veda counters by saying that she does not believe anything will help; she fears that her life will derail again. The discussion follows earlier scenes. Veda sits in a wheelchair, facing camera, while the filmmaker is sitting on a nearby bench, gazing up at Veda in a side profile. The filmmaker sits at a lower level and she must look up at Veda, which gives Veda the power position in the scene. The visual composition, again, prioritises Veda's experience as something that others seek to understand.

The film ends with a birthday sequence of Veda turning twenty. At the birthday party, Veda is shown in a lively discussion with her family, and she is more comfortable participating in the conversation as an equal member of the group, both voicing her opinions and listening to those of others. For the filmmaker, Veda admits that she is happy and while she does not know what has changed, she does not want to go through assisted dying right now. From this, the film cuts to an interview with the psychiatrist, who argues that assisted dying wishes are often discussions on suffering. With mental health issues, the patients are commonly urged to do something about this suffering by themselves, whereas their suffering should be better understood and supported. Then, perhaps, there would be less of a need for assisted dying services. This argument frames the visual and narrative choices of the film. Dialogism adds voices, but Veda's voice is prioritised as an attempt to provide understanding and support for Veda. The closing suggests that perhaps suffering, in some cases, can ease if one is heard and understood.

Ethics of Listening

Nichols's article *The Voice of Documentary* (1983, 281) made 'voice' a key concept in understanding how documentary films allow space for various perspectives. Since then, giving voice to people in a marginalised position has been considered filmmakers' key ethical act. Kim Munro (2018), however, maintains that this is not enough. Munro argues that there are so many competing voices in the contemporary media that while there are plenty of opportunities for speaking, the most ethical act would be to listen. This act of listening can provide documentary filmmaking its critical and ethical engagement, because it moves the viewer beyond self-concern towards responsibility over the other (Munro 2018, 279–82). Consequently, while dialogism which allows voices such as Eelco's and Veda's and those of their loved ones to be heard, the ethical act on the viewer's part would be to listen to the multitude of voices. Jennifer Malkowski (2017, 83) argues that the practice where the camera provides a listener to a dying person also highlights the person's individual status. From the viewer's perspective, then, we should talk about the 'ethics of listening', which participates in the understanding process provided by these documentaries.

The ethics of listening unfolds in the documentary *Nathan – Free as a Bird*. Roel Nollet, the director, says on the film's co-fund page that the documentary started from the idea of filming the transgender process of Nathan. When the process failed Nathan's expectations, he became depressed, and the story took another direction. When Nathan asked Nollet to document his process of assisted dying instead, Nollet had to consider whether he was comfortable with the topic. A few days later, Nollet phoned him back, and Nathan reasoned that it was his legal decision and that he wanted the world to know his tale (Nollet 2014b). The filmmaker did not want to tell people what they should think about euthanasia, so he focused on Nathan's, rather than his own, experience:

> When we look through his eyes, we can get a glimpse of his mind too. Away from all the pro and contra lobbies, we can only try to understand what made him decide to do this, and why – for him – this was the only option at that given moment in time. (Nollet 2014b)

In this quote, Nollet uses the word 'understanding' as a key element for the film, where both he and the viewer can search for answers.

In the film, the director places himself in the role of a mediator who listens and asks the viewer to listen with him. Munro (2018, 289–91) argues that a documentary film can engage with active listening by acknowledging, implicating and modelling acts of listening for the viewer. In *Nathan – Free as a Bird*, this happens already during the first shots, where the filmmaker sits by a computer, listens to Nathan's voice recordings and writes his story posthumously. A clip

DIALOGICAL DOCUMENTARIES

of Nathan's recordings plays over the image: 'I'm going to talk to you about what is going on in my head.' A close-up of the filmmaker's focused expression, when Nathan's voice declares that he wants to die, emphasises the act of listening, before the filmmaker-narrator declares that this is the story of 44-year-old Nathan who asked for assisted dying because he felt imprisoned inside a female body. This opening confession places the filmmaker (and the viewer) as a listener. It is this person that Nathan talks to and would like to understand him.

The same way as in Eelco's and Veda's stories, the interviews of Nathan's friends and media segments add dialogism to the circles of understanding. The media segments provide background information to Nathan's story and contextual discussion on the ethics of assisted dying. In dialogue with media material, Nathan confesses that his identity traumas go beyond transgender issues. He was a victim of incest as a child; his mother failed to support him and instead humiliated him about his looks. There are newspaper clips where the mother calls Nancy an ugly child and denies that Nathan's death would make her sad. The friends, however, serve as models of understanding. They are sad to lose Nathan, yet they have listened to Nathan's requests and support him. One of them even speculates that Nathan may have wanted to become a man because he was rejected as a daughter; maybe he thought he could become lovable as a man. These dialogical scenes enhance the viewer's understanding of the traumas behind Nathan's mental suffering.

The plurality of dialogism provides the viewer with different perspectives that can make the whole of Nathan's experience understandable, but it is the private moments of the film that emphasise the viewer's responsibility of listening. Munro (2018, 285–6) adds that listening builds on affective responses to the other, because the listener is willing to give up a power position in favour of reaching beyond oneself and engaging with the other. Listening, as Jan Grue (2022, 11) argues, adds truth value to experiences and makes it difficult to question these arguments. In *Nathan – Free as a Bird*, the affective relationship with the viewer is emphasised in the private moments at his home, where the filmmaker and the viewer become his trusted listeners.

The first intimate section takes place quite early on the film. The sequence starts with Nathan organising his home and belongings to be donated after his death. At the same time, he explains to the filmmaker why he seeks assisted dying to escape his suffering. He tells about his failed penis operation. The film includes a few pictures of his deformed penis, to confirm the claim, not to linger. Nathan argues that every time he goes to the bathroom, he needs to encounter this failure: 'You don't feel like a human. You feel like a freak.' The sequence continues in the bathroom, where Nathan stands in front of a mirror, removes his shirt and looks at himself in the mirror. After some dialogical jumps, where a friend, for example, says that suffering cannot be seen on the outside, the narration returns to the bathroom, where Nathan confesses being

185

disappointed by his looks. An extreme close-up of his eyes returns his gaze before the framing readjusts, showing Nathan talking to his mirror reflection and pointing out his flaws, such as the deformed result of breast removal.

Glen Donnar argues that mirrors are important for constructing, strengthening and performing an identity, because they function in-between public and private. While the bathroom refers to privacy, the mirror opens up to other spaces, how others see you. Mirrors connect private performances of self to public constructions of self. In (fiction) films, Donnar continues, mirrors tend to mark male inadequacy and self-doubt related to the performed self (Donnar 2015, 181, 188–9). This argument resonates with Nathan's experience as he appears to feel imprisoned by his body. The bathroom scene also reveals the discontinuity of Nathan's public and private self. Out in public, among his friends, Nathan appears functional and well spoken, but when the layers of clothes and public masks are removed, he finds no peace with himself. When the viewer is allowed to access this private space, the viewer is also given responsibility to listen to these personal confessions.

Further along the film, the affective and private relationship between Nathan and the viewer deepens. Nollet says that Nathan sank into a deep depression after his failed gender construction operations:

> There were times when I called him he said he was so depressed he had locked himself up and didn't want to talk to anyone. I suggested to give him a small camera, so Nathan could record himself on the moments he needed to talk to someone the most, and no one was there. He agreed. (Nollet 2014b)

Figure 9.1 Nathan in his bathroom, looking at himself in the mirror, tears in his eyes (Nollet 2014a).

DIALOGICAL DOCUMENTARIES

Some of these privately filmed scenes are part of the documentary. For Munro (2018, 283), such self-recorded testimonials serve as evidence that there is someone one can talk to and that someone is listening. Thus, without even the filmmaker's presence in the scenes, the viewer becomes the most trusted confidant and listener, which highlights the ethical requirements over these encounters.

One night, when Nathan has trouble sleeping, he films himself in a walk-in closet. The dark and shaking image of a close-up of his face emphasises the emotional tension of the moment. Nathan says that he cannot find peace, nor does he feel joy. In another self-filmed scene, Nathan declares that he prefers keeping his suffering to himself, because he does not force others to share his sadness, anguish and suffering. A tear runs down his face, when he says people cannot know how he experiences things, how broken he is. These self-confessionals, filmed in privacy and revealed for the viewer give the viewer the privilege and the burden of being the one who Nathan trusts to share his suffering with.

The last sequences of the film focus on Nathan leaving his goodbyes and preparing for death. Here, the dialogism between Nathan and his friends intensifies when some of his friends ask Nathan to change his mind, but Nathan sticks with his decision. In the parking lot of the hospital where Nathan goes to die, the filmmaker captures Nathan in a close-up, with tears in his eyes, when he says that he is looking forward to being free. This comment appears to be directed towards the viewer who has seen and heard his private confessions, and thus, might be able to understand why Nathan does not want to back down. The viewer is placed into a position where the circle of understanding is well-constructed, perhaps even better than with the people in his life.

Around Nathan's deathbed, however, any doubts are set aside. A friend reads a poem that speaks to the friends' desire to understand Nathan's feelings and decision: 'You felt lonely, and that's why we let you leave.' When a cannula is inserted into Nathan's hand, the viewer hears his voiceover giving life instruction. He instructs people to enjoy small things about life, to make room for affection and to respect others. These are the last messages Nathan wants everyone, including the viewer, to listen to. A close-up of dripping medicine indicates that the moment of death is close. Nathan bids farewell. His death follows in seconds, leaving the friends standing solemnly by his bed before the image fades to black.

After Nathan's death, the film repeats the opening scene. The filmmaker sits in his study, writing a book and listening to Nathan's recordings. One last time, the scene draws attention to the act and the ethics of listening. The filmmaker's words on the film's co-fund page emphasise the importance of listening: 'I felt like his [Nathan's] voice was being heard for the first time. On the day he died, I found a short note in my camera bag. He thanked me for listening to him' (Nollet 2014b). This anecdote reveals the ethical power of listening – while many of us can talk, perhaps more of us should be able to experience being listened to. Perhaps it is the act of listening that has the power to transform us and our preconceptions.

REFUSING TO LISTEN

In *The Good Death*, the ethics of listening takes another turn. Whereas Eelco's, Veda's and Nathan's stories take place in contexts where assisted dying is legalised, Janette lives in England, where assisted dying remains illegal. This contextual information adds a twist to her story. To be able to die assisted, she says, she has told so many lies to so many people. She has had to strategise how to make people see that there is really no alternative. The film, indeed, includes plenty of scenes where others refuse to listen to and understand Janette's choice. For example, her physicians have refused to help her and have instead threatened to admit her to hospital for her psychological issues, and Janette had to lie that she had changed her mind about assisted dying. She also lies to some friends that she will go and live with her son, whereas in reality, she is packing up her things to die in Switzerland. Janette's biggest struggle for understanding is with her daughter, who asks her mother to change her mind until the very end. The daughter claims to understand but keeps offering alternatives. Janette confesses to the camera that 'all they [her son and daughter] are now doing is they are making me angry and upset'.

The desire to change Janette's mind continues in Switzerland, where both of her children accompany her. When she meets with the physician from the clinic that offers assisted suicide, Janette clings to her. She cries and repeats the words 'thank you', not only thanking for the assistance, but for understanding. The physician even explains to Janette's children that their mother is prepared to die and is in her right mind. The doctor defends Janette's decision for her, while the children sit quietly and listen. They also promise that they will not stop Janette. However, the daughter, who promises to support her decision, asks her mother to consider postponing the death. Janette remains calm and once again explains her decision to her children, who keep interrupting. Here, Janette takes a position of active listening. She supports her children by saying that she knows her decision is difficult to accept and that she is sad to cause misery to others.

Janette becomes the one who listens to others and tries to adjust her explanations so that the others could accept them. This context emphasises the viewer's role. For Janette, the viewer becomes a confidant, a listener who might be able to understand her. At the level of narration, the desire to win the viewer over is evident in the constant use of Janette's voice. While the filmmaker films Janette in everyday activities, such as gardening or getting the mail, Janette's voiceover keeps asking for a listener. In a calm and carefully pronounced

DIALOGICAL DOCUMENTARIES

manner Janette talks about her daily difficulties and her wish to avoid further suffering. As a solution, she wants to have control over her own death. The explanations are probably similar to those that she has offered to people in her life, but this time, she asks if the viewer could understand her experiences and reasoning.

The visuals of the film support Janette's experiences of being left alone with what she wants. The narration repeats shots of waking up. This is an overhead image, shot from the ceiling above the bed. The first time, it shows Janette waking up alone in her bed. She breathes heavily and stares at the ceiling before slowly and carefully placing her feet on the floor. She needs support from a cane and the wall to move towards the bathroom. Her voiceover says that life is not fair, but she has learned to accept her disability. The intimate space, the bed and the bedroom, reveal her physical fragility, but also her resilience and determination. Soon, there is another bed scene, of Janette's son waking up. The camera, once again, takes an overhead shot. The image shifts to an eye-level shot when the son places his feet on the floor, more agile than his mother, and easily slips his feet in a pair of jeans. The son is physically more able, yet the comparison of the images reveals his potential future of a fragile physical condition. Bed scenes feature again in the latter half of the film when Janette and her children travel to Switzerland for Janette's death. On her last night at home, after packing her bags, Janette goes to sleep. In the dark bedroom, the camera again gazes from overhead, offering a last moment of considering of staying at home, in your own bed.

The overhead shots add dramatic visualisation to the film, but also guide the viewer's attention to the privacy of experience and the role that the viewer has in witnessing these intimate moments of waking up, the moments between being vulnerable while sleeping and moving towards the public parts of day. The scenes also prepare the viewer for Janette's deathbed scene. During the assisted death, the camera stays on eye-level, which highlights the role of the observer rather than that of an intimate listener. After Janette opens the valve to receive medication, she lies on a bed, quietly smiling, while her daughter caresses her hand and her son sits on a sofa. When she starts breathing heavily and closes her eyes, the image fades to black and quiet music starts.

The bed theme returns once more. After Janette's death, an overhead image of the son sleeping on a bed is repeated. This returns the viewer's mind to the increasing fragility of Janette, which might be the son's fate as well. After waking up, the son admits that he is sad to see his mother gone. He hopes that the choice for assisted dying will be understood and acknowledged when his own condition has reached that stage. He does not know what his choice will be, but he hopes there is a choice. The film ends here, with images of the sea and sky juxtaposed to being confined in one's own body and bed. 'Euthanasia', Greek for good death, is written over the scenery as closure.

Conclusion

The dialogical documentaries discussed in this chapter provide personal justifications for choosing assisted dying. Through stories of a person's journey, these films serve as models of understanding. The narrative approach highlights these end-of-life decisions as individual and singular choices. The viewer is not expected to make a similar choice, or even accept legalisation of assisted dying at a general level. Instead, the viewer is presented with models of understanding to see why this particular person ended up in this situation and this particular choice. From the perspective of the filmed subject, the desire of being understood also relates to alleviating anxiety. The protagonists do not fear death, but see it as a relief. What they fear is not being understood. In comparison, understanding adds value to their life and death.

In order to emphasise the polyphony and to acknowledge the mixed attitudes towards assisted dying, these documentaries utilise a dialogical format. The viewer has access to the voices of those who wish to die, but also to voices of their families and friends, and occasionally of authorities, such as physicians. These voices add contextual understanding of the situation, but also provide personal models for listening. In total, the dialogues contribute parts to the whole, and increase the potential for the viewer to understand the complexity of the situation. While the focus is on the personal experience of the filmed subject who seeks to die, none of the films denies that death and loss give rise to difficult emotions. Instead, they openly address that it can be hard to let go, even when you want to understand and support the person you care about.

Thus, the argumentation in dialogical documentaries about assisted dying draws from affective and emotional processes of understanding, instead of focusing on rational reasoning for or against assisted dying. The personal becomes political through emotions and experiences. As such, the ethical connection to assisted dying builds through the ethics of listening instead of debating normative ethical guidelines. In dialogical documentaries, listening takes place on various levels. First, the person wanting to die talks, and their friends and families listen, try to understand and bring their perspective to the dialogue. Their reactions can model listening and understanding for the viewer, or in some cases, challenge this process, which allows the viewer to see how the refusal to listen can be difficult for the person seeking understanding. Second, the filmmaker provides the position of a listener, either explicitly in the images or as a narrative position to whom the main subject talks. The filmmaker also represents the viewer, who is invited to listen and to understand. In some cases, where the filmed subjects have self-recorded their experiences, the viewer's role as an ethical listener is enhanced. The viewer is asked to prioritise the dying person's experience before making any moral judgements.

While there is no obligation to transform one's values related to assisted dying, these films ask the viewer to understand singular contexts where a desire for assisted dying can emerge. The 'ethics of listening' becomes an affective and emotional process, with a potential for transformed thinking and feeling. Instead of demanding, these dialogical documentaries gently ask the viewer to understand, and then perhaps (re)consider how they feel about assisted dying.

REFERENCES

2Doc.nl. 2019. 'Veda beslist zélf'. 2Doc.nl. 24 April 2019. https://www.2doc.nl/docu mentaires/2019/04/veda-beslist-zelf.html. Last accessed 25 January 2023.

Abulad, Romualdo E. 2007. 'What Is Hermeneutics?' *Kritike* 1 (2): 11–23.

Bakhtin, Mikhail. 2011. *The Dialogic Imagination: Four Essays*, edited by Michael Holquist. Translated by Caryl Emerson and Michael Holquist. First published 1981. Austin: University of Texas Press.

Cineuropa. 2020. 'Tomáš Krupa, Producer, Hailstone: "Emotions Are the Only Thing We Have"'. *Cineuropa – the Best of European Cinema*. 20 February 2020. https://cineuropa.org/en/interview/385611/. Last accessed 25 January 2023.

Donnar, Glen. 2015. 'Monstrous Men and Bathroom Mirrors: The Bathroom as Revelatory Space in American Cinema'. In *Spaces of the Cinematic Home: Behind the Screen Door*, edited by Eleanor Andrews, Stella Hockenhull, and Fran Pheasant-Kelly, 180–93. London; New York: Routledge.

Eliot, T. S. 1928. 'A Song for Simeon'. In *Ariel Poems*. London: Faber and Gwyer.

Fariña, Juan Jorge Michel, Irene Cambra Badii, and Ailen Provenza. 2016. 'Euthanasia and Assisted Suicide: A Cinematographic Approach to the Death That Hurts the Most'. *Jahr: Europski Časopis Za Bioetiku* 7 (2): 293–305.

Gadamer, Hans-Georg. 1998. *Truth and Method. Second, Revised Edition*. First published 1960. New York: Continuum.

Grue, Jan. 2022. 'The Death of Others. On the Narrative Rhetoric of Neoliberal Thanatopolitics'. *Disability Studies Quarterly* 42 (1). https://doi.org/10.18061/dsq.v42i1.7799.

Heidegger, Martin. 1978. 'Being and Time'. Oxford: Blackwell.

Ihde, Don. 1986. *Hermeneutic Phenomenology: The Philosophy of Paul Ricoeur*. First published 1971. Evanston, IL: Northwestern University Press.

Kennedy Schmidt, Lawrence. 2016. *Understanding Hermeneutics*. London; New York: Routledge. https://doi.org/10.4324/9781315539331.

Krupa, Tomáš. 2018a. *The Good Death*. Documentary. ARTE; Czech Television; Golden Girls Filmproduktion.

———. 2018b 'Director's statement'. The Good Death by Tomáš Krupa. 2018. https://gooddeath.net/. Last accessed 25 January 2023.

Laverty, Susann M. 2003. 'Hermeneutic Phenomenology and Phenomenology: A Comparison of Historical and Methodological Considerations'. *International Journal of Qualitative Methods* 2 (3): 21–35. https://doi.org/10.1177/160940690300 200303.

McAdams, Dan P. 2011. 'Narrative Identity'. In *Handbook of Identity Theory and Research*, edited by Seth J. Schwartz, Koen Luyckx, and Vivian L. Vignoles, 99–115. New York: Springer. https://doi.org/10.1007/978-1-4419-7988-9_5.

Malkowski, Jennifer. 2017. *Dying in Full Detail: Mortality and Digital Documentary*. Durham, NC; London: Duke University Press. https://doi.org/10.1215/978082237 3414.

Munro, Kim. 2018. 'From Voice to Listening: Becoming Implicated Through Multi-Linear Documentary'. In *Critical Distance in Documentary Media*, edited by Gerda Cammaer, Blake Fitzpatrick, and Bruno Lessard. Cham: Springer International Publishing. https://doi.org/10.1007/978-3-319-96767-7.

Nichols, Bill. 1983. 'The Voice of Documentary'. *Film Quarterly* 36 (3): 17–30. https://doi.org/10.2307/3697347.

———. 2016. *Speaking Truths with Film: Evidence, Ethics, Politics in Documentary*. Oakland: University of California Press.

———. 2017. *Introduction to Documentary, Third Edition*. Bloomington: Indiana University Press.

Nollet, Roel. 2014a. *Nathan – Free as a Bird*. Documentary. Coccinelle Film Placement.

———. 2014b. 'Nathan Free as a Bird'. Indiegogo. 2014. http://www.indiegogo.com/projects/975773/fblk.

Peters, Michael A., and Tina Besley. 2021. 'Models of Dialogue'. *Educational Philosophy and Theory* 53 (7): 669–76. https://doi.org/10.1080/00131857.2019.1684801.

Ricœur, Paul. 1969. *The Symbolism of Evil*. Translated by Emerson Buchanan. Boston, MA: Beacon Press.

Schleiermacher, Friedrich. 1998. *Hermeneutics and Criticism and Other Writings*, edited by Andrew Bowie. Cambridge: Cambridge University Press.

Sera, Mareike. 2016. 'The Value of Hermeneutics to Film Phenomenology: Michelangelo Antonioni's L'eclisse'. Unpublished paper. https://www.academia.edu/17522351/The_value_of_hermeneutics_to_film_phenomenology_Michelangelo_Antonioni_s_L_eclisse. Last accessed 27 January 2023.

Suddick, Kitty Maria, Vinette Cross, Pirjo Vuoskoski, Kathleen T. Galvin, and Graham Stew. 2020. 'The Work of Hermeneutic Phenomenology'. *International Journal of Qualitative Methods* 19 (January): 1609406920947600. https://doi.org/10.1177/1609406920947600.

Venrooij, Jesse van. 2018. *A Dignified Death*. Documentary. Film Moment.

———. n.d. 'A Dignified Death'. FilmFreeway. https://filmfreeway.com/adignifieddeath. Accessed 25 January 2023.

Villerius, Jessica. 2019. *Veda's Choice*. Documentary. BNNVARA & Posh Productions.

Wojnar, Danuta M., and Kristen M. Swanson. 2007. 'Phenomenology: An Exploration'. *Journal of Holistic Nursing* 25 (3): 172–80. https://doi.org/10.1177/0898010106295172.

SECTION III
PERSONAL VOICES

10. FIRST-PERSON DOCUMENTARIES

Filmmakers' Personal Journeys

On-screen, *Looking Death in the Face* (2003) begins with the funeral of a pet rodent. The pet is carefully covered in a box, camera close to the ground when the tiny box is placed in a small grave. Off-screen, the film began years before, when, at her mother's passing, the Finnish filmmaker Kiti Luostarinen found that death would not leave her be. She promised herself that one day she would find out about death.

The Canadian film *Griefwalker* (2008) opens with soft instrumental music and the sound of drops falling into water. The sounds are accompanied by images of melting ice and snow which morph into the image of a drip. Nature and the medical world interlace. In voiceover, filmmaker Tim Wilson tells the story of his close call with death after a routine operation gone wrong. Moving on, the film portrays Wilson standing in the bathroom, clearing the mist from the mirror and looking at himself. He asks, 'Am I really going to die?'

The opening title of the American documentary film *Living while Dying* (2017) fades to black before a forest road fills the screen. Filmmaker Cathy Zheutlin walks along the dirt road, and her footsteps crunch on the pebbles. In a voiceover she confesses: 'Somehow I've made it to my sixties and know very little about how to face mortality. But death is getting closer now. I can't ignore it anymore.'

In the British documentary *Terry Pratchett: Choosing to Die* (Russell 2011a), the fiction writer opens the film with a confession in a close-up. Pratchett talks about being a 62-year-old with Alzheimer's disease and wonders: 'Sometimes, particularly when I am depressed, I dread what the future may hold.' While Pratchett is not the director of the film, he is the narrator whose perspective guides the story, and an active figure participating in the filmmaking. In a blog entry, the film director Charlie Russell (2011b) reveals that Pratchett 'needs the minimum of guidance, so my role in filming *Choosing to Die* was often just to capture what he was experiencing'.

All four documentary openings raise the issue of death, dying and end of life. They do so from a personal perspective, where the filmmaker is the subjective narrator of the film. The filmmakers become the story, or at least part of the story. Yet, these films are not autobiographical in the sense that they would narrate the filmmakers' own deaths. Instead, the filmmakers introduce various terminally ill people from whose experiences they are trying to learn. In this chapter I study these documentaries – *Looking Death in the Face* (Luostarinen 2003), *Griefwalker* (Wilson 2008), *Terry Pratchett: Choosing to Die* (Russell 2011a) and *Living while Dying* (Zheutlin 2017) – as personal explorations of what death and dying are.

I interpret these documentaries through Alisa Lebow's concept of first-person films that speak from a subjective position. This definition allows us to see various narratives as subjective films, ranging from autobiographical documentaries to films where the events and other people are seen through the filmmaker's perspective (Lebow 2012, 1–3). First-person documentaries share similarities with performative documentaries. Stella Bruzzi (2010, 185, 187), for example, argues that performative documentaries emphasise either stylised performances of the filmed subjects or the filmmaker's emphasised presence. I discussed the stylised aspects of performances in Chapter 6, while this chapter turns to questions of the filmmaker's presence.

Bill Nichols, similarly, sees that first-person essays utilise performative modes: the filmmaker's voice organises the narrative and provides either an expressive testimonial or a personal essay. Because such documentaries use at least some degree of self-scrutiny, the topic becomes embodied and affective. When documentary film is understood to enable an ethical space, such intimacy allows for a meaningful transformation in attitudes. Yet, for Nichols, the subjective perspective can dissociate the documentaries from broad contexts and perceptions (Nichols 2017, 106, 109). I aim to show that the self-reflective mode has significance in making the topic of death and dying meaningful not only for the filmmaker, but also for the viewer and society. This argument garners support from the so-called subjective turn (Chanan 2007; Renov 2004) and the emotive turn (Helke 2016) in documentary filmmaking. These concepts refer to a trend where the subjective views, appreciation of personal emotions and glorification of the everyday are openly embraced and recognised as ways to create and share knowledge.

Some writers, such as Nichols (2017, 109, 149), have questioned the premises of constructing knowledge through subjective experience, but I argue that subjectivity enables an ethical and epistemological premise for documentary-making. Susanne Helke explains the interest in subjectivity through loss of faith in grand narratives. Instead of trying to explain experiences as homogenous, contemporary documentaries allow fragmented identities and varieties in which reality is experienced, felt and embodied (Helke 2016). When documentary filmmakers invite the viewer to experience the issue from an openly personal perspective, they allow space for the viewer to reflect on their own experiences and understanding.

While subjective, the interpersonal relationship with the viewer gives first-person films a societal aspect. Michael Renov (2004) maintains that subjective documentaries have roots in identity politics, where personal turns political. Thus, first-person documentaries, where the filmmakers embrace their influence on the films' argumentation, are not merely tools for the filmmakers' self-discovery or self-investigation. Instead, through a dialogical relationship between the filmmaker and the filmed subjects, and the dialogical relationship between the film and the viewer, these documentaries encourage conversations on the chosen topic. Similarly, first-person end-of-life documentaries abandon observational practices and favour personal, participatory, embodied and emotional approaches to death and dying. In this chapter, I claim that these documentaries offer their subjective approaches as ethical options to discuss the end of life. Subjective argumentation avoids preaching to, or lecturing, the viewer, and rather invites the viewer to explore the topic together with the filmmaker.

Journey Inspired by Fear

The four first-person documentaries examined in this chapter begin with the filmmakers' admissions of lacking understanding of death. They search for answers and knowledge. In these films, the metaphor of a journey emphasises the filmmakers' transformative self-discoveries about the end of life. In *Griefwalker*, after the revelatory mirror discussion with himself, the director starts a journey both metaphorically and literally. Wilson packs his clothes and literature on death studies in a suitcase and sets off to meet people with whom he can discuss mortality. *Terry Pratchett: Choosing to Die* has repetitive scenes where Pratchett and his assistant travel by car, train or plane to see people who have decided either against or for assisted dying. In the travel scenes, the men either contemplate their own emotions by staring into nothingness or reflect in conversation what they are witnessing. Similarly, in *Living while Dying*, Zheutlin visits dying people and travels abroad to learn from other cultures their ways of accepting and celebrating death. Journeying thus becomes a part of these documentaries' narrative structures, events and metaphors.

FILMING DEATH

Given the metaphor of a journey, these documentaries borrow elements from the genre of road movies. The connection is highlighted in repeated scenes where the filmmakers or their companions are driving a car to or from the meetings with dying people. In the cinema, being on the road serves as a learning experience for the main characters who are placed in unfamiliar settings, which either gives them freedom from their usual routines or places them in a liminal space (Laderman 2002, 13; Römpötti 2012). Similarly, in travel research, the experience of travel is conceptualised by liminality. People who are in transit can feel freedom, undergo migrancy or experience out-of-placeness (Andrews and Roberts 2012). In end-of-life documentaries, 'journey' offers filmmakers potential to learn through the experience of liminality.

Anthropologists Arnold van Gennep (2019) and Victor Turner (2011) introduced the concept of liminality in the early twentieth century. Turner, for example, sees liminality as one of three ritual phases. Rituals are transitions from one social status to another, such as being alive to being dead. The liminality refers to an ambiguous middle phase where the status is in transition and not clearly defined (Turner 2011, 95). Today, liminality is often used to describe the experiences of terminally ill people. The concept has also become a popular way of describing any states or experiences of 'in-betweenness' (Wels et al. 2011, 2). Liminality as in-betweenness assumes transition and transformation. In the case of end-of-life documentaries, the filmmakers' goal is to transform their attitudes about death and to learn to accept their mortality – at least on some level.

While the journey provides a liminal space for the filmmaker to engage with transformation, the film as a journey can potentially provide the same experience for the viewer. In an interview, Tim Wilson argues that *Griefwalker* was 'a learning'.

> I didn't intend to change anyone's mind or to change a practice in the culture. It is more an exploration, and it was more, I would not say a confessional, but it was a personal essay about ... Well, I was hoping that someone would see in my volunteering to display my naïveté that that might be them as well. And that it [denial of mortality] probably doesn't serve them. (Wilson 2019)

Thus, the film is a personal essay, which the filmmaker hopes will enable the viewers to reflect their thoughts in relation to the director's experiences. In the subjective approach, the invitation to learn together is not phrased as an obligation or a need, but as a suggestion through personal experience. As such, it gives the viewer space to think and feel.

Kiti Luostarinen, the director of *Looking Death in the Face*, emphasises a similar approach. Luostarinen's filming of her own process allows the viewer

198

to recognise a similar need in themselves. By using her own experiences, Luostarinen was able to voice common doubts and fears about death. While she hopes that the film encourages the viewer to recognise that death, or at least dying people, are not scary, she acknowledges that only those who are ready to transform will do so, and if the film helps even one person, it is valuable (Luostarinen 2020). The film does not make demands, but is one speech act among others to make death visible in society.

Whereas 'journey' has literal use in other documentaries, the liminal and transformative journey takes place at a symbolic level in *Looking Death in the Face*. Instead of travelling to different places, the filmmaker signs up as a volunteer at a hospice home, which – like travelling – provides a liminal space. She opens the door to the hospice home and begins the transformation. In the liminal space between life and death at the hospice, the filmmaker temporarily steps out of the hectic world that centres on producing and consuming. She slows down to engage with the dying people and spends time just sitting by their bedside. The lack of urgency offers time for self-discovery and self-reflection of emotions and thoughts. In an interview, Luostarinen describes that the filmmaking and, even more so, being at the hospice was a 'journey towards my own fears, towards breaking my own taboos'. She feels that these experiences changed her, encouraging her to live in the present and appreciate the beauty of life (Luostarinen 2020, translated from Finnish). As Luostarinen's argument shows, the personal transformation happens through the filmmaker's emotions and inner realities.

Emotions are not easy for documentaries to observe. Yet, Mette Kramer (2018) argues that various on-screen personal and emotional testimonies in first-person documentaries deepen the viewer's engagement with the films and their topic. Similarly, first-person end-of-life documentaries search for ways to witness the filmmakers' psychological processes. *Griefwalker* paints poetic images of nature to visualise the filmmaker's revelations of death's place in the world. *Terry Pratchett: Choosing to Die* applies the well-known fiction writer's talent to transform emotions and experiences into self-reflective monologues. *Living while Dying* uses dark animated scenes, and *Looking Death in the Face* turns towards diary writing.

Luostarinen describes in an interview how she kept a diary during the filming and how these reflections became part of the film narration. The diary entries give the film its structure and provide tangible elements for inner experiences (Luostarinen 2020). Indeed, autobiographical and intimate approaches, such as diary writing, are something that the audience can relate to and identify with on a personal level because of the emotional and affective qualities of the narrated and perceived experiences (Henderson 2019, 27). Throughout *Looking Death in the Face*, we see the filmmaker writing her diary. The diary also offers a visual cue. In the editing process, scenes of nature, particularly those involving water, snow and ice, are reflected on the diary pages. In an interview, Luostarinen (2020) also argues that nature added symbolical, unconscious and irrational elements to the narration by marking human beings as a part of nature and its cyclical nature. The visual images of diary pages are accompanied with the filmmaker's poetic and philosophical voiceover reflections. In one of the scenes, the filmmaker sits by a campfire, writing her diary, while a skeleton sits on another bench as a reminder of death's presence in life (see this book's cover image). In a diary voiceover, the filmmaker describes how a spirit cannot escape the body: 'This is the amount of space I take up in the world, and in the end, only white bones remain' (Luostarinen 2003, translated from Finnish). The skeleton makes visible the filmmaker's personal journey of growing comfortable with her own mortality.

Living while Dying captures the filmmaker's inner struggles and emotional transformation in animation. The film starts with a woman walking down a dark street in winter. Soon, this turns into a black-and-white animated scene with the dark, haunting figure of death in the background (Figure 10.1). We hear the filmmaker's voiceover: '[d]eath is a big mystery and yet the outcome 100 per cent certain. How do you plan for the unknown? Denial works wonders for a while, but death always shows up.' After the opening title, the animation makes way for the filmmaker walking on a forest road. The comparability of the figures underlines the connection between the filmmaker and the animated woman. Furthermore, the montage editing where the filmed scenes morph into animation and back marks the animations as entries to the narrator's inner emotions.

Figure 10.1 Animated opening of *Living while Dying* (Zheutlin 2017).

The black-and-white animations appear throughout the documentary, and particularly during the voiceover self-reflection. The stark contrasts, shadows, dark colours and the figure of a woman resembling the filmmaker help these animations to create an anxious, even a threatening atmosphere. The shadows close in. The filmmaker's stalker, death, is ever-present. The affective moments produced by the images and voiceover communicate effectively the fear of death to the viewer.

While animated images can be considered non-realist and imaginary, in documentary films they provide an intensive approach to reality. Animation adds breadth and depth into moments that can be difficult to represent through live-action images. In other words, animation is a mode of representation that emphasises metaphors, affective insight and anxieties of contemporary life (Skoller 2011; Takahashi 2011; Roe 2011, 229). It is a particularly useful tool for representing experiences such as trauma and fears, which are difficult to express through other means (Piotrowska 2011; Skoller 2011). In *Living while Dying*, animations mediate the filmmaker's affects and fears related to death and dying. Animated elements support speculative and subjective imagining, which further adds to their role in subjective documentary cinema. The animation's connection to the inner experiences, and particularly to death anxiety, is contrasted with bright scenes of the filmmaker's visits in other cultures to learn about death acceptance. For example, the images of the filmmaker's meeting with a shaman and a death doula in Australia are brimming with colour and visual arrangements. Serene-looking people are dressed colourfully, they are placed in a spacious landscape, and the scenery, with the sun shining from a blue sky, adds light and life to the personal relationships with death, an attitude that the filmmaker wants to adopt (Figure 10.2).

The contrast between the filmmaker's inner experience and what others have taught her is also pointed out. Midway through the film, the narrator asks if she is the only one who is afraid of death because she keeps meeting people who are prepared to die. While the filmmaker does not try to paint an overly beautiful image of dying – all the presented people have their moments of doubts – the people she meets emphasise that knowledge of their mortality has allowed them to focus on living. For example, Azul, a dying man, argues that awareness of death has made him more appreciative of life.

While Zheutlin's journey is personal, it is not lonely. For example, the filmmaker portrays the story of Clair, a family member who is dying. In a scene, Clair lies on his bed and describes listening to the sound of a ticking clock. The ticking seems to resonate with his pulse, perfectly timed. The filmmaker's voiceover frames Clair's death as something where time slips away. Clair's subjective experience becomes part of the filmmaker's subjective experience. After meeting with Clair for the last time, the filmmaker admits she has not learned enough about dying. She feels like death is a mystery worth exploring

FILMING DEATH

Figure 10.2 Colourful arrangement of a shaman and his disciples in *Living while Dying* (Zheutlin 2017).

and she needs to continue her journey in order to find new perspectives. She travels to meet other people to learn more, and these discussions, one by one, help her to change her attitude from denial to acknowledgement of death.

Living while Dying argues that we should talk more about death – and this is where the film ends. Towards the end, the filmmaker starts to talk about her expectations of death with her family members and encourages others to be similarly open about the topic. Death is still an emotionally challenging topic, but the filmmaker no longer denies its existence, and sees value in death awareness. The film finishes with a black-and-white animation of the woman as a crouching silhouette. By a pond, she touches the water with one hand while the other hand embraces a dark figure beside her. Rather than a stalker, death has become a companion. The voiceover assures, 'I know there is no right way to die. It just happens. But since it's unpredictable, I pray to be aware of the fleeting perfection of this very moment' (Zheutlin 2017). The filmmaker's journey has led her away from anxiety and enabled her to live fully.

The Other in Narration

In the context of first-person documentaries, Lebow introduces the concept of 'singular plural'. In singular plural, the concept of 'I' always includes an expectation of 'another'. In other words, one's individuality is interrelated to others and to society. Similarly, in first-person films 'I' functions in a context of 'we', and as such, '"I" is always social, always already in relation' (Lebow

2012, 3). In first-person end-of-life documentaries, the singular plural is used when the filmmakers use the stories of dying people to make the topic of death meaningful and understandable for themselves, and for the viewer. Their transformation is enabled by encountering the other on their journeys.

In all these documentaries, the filmmaker provides the curiosity to the narration; they want to learn about mortality, and to do so, they need someone to teach them. Lebow maintains that first-person filmmaking tends to focus on the other: a protagonist, group or collective, subject of the film or phenomenon. This focus requires dialogue, and in dialogue, the filmed objects (the other) become subjects as well. In this dialogical process, the filmmaker's subject becomes part of the film, something to be witnessed by the viewer. It also gives the filmmaker the role as a viewed object. The 'multiple positionality of subject/object', Lebow argues, splits the subjectivity. The split subjectivity allows singular plurality to take place (Lebow 2012, 4–5). This is a logic that the first-person end-of-life documentaries make active use of. While the films are framed as the filmmakers' personal journeys, the subjects and protagonists of these documentaries are the dying people they meet. The terminally ill add another layer to how mortality is experienced, tangible stories that both the filmmaker and the viewer can witness. The viewer, thus, follows a dual relationship with end of life, one where the filmmaker learns about the topic, and the other where the terminally ill share their experiences.

In *Looking Death in the Face*, director Luostarinen meets with death industry professionals, such as a grave digger, a casket manufacturer and a coroner. These professionals do not provide answers about mortality, rather they help the filmmaker to see death as a concrete, undeniable part of life. Apart from these few encounters, Luostarinen wanted to avoid institutional perspectives where (medical) professionals would explain death and dying. The subjective approach, she says, makes the film touching. Instead of factual information she searched for an understanding of how to live with the idea of being mortal (Luostarinen 2020, film quotes translated from Finnish). Because this is an emotional process, *Looking Death in the Face* finds that change comes through the other, the dying people, who serve as singular plural for the filmmaker's journey.

The film introduces two central characters, Jussi and Mari, patients at a hospice home. Jussi is a middle-aged man who yearns to live a normal life, to love and be loved. His child has reached adulthood and Jussi is supposed to have time for himself and his marriage. Death comes at the wrong time. Terminal illness has made him realise that people complain about the smallest things. He used to do that as well. Now, if he could go back, he would enjoy the world as it is. Jussi appears serene, calm and well spoken. There is nevertheless a certain melancholy about him: he misses the life and the future he could have had. From Jussi, the filmmaker learns about quiet acceptance of dying and priorities about living.

From Mari, a middle-aged woman with a terminal illness, the filmmaker learns about loss. The two women become good friends sharing everyday moments with Mari's husband and the couple's dog. The filmmaker listens to Mari's dreams and fears, comforts her and sits by her bed while she is sleeping. Such witnessing makes the filmmaker despair: 'What can you say, when there is no hope left?' The feeling of loss is palpable in a scene where the husband has once again come to see his wife. Mari would love to see their countryside cottage one more time, but the filmmaker's voiceover makes it clear that no one has the heart to tell her that she is in no condition to travel. Quiet and sad, the husband continues to rub Mari's feet without confronting the issue.

Mari, too, seems to have accepted her death at some level. She is open and even humorous about her funeral plans. She prefers doing the planning and organising herself, because she wants to make things easy for those mourning for her, and to be present in some way. Still, the thought about others missing her, and her missing the event, makes her cry. Her acceptance of the inevitable is both practical and emotional. The filmmaker goes through a similar process and tells the viewer that Mari has taught her how to say goodbye. The scene is shown to us through the filmmaker's diary. Mari is unconscious but still breathing. Diary pages fill the screen, and images of the filmmaker sitting by Mari's bed are reflected onto these pages (Figure 10.3). When the diary entry appears, the scene is framed as a memorial photograph. 'Death is relentless,' the filmmaker says. It bullies and tortures. At the same time, we see the filmmaker quietly caressing Mari. In a voiceover, the filmmaker refers to the

Figure 10.3 The filmmaker sitting by Mari's deathbed, reflecting her emotions through diary writing (Luostarinen 2003).

FIRST-PERSON DOCUMENTARIES

ticking clocks as being from this world, while Mari is already seeing another dimension.

Jussi's and Mari's stories are personal, yet their experiences are mediated through the filmmaker's eyes. The filmmaker's perspective is highlighted at the event of their death, which the filmmaker reflects in her diary. 'Jussi died today,' the filmmaker writes. The entry brings to mind the famous opening lines of Albert Camus's *The Stranger* (1942). 'Mother died today' signifies both the end and the beginning of this profound experience. The film then cuts to a close-up of Jussi's face. This close-up comes from an interview in the garden, where he sits among roses, his eyes closed and looking serene. He is not talking, only silence accompanies the image. Here, the filmmaker emphasises the person's face which has a symbolic meaning in the film, including the name of the documentary *Looking Death in the Face* (the Finnish title *Kuoleman kasvot* can also be translated as the 'face of death'). The filmmaker understands that the 'face of a dead person is like a map of their lives – their experiences, actions and emotions. Similarly, my face is transforming towards its final form at the moment of death.' Thus, a close-up of Jussi's serene face a few days before his death serves as a final form or final expression of his existence. The serenity that Jussi leaves behind him is both comforting and plaintive. The filmmaker describes for the viewer that we are all fragile and resilient at the same time. Accepting the forthcoming death does not necessarily translate to wanting to die.

In a similar manner, Mari's death is announced through a diary scene. A wintery image fills the screen, with sounds of nature, followed by the sound of pen on paper: 'Mari died today.' In Jussi's case, the film cuts to a frozen close-up of him still alive, but with Mari we see her deceased face, still and pale. It is this face that the filmmaker's hand caresses. The filmmaker observes in a voiceover how small Mari looks beneath the sheets. The scene ends with a distanced image of Mari lying in the middle of the hospice viewing room while we can hear the filmmaker's steps walking away from the room. This is the last time we see Mari. Even when we get glimpses of her funeral and grave, the filmmaker leaves the viewer with a symbolic idea of her face and death.

From these encounters, the filmmaker learns two main things. One, she abandons her wish for a sudden death, which now appears to her as dying in secret from the family and from oneself. Instead, dying can be about goodbyes, love and gratitude. Second, she sees time as merciless. Life will always fade away, regardless of whether we want to talk about it or not. The final images of the film are diary entries printed on a summery scene with a lake and a boat. In the nature's cycle, summer symbolises life and growth, whereas the previous images of winter had referred to death and loss. 'One day,' the filmmaker writes, 'there will be a hole of my size in this world. That's all. The wonderful certainty.' The diary closes, and the film ends. The self-reflection combined with her interpretations of the dying people's experiences highlight the film-maker's change of heart. None of this would have been possible if she had not followed Jussi and Mari through their end of life. By witnessing the other, the 'I' of the story can evolve and transform.

'WE' IN NARRATION

When Tim Wilson, director of *Griefwalker*, wants to unravel his close call with death, he contacts his friend Stephen Jenkinson to help him search for answers. Jenkinson, then a leader of a palliative care counselling team at Toronto's Mount Sinai Hospital, and nowadays a cultural activist advocating for recognition of ancestry and death acceptance, becomes the second main character of the documentary. Through him Wilson meets with terminally ill people, patients that Jenkinson counsels. Their experiences are used to exemplify his teaching. Jenkinson has a holistic and spiritual uptake on death and dying despite his medical background in palliative care. He talks about how the fear of death is limiting the way in which people live, and especially how they die. To him, death should make humanity and existence meaningful.

When I talked to Tim Wilson (2019), he described Jenkinson as 'charismatically intelligent' and able to cut into 'elegant words, mysteries and complexities that few of us express so well'. Jenkinson had a wealth of knowledge about end of life, but Wilson did not want to create an institutional film.

> I wanted it also to be the story of someone not as active, you know, not as experienced, maybe more like, general, that stands for someone who needs to learn something. It's interesting that the film board [National Film Board of Canada, the distributor of the documentary], with the prep for the current poster of the film, which used to be Steve standing in front of the canoe, is me looking kind of scared into the mirror. That's ok with me, that's fine. Because I think the story is of me learning. (Wilson 2019)

By framing himself as a naïve learner about end of life, the filmmaker becomes the viewer's entry into the story and the topic. The viewer can share the feeling of not knowing enough about death, and as such, the filmmaker's first-person voice is a point of connection. The viewer can learn together with the filmmaker. While the narrator, or 'I', creates a singular plural connection with the other (Jenkinson with knowledge and the terminally ill with experience), a similar process can take place at the level of the reception. The filmmaker forms a 'we' relationship with the viewer. In these films, death is often represented as mysterious, something 'we' rarely think about in our everyday lives, yet something 'we' need to acknowledge. In this way, 'we' becomes a viewer position and a part of the film's organisational structure in 'our' desire to learn more about death and dying. In first-person documentaries, subjective truths can visualise how reality is experienced, felt and embodied in ways where the personal becomes relatable, and as such, social.

The filmmaker's subjective documentary voice mixes with Jenkinson's teachings. He shares what he has learned about mortality, while the filmmaker acts in the role of a student. However, the filmmaker does not merely adopt the offered points of view, but works as a critical evaluator as well. This is evident in voiceover comments, such as 'I have to confess, I am not convinced. What good is it to know that you are dying, let alone make it into "a prized possession". How can death at your door turn your life around?' (Wilson 2008) This question follows a scene where Jenkinson suggests that a terminally ill woman, Sandra, and her husband should try to embrace the idea of death.

The film provides a mix of critical distance and emotional embrace of Jenkinson's ideas about the spirituality of death acceptance. In this documentary, too, natural cycles gain symbolic strength. Jenkinson often talks in metaphors of nature. He sees that western cultures have distanced themselves from natural cycles, which has made death a difficult topic. When death is understood as a part of nature, people might be able to recognise death's role in ancestry lines and human heritage. These discussions are framed by poetic images of nature, changing seasons and indigenous rituals. Jenkinson searches for acceptance of mortality in spiritual traditions, and while the filmmaker finds comfort in nature and rituals, he also criticises this view for romanticising death. As such, the filmmaker offers space for transformation, but does so with a pinch of salt. The viewer is invited to embrace his approach, but at the same time, the self-reflective approach encourages the viewer to question whether this is the only way of understanding the meaning of death.

The scenes where the filmmaker challenges Jenkinson's teachings, and the scenes where he reflects on the meaningfulness of Jenkinson's view of mortality, function as narrative tools to include the viewer into the story. The filmmaker asks questions for himself and for the viewer. The narrative style positions the filmmaker and the viewer together as 'we' who learn, but who also critically evaluate the teaching. At the end of the film, the filmmaker (and perhaps the viewer as well) appears to be fairly comfortable with the idea that grief over one's own inevitable death and the death of others is part of life. Consequently, death awareness becomes a skill to celebrate life, something that completes life rather than robs life of its value.

RELATIONAL KNOWLEDGE OF PERSONAL EXPERIENCE

Mette Kramer (2018) discusses the forms of knowledge in first-person documentaries and argues that they offer relational knowledge which is based on embodied reality and is performed through emotional and cognitive levels.

Relational knowledge, for Kramer, is a dual system. It is both automatic (implicit) and declarative (explicit). Because this knowledge is embodied in film, it is at least to a certain degree a declarative performance for the filmmaker. Thus, relational knowledge arises from filmmakers' experiences which are enacted on-screen (Kramer 2018, 244–58). The above examples from end-of-life documentaries show how these subjective experiences morph towards the other, including both the dying people and the viewer. Consequently, the relational knowledge of first-person documentaries includes societal aspects. Particularly, the declarative parts of first-person experiences add to a public understanding of end of life, they make the affective, personal and implicit visible in public space.

The societal aspects of subjective views as relational knowledge are underlined in the reception of *Terry Pratchett: Choosing to Die* in the UK. This documentary explores the experiences related to assisted dying. In the UK, assisted dying is illegal, yet many British citizens have sought help from Switzerland, which allows foreigners to ask for assisted suicide. The narrator, Pratchett, explores why some people have chosen to use this option or have opted out of it. He uses his own situation as a starting point because he doubts that Alzheimer's disease will allow him to die a dignified death. At the same time, he wants to enjoy life as long as possible. How to decide when the time is right to make decisions about end of life? The internal struggle and a fear of suffering inspire his search for answers.

Pratchett meets the widow of Hugo Claus, a Belgian author who died by euthanasia, which is legal in Belgium. The widow recalls the moment of Claus's death and assures that those last moments together were beautiful and loving. Claus got an ending he wished for, and the wife wanted to support that request. Pratchett also meets with Mick, who chose hospice care after considering assisted dying. Mick is happy with his choice but emphasises that everybody should have the right to choose for themselves. Pratchett also meets Peter and Andrew who both decide to travel to Switzerland for assisted dying. These two stories become the key experiences for Pratchett to reflect on, and he and his assistant travel to witness Peter's and Andrew's last days in Switzerland.

The closer Pratchett gets to witnessing assisted dying in practice, the more agitated and conflicted he becomes. The self-reflective discussions, either in voiceover or with the assistant, voice doubts because Pratchett feels these men are dying too early. When Pratchett meets Andrew, a 42-year-old man with multiple sclerosis, a day before his scheduled death, Andrew talks about falling in love with Zürich, hoping he would not need to die right now. Pratchett suggests that Andrew should consider postponing his death because he seems to be so full of life. Andrew stands by his decision, arguing that if he does not do it now, it might become too late. The dying persons need to be physically able to take the medication by themselves. The next morning, at their hotel, Pratchett and his assistant are melancholic. They listen to the music Andrew has chosen for his death, raise a glass to his memory, and Pratchett cries.

The documentary's culmination point comes at the end of the documentary when Peter allows Pratchett and the film crew to accompany him to his last moments. These scenes emphasise Pratchett's role as a subjective witness. Peter, his wife and two staff members from the death-aid clinic sit at the coffee table, having drinks. The moment appears mundane, yet at the same time, the staff members confirm multiple times that Peter is sure about his decision. Peter is rather matter-of-fact in his affirmative responses. The camera cuts between this discussion at the coffee table and Pratchett, who stands in a corner of the room. The distance between these two groups, and Pratchett's uncomfortable posture, show his struggle to witness. He is mostly quiet, looking down as if wanting to avoid what is taking place in the room. His quiet words, such as 'I can't believe', stress the disbelief about what will happen. In this way, Pratchett offers a position that the viewer can share – witnessing yet questioning the morality of the moment. Whereas Peter's process towards assisted death is informative, Pratchett's humane and tangible reaction embodies the emotions related to the situation. As such, the created knowledge is relational and is transmitted through a first-person approach. The knowledge about assisted dying as a practice is both embodied and performed for the viewer.

In the next scene, the group has made its way to a living room, where Peter takes a seat on the sofa, and his wife sits next to him. The wife is slightly hesitant at first, as she cannot in any way participate in helping with the dying process. When the professionals assure that it is 'proper' to offer emotional support, the wife holds Peter's hand and Peter reassures her, before he drinks the medicine. Peter does not hesitate, but when the medicine makes him gag, the camera cuts to Pratchett, who is again looking down at the floor and is slightly removed from the situation. Peter's gagging sounds turn to snoring, and the assistant staff says that now that Peter is sleeping, he will stop breathing first and then his heart will stop. The camera turns back to the now peaceful-looking Peter, and his wife sitting next to him. Pratchett takes a deep breath, 'It is hard to believe, I've seen death.' In the following scenes, Pratchett stands outdoors, where snow is falling, and is clearly moved. He describes Peter's death as a happy occasion because he died peacefully in his wife's arms. He also praises Peter for his courage. Yet, he admits, he is not sure whether he is able to follow in Peter's footsteps. Despite his misgivings about whether he wants to choose assisted dying, Pratchett remains convinced that people should have this option.

In a blog, Charlie Russell, the filmmaker, argues that they wanted to make an honest film about assisted dying, and that honesty included filming the death as well, and to film it 'respectfully, sensitively but most of all truthfully'. Russell shares this responsibility with the viewer: 'It is up to you to decide whether his last moments are deeply moving, distressing or rather ordinary' (Russell 2011b). The audiences latched onto this possibility to decide for themselves, and at its television premiere, the film was deemed controversial. The controversiality arose partly from the contested legality of assisted dying. However, it was also linked to the relational knowledge provided through Pratchett's subjective position. Particularly those who oppose the legalisation of assisted dying accused the film of bias because it chose to follow Pratchett, a public figure and known advocate for assisted dying (Blake 2011; Laughlin 2011). The BBC's commissioning editor for documentaries, Charlotte Moore, defended the decision to produce this documentary. In a BBC blog, she argues that because death is a controversial issue, 'it's not something that we'd ever take the decision to show lightly'. She also emphasises that BBC documentary makers 'faithfully documented his personal journey', and while 'not everyone will feel comfortable watching *Terry Pratchett: Choosing to Die*, [...] we hope that all would accept that it's important that the BBC tackles the difficult subjects that we're often faced with in life' (Moore 2011). Thus, Pratchett's subjective perspective is also seen as an enabler for debating the controversial issue.

These aftermath discussions use the narrator's subjectivity to interpret the film either as having an ethical or an unethical approach. The ethical perspective praises the first-person narrative for making visible the etymological aspects of knowledge: the film does not hide its personal view nor does it offer this view as an objective truth. Blaming the narrative structure as unethical arises from the notion that subjectivity offers misleading or biased information. What we see is therefore not a trustworthy representation of the issue. These arguments also reveal the first-person documentaries' ethical potential, which calls the viewers to think about end-of-life choices, but does not demand that they align their thinking with the represented perspective.

However, it is interesting to compare the contradictory reception of Peter's death in *Terry Pratchett: Choosing to Die* to the death of Don in *Living while Dying*. The latter film does not focus on assisted dying, but assisted dying is represented as an option given to Don, a patient with cancer. If he wants to live longer, he needs to go through aggressive treatments. Instead, he chooses to live for only fifteen days after the diagnosis and to take part in the Death with Dignity programme in Portland. Don denies this is a sad process. Rather, it is one that he can control and say his goodbyes and die surrounded by the people he loves. The film also includes the events before death, Don taking his medication and saying his goodbyes calmly. Shortly after, his loved ones hold his hands when he lies unconscious in his bed.

Unlike the portrayal of Peter's death, Don's death scene has not created controversy, even if both are represented from a filmmaker's subjective perspective. Yet, there are significant differences between the scenes. Peter dies far away from home, in a death-aid facility that is in the middle of an industrial area, in the shadow of a factory. His death is administered by professionals who guide Peter through pre-meditated steps. These elements further add factory-like symbolism to the scene, where Peter's death becomes another product on a conveyor belt. Don, in turn, dies at home. The scene conveys warmth and love. In both cases, the filmmakers are witnessing the situation from a few metres away, but whereas Pratchett's reaction speaks of disbelief, Zheutlin's use of intimacy and soft music conveys support to Don's personal decision. In a way, Peter's death scene in *Terry Pratchett: Choosing to Die* is aimed towards the viewer, who sees Pratchett's discomfort. This calls for an evaluative 'we' position and a critical evaluation of the knowledge provided on the topic. In comparison, Don's death scene is aimed towards the other and their embodied knowledge. The camera focuses on Don's experience, which encourages the viewer to share an emotional and a liminal moment instead of evaluating its morality.

These differences in embodying the relational knowledge invite different reactions from the viewer. Pratchett frames his search for answers and his witnessing of Peter's death as a moral dilemma. Pratchett questions whether we can ever know the right time to die, and thus, while assisted dying should be allowed to be a personal choice, the right to choose will never be easy nor straightforward. Pratchett's embodied doubt stands in for the viewer's doubt as well. The viewers are asked to form their own subjective understanding of what has just happened. Zheutlin's approach to Don's death does not question his right to make this choice but aims for understanding. Assisted dying is legal in Portland, and its status is not contested in a similar way as is Peter's death in the UK context. Also, Zheutlin's own acceptance of her friend's decision embodies an accepting attitude for the viewer. Zheutlin asks the viewer to look at the beauty of the moment, instead of its morality. Thus, from the viewer's perspective, the filmmaker's performance of knowledge can influence how the viewer engages emotionally and cognitively with the film and its characters. In this way, as Kramer (2018, 244–58) argues, the directors transmit their experience for the viewer and their subjective experiences become intersubjective. In the end-of-life context, the personal experiences of the filmmakers can turn into a social understanding or debate of what death and dying are or should be.

Conclusion

In first-person end-of-life documentaries the filmmakers narrate their own personal experiences and transformations of encountering stories of dying people. Instead of seeking help to understand the medical or physical aspects of death and dying, they hope to see personal growth take place on an emotional level. The filmmakers seek to mould their attitudes and values in such a way that an idea of mortality becomes bearable and that they find some ways to cope with death-related fears. However, it is important to ask why we should care about their experience. Why do we need hear personal stories from people who are not dying themselves and who are not experts in the field of death and dying?

The answer is found in the inclusive aspects of intersubjectivity. The viewer is invited to share the transformative experiences of the filmmaker, and as such, these documentaries also aim for a wider understanding of death and dying in their sociocultural contexts. When the filmmaker becomes an entry into the story, it provides a position for the viewer to relate with. Thus, the singular plural of first-person narratives works in two directions. First, the sense of 'us', the sense of a shared experience, is created together with other characters in the documentaries, the characters whom the filmmakers are learning from. Second, another sense of 'us' is created together with the viewer, who is recognised as having the same need or desire to learn about end of life.

In this process, the filmmaker, the 'I' of the story, becomes the mediator in a process where various fears, expectations and experiences about death and dying are socially shared and constructed. Thus, these documentaries create intersubjective, socially situated and historical insights into emotional practices regarding end of life (e.g. Kiernan 2020). The filmmakers' personal journeys and performances of subjective emotions about death and dying can emotionally engage the viewer with the film, its characters and themes. When they succeed in this, the first-person experiences can turn into intersubjective coping mechanisms with death anxiety. These films also show how the relationship between 'I' and the other can transform the narration and the viewer – an 'us', a public – and how the internalised ethical encounter turns to having political power.

References

Andrews, Hazel, and Les Roberts. 2012. 'Introduction: Re-Mapping Liminality'. In *Liminal Landscapes: Travel, Experience and Spaces In-Between*, edited by Hazel Andrews and Les Roberts, 1–17. London: Routledge.

Blake, Daniel. 2011. 'Terry Pratchett Pro-Euthanasia Documentary Blasted for Death Show'. *The Christian Post*. 14 June 2011. https://www.christianpost.com/news/bbc-condemned-for-death-scenes-in-unbalanced-euthanasia-documentary.html. Last accessed 17 December 2022.

Bruzzi, Stella. 2010. *New Documentary*. First published 2000. London; New York: Routledge.

Chanan, Michael. 2007. *The Politics of Documentary*. London: British Film Institute.

Gennep, Arnold van. 2019. *The Rites of Passage, Second Edition*. Translated by Monika B. Vizedom and Gabrielle L. Caffee. First published 1909. Chicago, IL: University of Chicago Press.

Helke, Susanna. 2016. 'In Pursuit of Emotions: The Emotive Turn and Post-Political Sentiment in Finnish Documentary Film Culture'. *Studies in Documentary Film* 10 (2): 183–97. https://doi.org/10.1080/17503280.2016.1225356.

Henderson, Desirée. 2019. *How to Read a Diary: Critical Contexts and Interpretive Strategies for 21st-Century Readers*. London; New York: Routledge.

Kiernan, Frederic. 2020. 'Emotion as Creative Practice: Linking Creativity and Wellbeing through the History and Sociology of Emotion'. *International Journal of Wellbeing* 10 (5). https://internationaljournalofwellbeing.org/index.php/ijow/article/view/1517. Last accessed 30 March 2022.

Kramer, Mette. 2018. 'The Communication of Relational Knowledge in the First-Person Documentary'. In *Cognitive Theory and Documentary Film*, edited by Catalin Brylla and Mette Kramer, 243–60. Cham: Palgrave Macmillan.

Laderman, David. 2002. *Driving Visions: Exploring the Road Movie*. Austin: University of Texas Press.

Laughlin, Andrew. 2011. 'BBC Criticised over Assisted Suicide Film'. *Digital Spy* (blog). 13 June 2011. http://www.digitalspy.com/media/a324580/bbc-criticised-over-assisted-suicide-film/. Last accessed 17 December 2022.

Lebow, Alisa. 2012. 'Introduction'. In *The Cinema of Me: The Self and Subjectivity in First Person Documentary*, edited by Alisa Lebow, 1–11. New York: Columbia University Press.

Luostarinen, Kiti. 2003. *Looking Death in the Face (Kuoleman Kasvot)*. Documentary. Pirkanmaan elokuvakeskus.

———. 2020. Personal interview by Outi Hakola.

Moore, Charlotte. 2011. 'Terry Pratchett: Choosing to Die'. *BBC Blog*. 15 April 2011. https://www.bbc.co.uk/blogs/aboutthebbc/2011/04/terry-pratchett-choosing-to-die.shtml. Last accessed 17 December 2022.

Nichols, Bill. 2017. *Introduction to Documentary, Third Edition*. Bloomington: Indiana University Press.

Piotrowska, Agnieszka. 2011. 'Animating the Real: A Case Study'. *Animation* 6 (3): 335–51. https://doi.org/10.1177/1746847711418566.

Renov, Michael. 2004. *The Subject of Documentary*. Minneapolis: University of Minnesota Press.

Roe, Annabelle Honess. 2011. 'Absence, Excess and Epistemological Expansion: Towards a Framework for the Study of Animated Documentary'. *Animation* 6 (3): 215–30. https://doi.org/10.1177/1746847711417954.

Römpötti, Tommi. 2012. *Vieraana Omassa Maassa: Suomalaiset Road-Elokuvat Vapauden Ja Vastustuksen Kertomuksina 1950-Luvun Lopusta 2000-Luvulle*. Jyväskylä: University of Jyväskylä.

Russell, Charlie. 2011a. *Terry Pratchett: Choosing to Die*. Documentary. BBC Two.

———. 2011b. 'BBC – BBC TV Blog: Terry Pratchett: Choosing To Die'. 14 June 2011. https://www.bbc.co.uk/blogs/tv/2011/06/choosing-to-die.shtml. Last accessed 15 December 2022.

Skoller, Jeffrey. 2011. 'Introduction to the Special Issue Making It (Un)Real: Contemporary Theories and Practices in Documentary Animation'. *Animation* 6 (3): 207–14. https://doi.org/10.1177/1746847711422496.

Takahashi, Tess. 2011. 'Experiments in Documentary Animation: Anxious Borders, Speculative Media'. *Animation* 6 (3): 231–45. https://doi.org/10.1177/1746847711 417934.

Turner, Victor. 2011. *The Ritual Process: Structure and Anti-Structure*. First published 1969. New Brunswick, NJ: Aldine Transaction.

Wels, Harry, Kees van der Waal, Andrew Spiegel, and Frans Kamsteeg. 2011. 'Victor Turner and Liminality: An Introduction'. *Anthropology Southern Africa* 34 (1–2): 1–4. https://doi.org/10.1080/23323256.2011.11500002.

Wilson, Tim. 2008. *Griefwalker*. Documentary. National Film Board of Canada.

———. 2019. Personal Interview by Outi Hakola.

Zheutlin, Cathy. 2017. *Living While Dying*. Documentary. Peace Films.

11. COLLABORATIVE DOCUMENTARIES
Intimate Testimonials of End of Life

From The Bedroom to The Bathroom (Rawlence 2015) tells the story of Sue, who has motor neurone disease, and, as a result, limited mobility and difficulty speaking. Filmed in collaboration with Myton Hospices in the UK, the short documentary is a part of art therapy where interpretative dance and poetry help Sue to describe her daily battle of going to the bathroom. To her, this everyday act that many take for granted is a daily physical struggle. While she is not filmed in the bathroom, the necessity of making one's way there is relatable and invites compassion for her experience.

Sue's slow and laboured movements are captured in detail when she inches her way towards the bedroom door. Little by little, she moves her hand or takes a slow step. In voiceover, an assistant reads Sue's poetry that translates the experience into words: 'My recent history is written on the bedroom wall. By my own fair hands, quite literally, the layers of my days recorded. Visual echoes of hand to wall, hand to wall.' Her painstaking movements are edited together with art sessions and the sound of her slurring voice. With assistance, she is able to wave her arms and looks happy. The blissful ability to express oneself contrasts with her slow and uncertain movements and her solemn expression during the time it takes for her to reach the bathroom. In this short film, an everyday act, and particularly an act that is connected to intimacy and personal bodily functions, becomes a sign of loss and fragility, and summons the viewer to relate with the agonies of her struggle.

From The Bedroom to The Bathroom is an example of collaborative end-of-life documentaries. It was produced by Rosetta Life, a British organisation that creates collaborative art projects with terminally ill people and people living with disabilities and illness (Rosetta Life 2022). Filmmaking, engaging filmmakers to help patients tell their life stories, is one of the art resources in the programme. According to Lucinda Jarrett, co-founder of the organisation, the project started as a celebration of people living with illnesses. Collaborative art projects, Jarrett says, helps the vulnerable subjects to take ownership of their own stories (Jarrett 2007, x–xiv). Elizabeth Coffman (2009, 66–74), similarly, argues that collaborative projects include the voices of marginalised people and communities in a way that increases authenticity of the stories. From the perspective of the filmed subjects, the collaborative approach is all about engagement, agency and empowerment.

In collaborative documentaries, the terminally ill and dying people become more than filmed subjects: they actively participate in the planning, screenwriting, filming and/or producing. The collaborative subjects share authorship with the film director. As such, they differ from performative documents, although they have much in common when it comes to questions of empowerment and agency (Chapter 6). Ethnographic documentary in the 1950s launched the collaborative approach to documentary filming. Particularly, Jean Rouch, a French anthropologist and early *cinéma vérité* filmmaker, used the collaborative approach – or 'shared anthropology' as he called it – to give voice to the filmed subjects. Rouch argued that shared authorship and authority between the filmmaker and the participating subjects would allow polyphony of subjects' voices. These voices create a more honest, complex and open approach to the topic when compared to the authoritative and monologic voice of the filmmaker alone (Scheinman 2013; Henley 2009).

In end-of-life documentaries, Broderick Fox maintains, the collaboration can make the dying subjects appear as something different to 'other' whose experience can be dismissed as symbolic or as someone else's problem. When a subject participates in filming their own story, the experience comes close to the viewers and asks them to open up. The intersubjective space of collaboration, Fox argues, extends to and includes the viewer. These films which borrow elements from home movies and diary writing blur the limits between private and public spaces (Fox 2011, 5, 56–8). The co-authorship translates into an on-screen consent that promises the viewer that the filming respects the wishes and control of the filmed subjects (Porst 2007). The viewer is called to trust the film's ethical filmmaking practices and the priority given to the voices of dying people.

In this chapter, my focus is on the ethical aspects of collaborative end-of-life documentaries, which I will first discuss through an analysis of the American documentary film *The End* (2004). In the making of this documentary, the filmmaker Kirby Dick gave five terminally ill people and their families cameras to film their experiences. This is followed by an examination of the camera as an extension of the intimate relationships between the subjects in another American documentary, *The LuLu Sessions* (Wong 2011). Third, I will analyse collaborative documentaries on assisted dying, and particularly, the death scenes of these films. Here, four films provide the material: *Live and Let Go: An American Death* (Spain 2002), where twins Jay and Gretchen Niver fulfil their father's wish to make a story of his quest for a dignified death; *All in Her Stride* (2014), a co-production of the director Fiona Cochrane and actor Leverne McDonnell, who wants to make a statement for legalisation of assisted dying in Australia; the Australian film *Laura's Choice* (2020), which Laura's daughter Cathy Henkel and granddaughter Sam Lara directed about the 90-year-old matriarch travelling to Switzerland to end her life; and American film *Last Flight Home* (2022), where the filmmaker Ondi Timoner films her father's assisted dying during the Covid-19 pandemic.

Shared authorship does more than enhance the viewer's trust in the ethics of filmmaking and the authenticity of the story. I argue that co-authorship also translates into increased intimacy on-screen and off-screen. The collaborative end-of-life documentaries tend to be told by family members and friends, which emphasises intimacy between the filmed subjects and those making the film. The embodied camera work, where the camera becomes a technology of intimacy, includes the viewer in these intimate relationships. The intimacy encourages ethical viewing, which connects the viewers with the dying person, instead of leaving them to observe the death of the other from a distance. Being close with the filmed subjects, in turn, affects these documentaries' representations of end of life, and particularly, the emotional turmoil of end-of-life experiences.

Ethics of Collaboration

In collaborative documentaries, the dying subjects are members of the film crew. The collaboration means different things in each project (Coffman 2009, 67). The films to be discussed in this chapter were directed by family members and friends, which serves to increase the intimacy of the collaboration and narration. The only exception is *The End* (2004), directed by Kirby Dick, a well-known documentary maker. Dick's earlier film *Sick: The Life and Death of Bob Flanagan, Supermasochist* (1997) established him as a director who is not afraid of taboo or marginalised topics. In *Sick*, Dick uses Flanagan's home movies and video diaries to display the last years and death of the performance artist. In *The End*, Dick returns to the topic of death with an intimate personal approach. He gives cameras to five hospice patients and their families to take

COLLABORATIVE DOCUMENTARIES

home and record their experiences. He follows the common collaborative practice of the filmmaker's mixing subject-generated content with other materials to enrich the documentary (Cardillo 2022). The result is a five-episode film, where most of the footage is shot by the family members of the dying people. This gives the film an insider perspective. Paola Bilbrough (2013, 182) argues that collaborative practice can provide a buffer against a negative impact, particularly when dealing with sensitive topics. When the participants choose to be honest, the process leaves less room for the viewer to raise the alarm of vulnerable people being taken advantage of.

End-of-life documentaries, such as *The End*, can be brutally honest about the emotional turmoil that the dying and their families go through. *The End* opens with Phil and his family not in a scene of gentle serenity but embroiled in an argument. Phil takes out his anger on almost everyone in the room: because he is the one dying, his suffering matters the most, and others are not allowed to complain. He yells at his wife: 'I don't give a fuck how you feel, I'm the one who is dying.' The wife is upset, and so is the daughter holding the camera. She puts the camera down, blurring the image and leaving the viewer to witness the angry sounds of the commotion. The daughter threatens to leave if her father continues in the same vein, to which Phil responds: 'Leave! When your father is dying.' Later, hospice provides Phil and the family psychological help to deal with the situation. Phil admits that he is angry because he feels he is losing control of his life. Ordering others around is his only way to hold onto his independence and dignity.

At home, Phil admits to a hospice physician that he is becoming weaker by the day. He feels like he is dying. The doctor reassures him that all this is natural and that Phil has not done anything wrong, that his dying of cancer is not a punishment. With a hand-held camera, the daughters film the family's responses to the devastating news that the end is near. During the night, the wife, who has not taken well to being filmed, records a section on her own. Phil has weakened quickly and keeps fighting for his dignity. She confides in the camera how humiliated he was to wet his pants. She understands his anger and anguish. She takes the hand-held camera closer to Phil, who looks like he is suffering even in his sleep. This is the only sequence filmed by the wife, and it is a telling piece of footage of her trying to cope with Phil's transformation from a strong and capable man to a fragile dying man.

In these scenes, the family share their intimate responses with the camera and the viewer. The camera becomes something of a therapist, while the viewer listens to the family members' emotional confessions. Fox argues that the dying and their loved ones can find collaborative projects both empowering and therapeutic. The filming gives them an outlet and enables them to make sense of their own experiences. Fox calls this 'a healing process', which removes any sense of victimhood often associated with public representations

217

FILMING DEATH

of dying (Fox 2011, 56–60). Phil's dying is a struggle for him and his family. They use the camera and the viewer for their own agency and purposes, while the viewer is asked to witness and understand their battle.

In another story, Mike films the last days of his father, Stan, who seems barely tolerant of the camera and calls the whole thing 'crazy'. Using the camera thus turns into a power play. The son records his own testimonials and his increasingly vulnerable father, yearning for his acceptance. The camera becomes Mike's ally in this quest. He hopes that if he takes care of his father, who has remained distant throughout Mike's life, his father may finally appreciate him. In the name of documenting the process, Mike also records scenes such as physical examinations and going to the bathroom where Stan's autonomy is removed. In a bathroom scene that the son calls a 'Stan-cam', the camera captures Mike pulling down Stan's pants. The wrinkled skin on the bottom of an old, sick man, creates intimate privacy turned into discomfort. For terminally ill people, the fact that they need help to go to the bathroom and are deprived of body privacy raises questions of autonomy and dignity. Help and assistance can thus feel demeaning (Ferri, Muzzalupo, and Di Lorenzo 2015; Walsh and Kowanko 2002; Chochinov et al. 2002). That Mike includes the viewer in such private moments symbolises processes of loss at the end of life, and while it can foster compassion, Mike's power play may also invite distress.

Throughout this segment, the viewer hears Mike's heartbreaking desire to be loved. When he fails to get the response he seeks from his father, he turns his quest towards the viewer. Naomi Richards argues that end-of-life testimonies always require a witness. The idea of the viewer adds meaning and depth to the performance (Richards 2011, 47). During the last night of Stan's life, Mike continues to film and asks whether he is Stan's number-one son. At least on film, Mike never gets the confirmation he yearns for. Later that night, when Stan's body is moved on stretchers, Mike admits to the camera that he does not know what to do without his father. By being honest about his emotions, Mike seeks acceptance from the viewer. His intimate and at times uncomfortable filming gives voice to him in ways that might be questioned if the scenes were filmed by an outsider. Kate Nash argues that in documentary projects, the filmed subjects often see themselves as active and creative contributors influencing the filming with their own goals. However, as Nash points out, the filmed subjects are often excluded from post-production, which requires them to trust the filmmaker. This can be an unsettling experience (Nash 2012, 325, 328). Trust has a special place in the making of end-of-life documentaries, because the filmed subjects, such as Stan, have died before post-production.

In *The End*, Dick edits the footage together with his own material. Collaboration practices promise that shared authorship is honoured and respected throughout the process, including the phase where the filmmaker reclaims the footage (Bilbrough 2013, 181; Thomas 2012, 338, 342; Porst 2007). While the filmmakers' influence in the editing process can limit the transparency of the film, Jennifer Porst (2007) argues that their input is also needed to bring various voices together in such a way that the desired polyphony does not turn into indistinguishable cacophony. In *The End*, the filmmaker uses his own footage of the home hospice team that attend to the families to frame and explain their experiences. For example, the professionals of hospice and palliative care normalise Phil's anger and Mike's reluctance to let go as typical reactions to physical decline.

In most cases, Dick uses the hospice team's explanations to validate the experiences of the filmed subjects. However, there is one story where the filmmaker uses the hospice team scenes to challenge the subject-provided footage. Rosalie's story is about pain and suffering. Her friend Sonia is sympathetic and encourages Rosalie to find medication and alternative treatments, such as blessings, energy treatments and angelic healing practices for pain. While Rosalie takes part in the filming, the events are seen from Sonia's perspective. Sonia does most of the filming and makes herself visible through mirror shots, by giving testimonies to the camera and by adding running commentary to the scenes. Her footage is optimistic, full of partnership and care. The filmmaker, however, provides an alternative view of the events by including conversations among the hospice team members. They complain that Rosalie's demand for drugs, and particularly a certain brand of medication, is unusually high, and that the prescribed medications seem to disappear immediately. When the hospice team replace an opium-based medicine with methadone – which only has value to Rosalie herself – conflict ensues. Sonia, particularly, gets upset. She asks Rosalie if she wants to go on as the 'hostage' of the hospice team. These scenes make the viewer question whether Sonia's footage is really about care, or indicates addiction issues and misuse of medicines (either by Rosalie, Sonia, or both).

At the end of this segment, Sonia tells the camera that Rosalie left her behind and moved to live with her daughter. Rosalie dies a month later, but in the film her story ends with Sonia. By removing Rosalie from the situation, the hospice team's perspective wins in the end. In the following short scene, the team takes a short break to celebrate the birthday of a colleague. The scene's placement in the film suggests a celebrative mood after Sonia's defeat. Bilbrough (2013, 189) argues that in a collaborative context, especially when dealing with sensitive topics, representing the events through the filmmaker's framing creates a variety of 'truths' and expands the potential meanings of the story. In the same way, while the filmmaker never blames Sonia outright, he frames the material in a way that suggests different interpretations of the situation.

The End portrays the complexity of ethical aspects in collaborative ventures, which require trust and respect throughout the project. These questions extend to the film-viewing experience in that the viewer becomes the trusted listener with almost an obligation to respect the intimacy of the filmed scenes. At the same time, the collaborative approach gives those involved in the dying process a unique position to share their insights and reflections of death with the viewer (Fox 2011, 56–60). Richards, based on an ethnographic study on Rosetta Life, recognises an inward and outward transformation in collaborative projects. The inward transformation refers to how the filmed subjects use the filming to manage their complex emotions and to pursue meaning, whereas the outward transformation refers to the processes of how these representations and performances create public statements about dying (Richards 2011). In *The End*, the families' intimate revelations help them to manage their emotions, but their confessions also paint a picture of the emotional complexity of end-of-life experiences. These stories do not feature quiet acceptance and stoicism. Dying and loss are pictured as devastating events in the lives of the families.

Camera as a Technology of Intimacy

In *The LuLu Sessions* (2011) director S. Casper Wong records the last fifteen months of her friend. On the film's home page, Wong says that the film was not planned. She was with LuLu when the oncologist called with biopsy results. Wong, who had just started in a film school, began filming and continued until the end (Wong 2021). The documentary grows into an exploration of cancer, dying and friendship. Wong mostly stays behind the camera, but the camera's position and movements mediate an intimate interaction between the friends. For example, when LuLu calls her family to tell them about the cancer, the filmmaker starts crying. Her sniffling and the shaky camera movements embody the impact of the diagnosis on those close to the person who is ill. In this scene, LuLu stays quite calm, dries her tears with a napkin and promises that 'it is gonna be okay'. The viewer cannot see the tears, but again the (involuntary) movements of the camera and LuLu's hand that stretches outside the frame with a tissue serve to create a powerful testimony of emotions. The camera embodies intimacy in ways that invite the viewer to experience what it means to lose someone.

Wong, thus, becomes the story's other main character, although she is rarely seen on-screen. Photographs of the friends become the main mediator of her corporeal being. A few times, such as catching her reflection in the mirror or when LuLu takes over filming, the camera turns on the director. The viewer seldom sees her, but her on-screen embodied presence is strong all the same. Her voice is audible in voiceovers and discussions with LuLu. In several scenes, LuLu speaks directly to the camera, not because of the viewer, but because her friend is behind the camera. The camera becomes the focal point of the affective connection, enabling the viewer to hear Wong's responses in dialogue. Her tone and embodied emotions, such as crying and sniffling, convey to the viewer her affective state of mind, as do the shaking frames of the hand-held camera.

The ways in which the camera and the filmmaker/friend are joined together throughout the segment recalls Porst's notion of subject-generated content. She argues that subjects' footage diminishes the distance between the subject and the camera. The viewer starts to view the eyes of the subject and the eye of the camera as the same, even when the persons turn the camera on themselves and speak directly to the camera (Porst 2007). This connection between the subject and the camera highlights the commitment to the intimate and personal experience and provides a unique opportunity to engage with the lived experience of others. In *The LuLu Sessions*, the director weaves her own emotions into the story, which becomes a shared exploration of what dying and loss are like. In the opening of the film, Wong frames the story as 'an adventure that not only brought us face to face with our deepest fears but gave us a most unexpected transformation of our lives' (Wong 2011). The use of pronoun 'we' further emphasises the shared authority and experience of the filming process.

The intimate connection between the filmed subject and the filmmaker translates into mutual trust and intimacy. LuLu, a cancer researcher herself, embodies sickness and performs the bodily aspects of her illness. She happily invites the camera to medical procedures and scientific analyses of images of cancer with her students. In one of the scenes, LuLu reveals that she has taped a Maxi Pad on her chest as a replacement breast. She unbuttons her shirt and allows the viewer to see her skin. These almost scientific scenes show how she uses her expertise on cancer to create distance to the illness and to gain a sense of control over the situation. Still, in other scenes, she has emotional breakdowns that show her struggle to cope with her illness. For example, at one point LuLu disappears from the hospital, and Wong is called in. She films her empty bed before finding her in the bathroom. The camera first peeks in by the door that is cracked open, as if asking for permission to enter. LuLu smiles and waves and explains in scientific terms that her lungs were filled with liquid. The cinematic uses of the bathroom emphasise vulnerability, and private bathrooms, in particular, become spaces of privacy, autonomy and control of access (Donnar 2015; Myers 2018; Fraiman 2022). Similarly, LuLu's escape to her own bathroom communicates both her need for agency and her vulnerability in the difficult situation.

There are two more bathroom scenes in the documentary, both further highlighting the intimate space as a place where easy-going LuLu lays bare her fears and concerns. In the second bathroom scene, LuLu is having a break from the hospice. She shares a hotel room with Wong while the two are travelling together. In the hotel room, Wong, or the camera, finds LuLu smoking marijuana in the bathroom. LuLu justifies this both to the camera and to Wong as being medically required for pain and nausea, as if asking for permission. In cinematic imagery, private bathrooms appear as liminal spaces, where bodily functions, private emotions and any functions related to shame can take place away from prying eyes. Thus, allowing a camera in these spaces heightens the intimacy of the scene and provides revelatory moments of both bodily functions and the characters' inner lives (Donnar 2015; Myers 2018; Fraiman 2022). Once again, the bathroom emerges as a space where LuLu can escape, not only to break the moral codes of society in secret, but also to reclaim some space and independence for herself. The third and final bathroom scene takes place on New Year's Eve, when the camera records the sounds of the breathing machine and finds LuLu reading a book in the bathroom. The stolen moment speaks volumes about her physical decline, as the image of her smoking turns to that of the breathing machine. The bathroom scenes also show the intimate connection between LuLu and the filmmaker. Not everyone is allowed to share bathroom spaces, but with the filmmaker the viewer is allowed to witness these personal moments.

LuLu's dying process is not a smooth journey towards acceptance of death, gracious goodbyes and personal growth. Instead, the intimate nature of film-making reveals her as an emotionally and socially complex person. It takes more than a terminal diagnosis for her issues to disappear. Wong says that their relationship has suffered from LuLu's drinking problem. While the friends make their amends during the film, LuLu does not stop drinking, smoking and cursing her days away. This causes a rift between her and her family; LuLu feels that her sisters are moralising instead of supporting her. She never manages to repair these relationships. Such honesty about negative emotional situations is rare in end-of-life documentaries. The honest approach makes it clear that LuLu would never want to turn into an angelic character. She readily admits to camera, and to Wong, that she has made mistakes, but she has had a wonderful life, and she imagines that she can continue her 'hard and fast' lifestyle in afterlife. Yet, LuLu's (morbid) sense of humour and outrageous personality, such as her response to withdrawal of treatments as 'why fuck a dead duck', endear her to Wong. LuLu's honesty and openness about her flaws, together with the filmmaker's loving gaze endear LuLu to the viewer as well. In Wong's (n.d.) own words, the film serves as testimony of how love can push past limits 'in the face of impending mortality'. This lets the viewer witness an alternative approach to end-of-life narratives where difficult emotions or flawed persons are not sugar-coated. The narrative promises that even 'negative' emotions can become accepted and normal, and they do not make anyone a failure or less lovable.

COLLABORATIVE DOCUMENTARIES

INVITATION TO WITNESS ASSISTED DEATHS

The collaborative approach to the stories on assisted dying create a continuation from internal transformation to external changes in attitudes and politics over legalisation of assisted dying. The films' subjects use their own stories to normalise practices of death assistance and admit wanting to use the film to make a difference. This follows Elizabeth Coffman's (2009, 62) notion that collaborative projects tend to blur the boundaries between advocacy work and storytelling. For example, *Live and Let Go: An American Death* (Spain 2002) was filmed when assisted dying was rarely accepted in western countries. The film proceeds to use a collaborative approach to emphasise the authenticity and intimacy of the story, but also to shock the viewer with the intensity of the dying process. The film opens with a warning: 'The following story deals with death in an open, candid way. Some viewers may find certain scenes objectionable.' What follows is the story of 76-year-old Sam Niver who has prostate cancer. Sam is afraid of losing his autonomy and dignity, and has decided that he wants an assisted death. When this is not available, he chooses a planned suicide as an alternative route to dignified death. The above warning refers to the final scenes where the filmmaker captures Sam's suicide on film as if to warn what happens when assisted dying is not available.

The film is produced by Sam's twins, Jay and Gretchen Niver who asked Jay Spain, a family friend and filmmaker, to help them. In an interview for *Los Angeles Times*, the son says that Sam had asked him to make a story about his conviction of the right to physician-assisted suicide, but Jay felt that he would be more comfortable creating a video that memorialises his father (Parsons 2002). The result is a compromise. The first half of the film is about Sam's personality and his lived life. The stories portray Sam as an active member of the community and a proud patriotic man who stands for American values such as liberty. In a nostalgic photo from the local Independence Day parade, Sam appears dressed up in the costume of his namesake Uncle Sam. The image – and his name – connect Sam to the national personification of patriotic fervour. Sam's request for a dignified death gains the symbolic weight of fighting for freedom to choose. His inner personality traits serve an outward function as he symbolically fights for the right to die. Yet, the film avoids a preaching tone, and all the argumentation for and against assisted dying takes place in the private circle of family and friends also voicing their opinions. Thus, instead of following the legalisation debate route, Sam frames his suicide as an individual choice: 'I have decided that I am going to decide when I have had enough.'

The latter half of the film builds on the process of dying. Sam declares that he is a member of the Hemlock Society, a right-to-die organisation from the

223

1980s to 2003. In addition to advocacy work, the Society was known for providing instructions on how to commit a suicide. It is this material that Sam relies on to make sure that his children will be protected from any legal consequences of his death. Until this point, the film has consisted of interviews with Sam, family and friends. However, the last day of Sam's life is filmed in an observational mode, inviting the viewer to witness the events. The final sequence opens with an image of Sam's house, an ambulance parked on the road and his son talking with police officers. Background noises, such as the mumble of conversation, birdsong and the rustle of the wind on the microphone communicate a non-edited, authentic approach to the scene after Sam's death, when emergency personnel invade his home, investigate his death and question the children. The son, particularly, gets increasingly frustrated and asks whether there is any dignity left in this show.

The narration then returns to the events on the porch earlier that day. The twins are sitting on chairs in front of their father. Sam is filmed from behind, stooped in his chair. When he asks if they are all ready, the camera's position changes, and the scene of his suicide becomes detailed (Figure 11.1).

Figure 11.1 Sam Niver taking the first steps towards his suicide in *Live and Let Go: An American Death* (Spain 2002).

COLLABORATIVE DOCUMENTARIES

Sam's seat is protected by plastic, he has a suicide note taped onto his chest and there is a table with various medications next to him and another with a plastic bag and rubber bands. The only sound in the background is birdsong when Sam holds his cup to take the final medication. He then eats a little to get over the nasty flavour of the drink. Next, he pulls a medical mask over his head. The mask covers his eyes. The son chuckles, when Sam fumbles with the suicide bag: 'It is supposed to cover your mouth.' Sam corrects the mask and throws a suicide bag over his head before stretching a rubber band around his neck. Both of his children are now on their knees, crying and holding their father's hands while telling him that they love him. Suffocation makes Sam gasp for breath, his hands in the hands of his son. Gentle soft music starts in the background, and after the gasping is over, the twins hold their father and each other. While Sam maintains his agency until the end, the scene is also a shockingly detailed description of a suicide. The viewer is asked to join the borderlands of legality. The unpleasantness of the moment encourages the viewer to think whether there should be legal alternatives for those wanting to die.

Another collaborative documentary, *All in Her Stride* (Cochrane 2014), shows another alternative for legal assisted dying. This is the story of Leverne McDonnell, an Australian actress, filmed by her friend Fiona Cochrane, who is also a documentary maker. Similar to Sam's introduction, the documentary first proceeds to tell Leverne's life story through memorialisation, photographs and videos. In the interviews and stories, Leverne comes across as a lively and charismatic woman. The latter half of the film, again, focuses on her dying process and adds an observatory mode to the mix. The observational half begins from the bad news that Leverne receives from the oncologist. In the presence of the film camera, Leverne explains to the doctor that the crew might be doing a film about euthanasia, the last word uttered in a hushed tone, as a secret. The following sequence draws from Leverne's video diary, where she cries that she does not want to die. At the same time, she is afraid of suffering, which prompts her to consider assisted dying as an alternative. The following scenes show her declining condition and increasing pain, but she is afraid of losing her personality if she takes any more pain medication. The palliative nurse tells Leverne's husband that a larger dose would make her more comfortable but could also hasten her death.

When Leverne becomes bedridden, she tells the camera that she is ready to die: 'As much as I want to be alive, I do not want to be alive under these circumstances.' She feels that her life has become a slow, torturous death. The filmmaker cuts to the husband's video diary, filmed after Leverne's death, where he discusses whether he regrets that Leverne's death was hastened. While they might have had more time together, that time would have been painful, not joyous for Leverne. This confession supports the viewer's understanding of her suffering and contextualises a short shot where Leverne is administered with more pain medication. The final images show Leverne on her bed, mostly unconscious, pained and frail with her slightly open mouth becoming a sign of distress (Figure 11.2). These images transform into the post-mortem shots, where Leverne lies on the bed looking pale, yet peaceful and pain-free. The pain medication merely hastened the death, it did not make her death quick and pain-free as the legal version of assisted dying promises.

The promised beauty of assisted death is realised in *Laura's Choice* (Henkel and Lara 2020). The two-part story starts when Laura takes a trip to Europe at the age of eighty-seven. She has a fun and lively trip with her granddaughter, but takes a bad fall and gets pneumonia. During the six weeks that she lies in hospital she realises that this is what her end of life might come to. A year later, she announces that she wants to die – immediately. She asks her daughter Cathy to assist her, but Cathy refuses to break the law. Laura turns herself into an activist who campaigns to legalise assisted dying in Australia. In the film, she jokes, 'It is a cause for which I am prepared to die.'

Laura was not terminally ill, so she could not get death assistance in Australia. Three years after her trip to Europe, then, she decides to travel to Switzerland. She invites her daughter Cathy and granddaughter Sam to accompany her and demands that they make a documentary about her decision to die. In an interview for *IF Magazine*, Cathy Henkel says,

> I'm not sure at what point she [Laura] was cooking up the idea for the film but I initially thought I would humour her by making a short

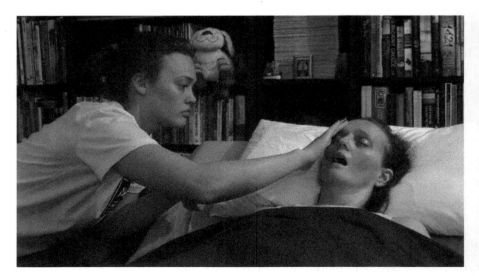

Figure 11.2 Leverne on her deathbed in *All in Her Stride* (Cochrane 2014).

tribute piece and that the footage of her saying she wanted to end her life in Ballina would not be seen by anyone. But as we progressed and she became more determined, Sam and I started to realise this was much bigger than Mum's story and had a far greater reach. (Slatter 2021)

The family has a strong background in film: Laura had an acting career in the 1950s, her husband was a filmmaker, and both Cathy and Sam have followed the filmmaking path in their lives. Telling the story through film is familiar to them to such an extent that Laura argues for the superiority of film in creating a compelling story when compared to other arts.

The collaborative filmmaking between three generations of women involves intimate negotiations over meanings. Both Cathy and Sam struggle with Laura's decision. They voice their doubts to each other, to Laura and to the viewer. These discussions show the complexity of losing a family member, and they make the story about Cathy and Sam as well. They use the documentary almost as a diary of their personal emotions and thoughts when they reflect on the events and turns of Laura's story. For example, when the ethical and legal debates on assisted dying are discussed in the first part of the documentary, Cathy and Sam ask experts for their views. While these scenes have something of an interview mode about them, the scenes are set up in a way that the interviewees rarely gaze at the camera. Rather, their gaze is slightly off-camera, cross cuts show them talking to Cathy and Sam, who listen carefully, nod along and ask the occasional question. When talking to the family, the advocates' tone is gentle. Instead of condemning Laura's choice, they focus on justifying their perspectives. Thus, they realise they are not talking about the death of other, but the death of a family member.

During the filming, Cathy and Sam learn to accept Laura's choice, but not without much soul-searching. Sam, for example, says that she believed that if they could just show Laura how much they loved her, she would change her mind. As a response to this, Laura talks directly to the camera, and Sam behind it, that they will not be able to have her forever. In this way, she gets to die the way she wants to. While Sam grows to support Laura, acceptance is still difficult. After Laura's death, Sam creates a video message to her grandmother to reflect her emotions. She tells the camera of having had to film uncomfortable things for the past years, and after rewatching the footage, she accepts that her grandmother still wanted to die despite how beloved she was. The film helps Sam to get closure when she realises that she did not fail her grandmother by not loving enough, but that Laura was ready to die because she was loved and able to enjoy that love until the end. Indeed, the latter part of the documentary focuses on warm and remarkable goodbyes, which take place in a private theatre performance of the Mad Hatter's tea party for Laura (instead of a funeral), accompanied by joyful moments of laughter with family and friends.

Laura is included in her own memorialisation and laughs at one point: 'I must die more often.'

The documentary also includes Laura's death scene, and following the style of the documentary, it takes a transparent approach to the filming. The filmmakers visit the room where Laura will die. They discuss where they will place the cameras, how they want to frame the images so that some of the duller elements of the room will not be visible in the picture. While they give these instructions to the cinematographer, the preparation also raises various emotions. At one point Sam announces that she cannot imagine that they are doing this. She half laughs, half cries, while her mother hugs her supportively. As a result, Laura gets her intimate portrayal of assisted death. Three cameras film her last moments, when she lies on the bed, her daughter on the one side and her granddaughter on the other (Figure 11.3). They have a glass of champagne and relax into a quiet moment of goodbyes. Laura, until the end, remains aware of her other audience, the viewer, and her last words to her daughter are 'you are going to make a good, good film'. The death is peaceful and beautiful and suggests what an assisted death can give to a family, a chance to prepare, to say goodbye and to leave in peace.

Last Flight Home continues along the same lines as *Laura's Choice* as both films highlight the importance of family relationships and make the filming a visible part of the narration. The director Ondi Timoner set up her cameras to follow the last fifteen days of her father's life after Eli Timoner had asked for assisted death. In several interviews, Ondi Timoner has explained how she wanted to leave a tangible memory of Eli for his family – with the family's

Figure 11.3 Laura's peaceful death scene in *Laura's Choice* (Henkel and Lara 2020).

COLLABORATIVE DOCUMENTARIES

blessing and collaboration. The cameras, however, should not intervene with goodbyes, and most of the footage is filmed by still and unattended cameras set up in the room (Carey 2022; Hemphill 2022; Hosoki 2022). Occasionally, however, either Timoner or some of her colleagues picks up a hand-held camera, increasing the sense of presence and participation in the situation. Timoner says her original intention was not to turn the footage into a public film, but the reception of the memorial service video encouraged her to edit a longer film which could serve as a compassionate way to support people's freedom to choose their care at the end of their lives (Carey 2022; Hemphill 2022; Hosoki 2022). In this way, the film became both intensely personal and social in its attempts to appeal to the public.

This documentary emphasises the intersubjective space of collaboration on the screen. The narration focuses on how Eli bids farewell to his friends, loved ones and family. Eli is in hospice care at home, but due to the Covid-19 situation, much of the farewell is done remotely via Zoom. While there is sadness related to this physical distance, this use of technology balances the viewer's position in the narration. The viewer becomes one of the included people who take part in events over the technological connection, over one more screen in the situation. The repetitive structure of numerous goodbye scenes can appear monotonous, yet they communicate the person's value of being loved and cared for. Combined with stories of Eli's life, these repetitive scenes invite the viewer not only to witness but participate in this intersubjective communication of love, as well as other emotions, such as grief and loss that the family members experience.

In this film, we see Eli's death when he drinks the drugs prescribed to him. The scene is almost brutally honest when Eli struggles to swallow and heartbreakingly dislikes the last taste he will ever sense. Yet, he is surrounded all the time by his family, who caress him and support him. Love and inclusiveness become the heart of assisted dying, not loneliness or hidden death. At the moment of his death, we see the filmmaker and her brother in the frame with Eli (Figure 11.4). The hand-held camera's framing and sense of intimacy bring the viewer similarly close to the deathbed. From this intimate position, the viewer can hear the siblings' whispers. 'His hand, you felt it? He squeezed my hand. His color changed too,' the son whispers in awe, to which the daughter replies, 'He turned blue. I think he is gone.' The quiet and ambient string music completes the moment, communicating devotion and wonder. The intersubjective space where Eli and his family share his moment of death with the viewer emphasises inclusiveness, where the viewer's ethical stance comes from openness to be included, to be moved, and to care. This inclusive intimacy refuses to keep Eli in the position of the other. Despite, or due to its affective potential, such intimacy can also feel challenging, as Carlos Aguilar's review reveals: 'But as much as one feels honored to be let into the innermost pain of a group of

Figure 11.4 Death of Eli Timoner in *Last Flight Home* (Timoner 2022).

strangers, perhaps some moments should remain sacred and only for the eyes of those directly involved' (Aguilar 2022). Thus, the ethical potential of the intersubjective space of collaborative end-of-life documentaries demands a willingness for challenging emotional intimacy.

None of the above documentaries shies away from the moment of death. Instead, they use the intimacy provided by collaborative projects as justification to show these deaths and use them as part of the argumentation. When the death is filmed by the loved ones and planned in collaboration with the dying subject, there are fewer questions about whether this can be filmed and shown, and whether the viewer can be sure about consent and respect for privacy. These deaths become the final testimonials of the subjects' lives, and their desire to make a difference in the world. In the face of mortality, these deaths also transform into intimate, inclusive experiences, and these techniques for extending intersubjectivity to the viewer can be either emotionally gratifying or difficult.

Conclusion

The collaborative documentaries where the filmmaker shares authorship with the filmed subjects have been argued to increase the viewer's trust in the authenticity of the narration (e.g. Pryluck 2005, 203–4). Similarly, in end-of-life documentaries, the promise that the filmed subject has been an active participant in planning the film assures the viewer that these documentaries are sensitive to the participants' needs and privacy. At the same time, this promise of trust deepens, which is further highlighted in these projects that are filmed, directed or produced by family members and friends. The collaborative projects do not shirk physical, emotional and social intimacy and do not evade moments of fragility and conflicts, either. Thus, the insider viewer appears to be more relaxed about protecting privacy than any outsider filmmaker would dream of being and often the camera (and by extension the viewer) is allowed into intimate experiences and private spaces, such as bathrooms, which are otherwise often inaccessible to the public. When the filmed subjects decide on their level of participation, they are not afraid to engage with detailed confessions. The viewer is included in a private circle of witnesses to an end of life. This position engages honest and raw encounters with loss, dying and death.

Collaborative end-of-life documentaries turn the film camera into a technology of intimacy, which changes the public image of death and dying. At best, collaborative documentaries blur the conventions of how dying people have been represented in many end-of-life documentaries. The previous chapters of this book indicate how various approaches to end of life tend to search for ways to manage death anxiety. In comparison, instead of explaining death anxiety, collaborative documentaries embrace it. Their filmed subjects remain as complex characters until the end, and they are allowed to argue and struggle if that is what they want and need to do. Similarly, family members and friends are allowed to show various negative emotions without the need of beautification. These documentaries promise that one does not have to turn into a better person; one is loved and accepted, warts and all. End of life, no matter what kind of route one decides to take, can include both beautiful and ugly moments, like life itself. Furthermore, in the inclusive space of collaborative end-of-life documentaries, the viewer is not allowed to keep a safe distance from the death of the other, and there are fewer emotional safety nets to experience not only love and care, but also discomfort and difficult emotions. The ethics of intersubjectivity has potential to transform our expectations for encountering mortality in our lives, but this potential can also be emotionally challenging in its rawness.

References

Aguilar, Carlos. 2022. 'Last Flight Home'. RogerEbert.com. 7 October 2022. https://www.rogerebert.com/reviews/last-flight-home-movie-review-2022. Last accessed 27 June 2023.

Bilbrough, Paola. 2013. 'The Process: Poetic Re-Presentation as Social Responsibility in a Collaborative Documentary'. *a/b: Auto/Biography Studies* 28 (2): 180–91. https://doi.org/10.1080/08989575.2013.10846826.

Cardillo, Susan. 2022. 'Collaborative, Crowd-Sourced and Interactive Documentary: The Voices of a Generation Through Campus Reboot'. *Interactive Film and Media Journal* 2 (1). https://doi.org/10.32920/ifmj.v2i1.1511.

Carey, Matthew. 2022. '"Last Flight Home": Filmmaker Ondi Timoner Documents Her Ailing Father's Wish To Go Out On His Own Terms'. *Deadline* (blog). 20 October 2022. https://deadline.com/2022/10/last-flight-home-mtv-documentary-films-director-ondi-timoner-interview-news-1235150396/. Last accessed 27 June 2023.

Chochinov, Harvey Max, Thomas Hack, Susan McClement, Linda Kristjanson, and Mike Harlos. 2002. 'Dignity in the Terminally Ill: A Developing Empirical Model'. *Social Science & Medicine* 54 (3): 433–43. https://doi.org/10.1016/S0277-9536(01)00084-3.

Cochrane, Fiona. 2014. *All in Her Stride*. Documentary. F-reel.

Coffman, Elizabeth. 2009. 'Documentary and Collaboration: Placing the Camera in the Community'. *Journal of Film and Video* 61 (1): 62–78.

Dick, Kirby. 1997. *Sick: The Life and Death of Bob Flanagan, Supermasochist*. Documentary. Lionsgate Films.

———. 2004. *The End*. Documentary. HBO.

Donnar, Glen. 2015. 'Monstrous Men and Bathroom Mirrors: The Bathroom as Revelatory Space in American Cinema'. In *Spaces of the Cinematic Home: Behind the Screen Door*, edited by Eleanor Andrews, Stella Hockenhull, and Fran Pheasant-Kelly, 180–93. London; New York: Routledge.

Ferri, Paola, Jennifer Muzzalupo, and Rosaria Di Lorenzo. 2015. 'Patients' Perception of Dignity in an Italian General Hospital: A Cross-Sectional Analysis'. *BMC Health Services Research* 15 (1): 41. https://doi.org/10.1186/s12913-015-0704-8.

Fox, Broderick. 2011. 'The Final Cut: End-of-Life Empowerment through Video Documentary'. In *Exploring Issues of Care, Dying and the End of Life*, edited by Sue Steele and Glenys Caswell, 55–62. Leiden: Brill. https://doi.org/10.1163/978184 8880580.

Fraiman, Susan. 2022. 'Bathroom Realism and the Women of Cable TV'. *Signs: Journal of Women in Culture and Society* 47 (3): 589–611. https://doi.org/10.1086/717698.

Hemphill, Jim. 2022. 'How a Family Keepsake Evolved Into One of the Most Moving Films About Death Ever Made'. *IndieWire* (blog). 1 November 2022. https://www.indiewire.com/features/general/filmmaker-toolkit-ondi-timoner-last-flight-home-interview-1234775066/. Last accessed 27 June 2023.

Henkel, Cathy, and Sam Lara. 2020. *Laura's Choice*. Documentary. Factor 30 Films; Virgo Productions.

Henley, Paul. 2009. *The Adventure of the Real: Jean Rouch and the Craft of Ethnographic Cinema*. Chicago, IL: University of Chicago Press. https://doi.org/10.7208/chicago/9780226327167.001.0001.

Hosoki, Nobuhiro. 2022. '"Last Flight Home": Exclusive Interview with Director Ondi Timoner'. Cinema Daily US. 13 October 2022. https://cinemadailyus.com/interviews/last-flight-home-exclusive-interview-with-director-ondi-timoner/. Last accessed 27 June 2023.

Jarrett, Lucinda. 2007. 'Preface'. In *Creative Engagement in Palliative Care: New Perspectives on User Involvement*, edited by Lucinda Jarrett, x–xiv. Oxford; New York: Radcliffe Publishing Ltd.

Myers, Robert. 2018. 'That Most Dangerous, Sacred American Space, the Bathroom'. *Anthropology Now* 10 (1): 40–50. https://doi.org/10.1080/19428200.2018.1437973.

Nash, Kate. 2012. 'Telling Stories: The Narrative Study of Documentary Ethics'. *New Review of Film and Television Studies* 10 (3): 318–31. https://doi.org/10.1080/1740 0309.2012.693765.

Parsons, Dana. 2002. 'In Film by Right-to-Die Advocates, Last Wishes Come First'. *Los Angeles Times*, 7 October 2002.

Porst, Jennifer. 2007. 'Awesome: I … Shot That!: User-Generated Content in Documentary Film'. Cinema and Media Studies, UCLA. http://web.mit.edu/comm-forum/legacy/mit5/papers/Porst%20Awesome%20Paper.pdf. Last accessed 19 February 2022.

Pryluck, Calvin. 2005. 'Ultimately We Are All Outsiders: The Ethics of Documentary Filming'. In *New Challenges for Documentary*, edited by Alan Rosenthal and John Corner, second edition, 194–208. Manchester; New York: Manchester University Press.

Rawlence, Chris. 2015. *From The Bedroom to The Bathroom*. Rosetta Life Production. https://www.youtube.com/watch?v=vSGmgbcIKZI.

Richards, Naomi. 2011. 'Promoting the Self through the Arts: The Transformation of Private Testimony into Public Witnessing'. In *Governing Death and Loss: Empowerment, Involvement and Participation*, edited by Stephen Conway, 45–52. Oxford: Oxford University Press.

Rosetta Life. 2022. 'Welcome to Rosetta Life'. Rosetta Life. 2022. https://rosettalife.org/. Last accessed 20 January 2022.

Scheinman, Diane. 2013. 'The "Dialogic Imagination" of Jean Rouch: Covert Conversations in Les Maîtres Fous'. In *Documenting the Documentary: Close Readings of Documentary Film and Video, New and Expanded Edition*, edited by Barry Keith Grant and Jeannette Sloniowski, 178–95. Detroit, MI: Wayne State University Press.

Slatter, Sean. 2021. '"We Started to Realise This Was Much Bigger": Sam Lara and Cathy Henkel on the Making of "Laura's Choice"'. *IF Magazine* (blog). 16 March 2021. https://if.com.au/we-started-to-realise-this-was-much-bigger-sam-lara-and-cathy-henkel-on-the-making-of-lauras-choice/. Last accessed 19 February 2023.

Spain, Jay. 2002. *Live and Let Go: An American Death*. Documentary. Fanlight Productions.

Thomas, Steve. 2012. 'Collaboration and Ethics in Documentary Filmmaking – A Case Study'. *New Review of Film and Television Studies* 10 (3): 332–43. https://doi.org/10.1080/17400309.2012.695979.

Timoner, Ondi. 2022. *Last Flight Home*. Documentary. MTV Documentary Films.

Walsh, Ken, and Inge Kowanko. 2002. 'Nurses' and Patients' Perceptions of Dignity'. *International Journal of Nursing Practice* 8 (3): 143–51. https://doi.org/10.1046/j.1440-172X.2002.00355.x.

Wong, S. Casper. 2011. *The LuLu Sessions*. Documentary. OO Media.

———. n.d. 'Director's Statement | The LuLu Sessions'. http://lulusessionsfilm.com/about/directors-statement/. Last accessed 30 March 2022.

12. CONCLUSION

When I first started to watch documentaries on end of life, I had no idea how many filmmakers saw death and dying as a significant social issue. As one of my interviewees articulated, 'the field is getting very crowded now' (Wilson 2019). Nor did I have any idea of the variety of approaches these documentaries take on the issue. For some reason, two notions had stuck in my head. The first came from the findings of Angela Armstrong-Coster's study: in the eyes of terminally ill people, positive and death acceptance-oriented documentaries can create false expectations of what being ill and dying is like (Armstrong-Coster 2001). The second notion came from Jennifer Malkowski's excerpt from the opening of the documentary *Silverlake Life: The View from Here* (Friedman and Joslin 1993), where the main character, Tom, has already died, and his partner describes his experience of not being able to close Tom's eyelids. He apologises to Tom 'that life wasn't like the movies'. Malkowski comments: 'Already having seen through Tom's dying process how little death is "like the movies", Mark feels renewed surprise that even this small detail – the ritual of closing the dead's eyes, restoring some sense of peaceful slumber – has been a fiction' (Malkowski 2017, 68). Together, these two observations encouraged me to hypothesise that cinematic representations of end of life might create cultural expectations of beautiful deaths. Such beautified deaths can cause disappointment, perhaps even a sense of failure, when people encounter deaths in their lives. I wanted to critically analyse what kinds of (potentially biased or harmful) narratives documentary films create on death and dying.

235

After spending hour after hour searching for and watching documentaries on end of life, I was pleasantly surprised: there was no one cultural model to be found. This book shows the range of ideas and approaches which filmmakers use to imagine and portray the end of life.

One thing that particularly caught my attention was the ever-present tension between public and private. Emily West (2018, 1483) writes that end-of-life documentaries 'make an ethical claim for showing death, by self-consciously moving it from the private sphere to media visibility'. Documentary filmmakers share an understanding that film is an influential communication channel, where art and the realm of 'real' can meet to tell a compelling and an engaging story. This has also been picked up by health communication. Research confirms that audiovisual health documentaries are persuasive because they appear as intimate and honest descriptions of life and because they promote emotional engagement. As a result, health documentaries of this kind meet with less resistance than do those which come across as educational or ideological (Borum Chattoo and Jenkins 2019; Niederdeppe, Roh, and Dreisbach 2016; Shen, Sheer, and Li 2015). The use of personal stories is similarly relevant in discussions of social and political constructions of end-of-life care options. Cultural and societal structures influence which aspects of end of life are topical social issues and how these questions are approached in documentary films, end-of-life films included. The private and public spheres thus overlap.

Discussions about private and public are also significant in the debates on cinematic ethics. Films provide space to exemplify, elaborate and examine moral themes, situations and conflicts. These examinations are public responses to an issue which is typically explored through personal stories. Even stories that do not openly approach an ethical or moral question can turn into an ethical experience if they encourage the viewers to re-evaluate their prejudices or preconceptions on other people, such as marginalised groups. The personal experience of the viewer on the story of others' experiences can therefore transform values, attitudes and beliefs. When films engage viewers to such an extent that they react to the discussed issue and think about it, their personal reactions may raise social, cultural or political awareness. At their most impressive, documentaries may become a part of social change, such as permanent attitude and legislative change.

A single documentary film can rarely claim to be a cause for social change. Documentaries, rather, work as part of campaigns and movements. Similarly, end-of-life documentaries function in the context of the death awareness movement, which aims to erase death's taboo role in western societies, advocates for death education and embraces death as a meaningful and natural experience (Incorvaia 2022). However, Lucy Bregman (2017) argues that while the death awareness movement has not been entirely successful at changing end-of-life care, it has provided people with a vocabulary to discuss social issues related to death and dying. This raises the question of whether the end-of-life documentaries have the social impact that they desire. Throughout this book, I have discussed 'the viewer', a theoretical assumption of the ideal viewing position and an openness to ethical transformation with the filmed subjects and the filmed material. I have argued that end-of-life documentaries see value in giving positions of agency and empowerment to the dying subjects; at the same time these documentaries expect the viewer to witness, to validate experiences, to embody, to understand, to listen and to care about the other. In other words, the caring gaze is key to the transformation towards acknowledging that we are mortal beings. As such, I have not analysed the impact of these documentaries, nor will I attempt to do that at this stage. However, I will return briefly to the film directors' interviews to discuss their views on the impact of their films regarding the two consistent themes of the previous chapters, the other and death anxiety.

DISTRIBUTION AND IMPACT OF END-OF-LIFE DOCUMENTARIES

Filmmakers want their documentaries to have meaning and impact. The film directors that I interviewed named several goals for their end-of-life documentaries. Giving death a place and dying people a voice in public conversations was the most common desire. The filmmakers argued that death and dying have been pushed to the margins of western societies, which has several implications, such as poor knowledge on the services and support that hospice and palliative care can offer and what assisted dying means. As a result, we also marginalise the dying people and cut them off from social networks and civil participation. The filmmakers saw their films as conversation starters that could potentially normalise death (including assisted death) and give voice to dying people, but visibility was not deemed to be enough as such. Documentary films should find ways to address, and perhaps alleviate, fears and anxieties, because fears prevent and limit open discussions about death. With lessened fears, the notion of mortality could encourage viewers to embrace their own mortality in ways that enable them to live life to the fullest.

To start a conversation, end-of-life documentaries need to find their audiences. The filmmakers often noted that a morbid theme can alienate viewers. If you prefer avoiding death, why would you want to watch a film about dying people? Compared to mainstream fiction films or to the most popular documentary films, end-of-life documentaries tend to have small and specific audiences. The documentaries that are broadcast on television or distributed through major streaming services such as Netflix and HBO reach the widest audiences. End-of-life documentaries are rarely distributed through mainstream cinemas, but the films (and the filmmakers) tour film festivals, which helps them gain visibility for their films. Festivals are used to market and promote the documentaries to the film industry, including international film distributors, broadcasting companies, film critics and bloggers. In addition, end-of-life documentary makers sometimes distribute their films free of charge online through such services as YouTube and Vimeo. They justify these decisions by wanting to maximise the audiences for the social issue they find important. They market these links through their own networks, but also through advocacy organisations and institutions, such as hospice and palliative care organisations, and right-to-die and right-to-live organisations.

While these distribution channels aim to maximise public visibility, almost all film directors recognise the significance of more private settings with niche audiences and potential for discussion. They have shown their films at academic conferences, in healthcare education, hospice and palliative care contexts and at community screenings in churches, advocacy institutions, hospices and community centres. The screenings, the filmmakers argue, add value to their filmmaking and the films because they enable on-site discussions where personal experiences and transformations of attitudes are shared with others. Here, too, personal experience can increase the awareness of death and dying. The on-site screenings also enable the filmmakers to get feedback, even if the audiences rarely want to discuss the narrative or aesthetic choices, but rather wish to share personal stories of how these documentaries move them and help them process their own past or present experiences. Claudia Tosi, for example, tells a story from a screening at the Finnish documentary festival, DocPoint:

> The moderator told me that Finnish audience is not like Italian audience, so probably no one will ask anything. So, I have questions for you in case this happens. At the end, she made one question, but there was this guy from the audience. He was explaining what happened with his father and how he felt about this. And then there was a Finnish girl who explained that she was going through the cancer treatments. So, even Finnish people became talkative after the film. (Tosi 2018)

It may be difficult to prove that end-of-life documentaries have led to major social changes, but the filmmakers offer plenty of stories of how their films touch individual viewers. This brings us back to cinematic ethics and the films' capability to encourage the viewers to be open to new experiences, face various realities and transform their ways of feeling and thinking about death and dying.

Alleviating Death Anxiety

For the filmmakers, alleviation of death anxiety emerges as a preferred emotional transformation. Death anxiety, however, is not one entity, but people can be afraid of different aspects of death and dying, such as the dying process and potential suffering, and the pain and loss of autonomy associated with it.

CONCLUSION

Some can feel threatened by existential questions, such as what being dead means to one's personality and individuality, or whether the awareness of mortality gives meaning to life or makes everything meaningless. Others may fear that death comes at the wrong time, either too early or too late or they can fear the loss of their loved ones more than they fear their own deaths. For many, death remains a great unknown – and breeds uncertainty and anxiety.

It is no wonder, then, that end-of-life documentary makers approach death anxiety in differing ways. Different types of films raise different issues and suggest different means to alleviate these fears. Medical documentaries suggest that accepting death as a natural part of life might ease physical, social and emotional suffering at the end. This would help the dying and their families to focus on what is meaningful – saying goodbyes and valuing quality over quantity. Hospice documentaries promise that holistic end-of-life care offers dying people and their families the support they need, including support to deal with death anxiety. Spiritual documentaries build on an understanding of afterlife where dying and death become transformations into another kind of being and thus alleviate the existential anxiety. Performative documentaries focus on the empowering aspects of being alive until the moment of death, and legacy documentaries suggest that by acknowledging one's impact on others through relationships and actions, one can be assured of their continued social existence after the death. Physical documentaries, in contrast, suggest that by observing the dying process itself, it becomes more familiar and less uncertain. Documentaries on assisted dying, similarly, focus on the dying process. For those in favour of assisted dying, suffering, pain, and loss of dignity and autonomy cause more anxiety than death. Here, death is painted as an inevitable event, and while it cannot be escaped, the dying process before death can be managed. For those opposed to assisted dying, life in any form appears as an ultimate value, and death as something that should be avoided and perhaps even feared. And finally, the personal journeys with filmmakers and dying people exemplify that familiarising oneself with the topic can help to manage, if not resolve, death anxiety. The interior view that the collaborative films provide of dying reveals that not overcoming one's anxiety and fears is as normal and acceptable as being able to embrace the idea of death at some level.

None of the approaches promises that there is a one-size-fits-all model to rid oneself of death anxiety. Instead, there are different perspectives on how to alleviate fears related to some aspects of death and dying. These documentaries offer suggestions on how to manage dying processes, existential fears and how to live a meaningful life until the end. While this study does not test whether these suggestions help the audiences to alleviate their fears, the filmmakers themselves found working with the topic meaningful. Claudia Tosi (2018) articulates that in her documentary *The Perfect Circle* (2014) she became the protagonist who went through the transformation when she experienced that 'it is possible to think about death in a peaceful way'. Some other filmmakers argued that their films helped them to understand death and dying better. Allan King notes that he cannot predict his feelings when the time comes, but he certainly knows and understands more about death. His cinematographer Peter Walker adds that filming *Dying at Grace* (2003), and seeing the process of dying, demystified death for him and made him less afraid of death, or at least the moment of death (King, Walker, and Hector 2008). Madeleine Hetherton, similarly, admits that the filming process, and particularly the witnessing of death, relieved her fear of death. Furthermore, it helped her to support others, because the filming alleviated her anxiety about being around people who are ill and dying. She also hopes that her film *Love in Our Own Time* (2011) would help the viewer to find a similar peace when just being with those who are dying (Hetherton 2020). The filmmakers went through a personal transformation while witnessing the death of others, and perhaps the viewer has similar potential for change through witnessing with the films.

To alleviate anxieties, the analysed documentaries also used different strategies to address their audiences. I recognised three main strategies that the documentaries used to engage their audiences – institutional voices, voices of the dying people and the filmmaker's voice. The methods to engage the audiences based on the narration's prioritised voices indicated what kind of ethical spaces these documentaries created.

The Death of the Other

In the context of end-of-life documentaries, several scholars have asked whether documentary films inspire transformation in the relationship with death and dying. In cinematic ethics, an ethical experience or transformation of thinking requires an embodied and affective connection with the image and engagement with the experiences of the filmed subjects. However, several scholars, including Jennifer Malkowski and Jan Grue, argue that documentary films portray deaths as individualised events that allow distance between the viewer and the image. These portrayals objectify the dying people, encourage the evaluative gaze and promise that the viewer does not need to worry, as this is a story about the death of the other, not about your mortality (Malkowski 2017, 86; Grue 2022, 18). As such, the desired emotional transformation is lacking. This argument, indeed, is visible in some of the institutional end-of-life documentaries that give voice to various authors and experts. These documentaries represent end of life as a (rational) problem that can be solved with expert help, such as proper end-of-life care, suitable end-of-life legislation or functional spiritual guidance. These documentaries also feature personal

CONCLUSION

stories of dying people. Yet, they are most often used as examples of argumentation, which allows the viewer to explore end of life from a distance and see the personal stories as deaths of the distanced others.

However, the variety of end-of-life documentaries builds intimate and embodied connections with the dying people in ways that highlight care, understanding and listening. Here, the understanding of the other in ethical theories becomes the key. While Malkowski and Grue see an insurmountable line between the viewer and the other, or the subject and the object, both Maurice Merleau-Ponty and Emmanuel Levinas, who have inspired discussions on cinematic ethics, see value in connecting with the other. Valuing the differences of the other, Merleau-Ponty argues, engenders an ethical encounter. The cinematic images of the other can invite the viewer to create meanings based on this respect (Merleau-Ponty 2002). There is therefore no need to erase otherness and make the other the same as the experiencing subject. This idea is further explored by Levinas for whom the moving image, and the constantly shifting facial expressions, carry particular ethical potential. The ability to see evolving expressions enables humane recognition and perceptual connection before the cultural and personal preconceptions kick in and limit the understanding of potential experiences and realities (Levinas 2011; 1991). For Levinas, the key to an ethical encounter lies in prioritising the other's experience over one's own. Both approaches see the other playing an important part in the subject's transformative experience.

Vivian Sobchack raises similar concerns of objectification as Malkowski and Grue, but she also recognises that the humane gaze which settles and focuses on the dying person aims to build a connection between the viewer and the other in ways that encourage affective embodiments (Sobchack 1984, 296). The potential of seeing beyond one's own subjectivity towards the other's experience is further developed by Margaret Gibson. Gibson argues that cinematic portrayals of death can construct sensibility and compassion towards the other by building an intimate interior view on the experience. When this happens, the death of the other can generate consciousness of one's own mortality as well (Gibson 2011, 928–31). These arguments show that while the viewer and the other do not become one, the intimate, embodied and affective access to the experience of the other can enable connection and that connection can enable transformation. I argue that this connection with the other takes place in the end-of-life documentaries that focus on the personal voices of dying people and those around them. These documentaries build on an embodied connection, inviting the viewer to feel and experience along with the dying or with those reflecting their own thoughts about death anxiety. This creates an interior view where death and dying become something more than a problem to be solved. Viewing becomes a transformative experience which invites the viewers to reflect on their own mortality. Instead of creating the same experience, then, the respect and understanding of the other's experience opens up to a world of potentials.

Final Words

When I started this research project, I had it titled as 'constructing good death'. I figured that I would be able to delineate the cultural models of good death promoted in western documentary films. Quite quickly I realised that a 'good death' is not a meaningful concept to approaching the documentary representations on end of life. While I do use the term occasionally, I do so in the context where the term was used in those documentaries. These discussions were not consistent, because a good death can mean very different things in the context of hospice and palliative care, in medical care, in spiritual approaches and in legalisation debates for assisted dying, for example. Consequently, I learned to recognise that good death is an empty concept, and it can mean whatever the person using it wants to mean.

Even when various parties continue to use the notion of good death in a normative manner or as a preferred cultural model, I was delighted to find that there is no singular model of end of life that the documentaries endorse. Instead, western documentary films create a complex image of death and dying, and the reluctance to understand death and dying in any certain way felt liberating. It means that there might be a documentary on the issue that resonates with each of our emotional, psychological, spiritual, social or physical needs. The lack of unified narration also promises that no one can fail society's or other people's expectations on how to die. We will die anyway, whether we accept it, rage against it or completely ignore it. In the meantime, we could do worse than let end-of-life documentaries give us some food for thought.

References

Armstrong-Coster, Angela. 2001. 'In Morte Media Jubilate [1]: An Empirical Study of Cancer-Related Documentary Film'. *Mortality* 6 (3): 287–305. https://doi.org/10.1080/13576270120082943.

Borum Chattoo, Caty, and Will Jenkins. 2019. 'From Reel Life to Real Social Change: The Role of Contemporary Social-Issue Documentary in U.S. Public Policy'. *Media, Culture & Society* 41 (8): 1107–24. https://doi.org/10.1177/0163443718823145.

Bregman, Lucy. 2017. 'The Death Awareness Movement'. In *The Routledge Companion to Death and Dying*, edited by Christopher M. Moreman. London; New York: Routledge.

Friedman, Peter, and Tom Joslin. 1993. *Silverlake Life: The View from Here.* Documentary. Strange Attractions.

Gibson, Margaret. 2011. 'Real-Life Death: Between Public and Private, Interior and Exterior, the Real and the Fictional'. *South Atlantic Quarterly* 110 (4): 917–32. https://doi.org/10.1215/00382876-1382321.

Grue, Jan. 2022. 'The Death of Others. On the Narrative Rhetoric of Neoliberal Thanatopolitics'. *Disability Studies Quarterly* 42 (1). https://doi.org/10.18061/dsq.v42i1.7799.

Hetherton, Madeleine. 2020. Personal interview by Outi Hakola.

Incorvaia, Aubrey DeVeny. 2022. 'Death Positivity in America: The Movement— Its History and Literature'. *OMEGA – Journal of Death and Dying*, April, 00302228221085176. https://doi.org/10.1177/00302228221085176.

King, Allan. 2003. *Dying at Grace*. Documentary. Alan King Associates.

King, Allan, Peter Walker, and Nick Hector. 2008. *Audio Commentary. Dying at Grace. Dir. Allan King*. DVD. Alan King Associates.

Levinas, Emmanuel. 1991. *Otherwise Than Being, or Beyond Essence*. Springer Science & Business Media.

———. 2011. *Totality and Infinity: An Essay on Exteriority*. First published 1969. Pittsburgh, PA: Duquesne University Press.

Malkowski, Jennifer. 2017. *Dying in Full Detail: Mortality and Digital Documentary*. Durham, NC; London: Duke University Press. https://doi.org/10.1215/9780822373414.

Merleau-Ponty, Maurice. 2002. *Phenomenology of Perception*. Translated by A. Landes Donald. First published 1945. Milton Park; New York: Routledge Classics.

Murray, Tom, and Madeleine Hetherton. 2011. *Love in Our Own Time*. Documentary. Tarpaulin Productions.

Niederdeppe, Jeff, Sungjong Roh, and Caitlin Dreisbach. 2016. 'How Narrative Focus and a Statistical Map Shape Health Policy Support Among State Legislators'. *Health Communication* 31 (2): 242–55. https://doi.org/10.1080/10410236.2014.998913.

Shen, Fuyuan, Vivian C. Sheer, and Ruobing Li. 2015. 'Impact of Narratives on Persuasion in Health Communication: A Meta-Analysis'. *Journal of Advertising* 44 (2): 105–13. https://doi.org/10.1080/00913367.2015.1018467.

Sobchack, Vivian. 1984. 'Inscribing Ethical Space: Ten Propositions on Death, Representation, and Documentary'. *Quarterly Review of Film Studies* 9 (4): 283–300. https://doi.org/10.1080/10509208409361220.

Tosi, Claudia. 2014. *The Perfect Circle*. Documentary. Movimenta/MiaFilm/Cobos Film/Petra Pan Film Production.

———. 2018. Personal interview by Outi Hakola.

West, Emily. 2018. 'Invitation to Witness: The Role of Subjects in Documentary Representations of the End of Life'. *International Journal of Communication* 12: 1481–500.

Wilson, Tim. 2019. Personal interview by Outi Hakola.

INDEX

A Dignified Death, 175–80
Adair, Camille, 72, 77
affection-image, 160–2, 165–6, 168–9, 171
All in Her Stride, 216, 225–6
assisted dying, 91–107, 174–91, 208–11, 223–30, 237, 239
awareness of mortality, 3, 53, 64–7, 239

Balzli, Res, 114, 119
Banci, Virginia, 53–4
Barens, Edgar, 136–41, 150
Beder, John, 30, 46
Beeler, Edwin, 72, 82–5
Before We Go, 113–19, 129
Being Mortal, 29–31, 44–7
Bouton, 114, 119–22, 129–30
Burnell, Matthew, 53, 61–2

cinéma vérité, 19, 115, 123, 215
cinematic ethics, 12–17, 236, 238, 240–1; *see also* ethical cinema
Cochrane, Fiona, 216, 225

Davidson, Paul, 3, 134–6, 141–4, 150, 163

death acceptance, 4–6, 37–40, 47, 71–2, 79, 87, 206–7, 235
death anxiety, 3–4, 13, 17, 47, 71–2, 87, 113–14, 117, 127–8, 148, 201, 238–42
death awareness movement, 7–10, 30–1, 53, 64, 71, 236–7
death denial, 4, 6, 31–2, 40, 47
death positivity, 9
Decommere, Alexander, 91, 93, 95–6
dialogical, 62, 175–6, 180–2, 185, 190–1, 197, 203
Dick, Kirby, 10, 216–19
Die Weisse Arche, 72, 82–8
discursive testimony, 77–80
Dunn, Kevin, 91, 93, 98–102
Dying at Grace, 154–5, 157, 159–66, 170–1, 240
Dying in Your Mother's Arms, 30–1, 46–7

Eastwood, Steven, 154–5, 160, 164, 167–8
Edge of Life, 30, 33–5, 44
The End, 216–20
End Credits, 91, 93, 95–8

244

INDEX

End Game, 53, 64–6
Epstein, Rob, 10, 53, 64–6
Ervine, Jeremy, 93, 103–4
ethical cinema, 12, 148–9; *see also* cinematic ethics
ethical space, 11–12, 15–18, 20, 74, 86, 88, 156, 157, 175, 196, 240
ethics of care, 53–60, 62, 65–8
ethics of listening, 175, 184–8, 190–1
Except for Six, 53, 59, 61–2
existential testimony, 80–2
Extremis, 30, 37–40, 44

Facing Death, 30–1, 40–4
Fade to Black, 93, 103–6
Fatal Flaws: Legalising Assisted Death, 91, 93, 98–104, 106
The First Wave, 30, 35–7
For One More Moment, 72–4, 87
Friedman, Jeffrey, 10, 53, 64–6

Gibb, Barbara, 3, 134–6, 142–4, 150, 163
Gispert, Oriol, 53
Griefwalker, 195–9, 206–7
good death, 37, 40, 42, 47, 92, 97, 147, 189, 242
The Good Death, 94, 174–5, 188–9

Hardie, Amy, 1, 114–15, 123–9
Heineman, Matthew, 30, 35–6
Helen's Story, 134–6, 141–4, 149–50
Henderson, Lily, 30, 32, 72, 74–5
Henkel, Cathy, 216, 226–7
Here & Now, 53–5
Hetherton, Madeleine, 3, 154, 156, 160, 170, 240
Hicks, Neal, 53, 60, 62–4
Hill, Mike, 7
hospice, 52–68, 73–5, 115, 123–31, 135–43, 145–7, 150, 208, 217–20, 237–9

immortality, 3, 134–5, 145, 149
individualism, 97, 175; *see also* individuality
individuality, 55, 98, 156, 202, 239; *see also* individualism

intersubjective, 11, 14, 16, 56–7, 211–12, 215, 219, 229–31
ISLAND, 154, 160, 167–9

Jennings, Thomas, 29–30, 44–6

King, Allan, 154–5, 159–61, 164, 166, 171, 240
Krauss, Dan, 30–1, 37, 39
Krupa, Tomáš, 94, 174–5, 188–9

Lara, Sam, 216, 226
Last Days of Life, 53, 56–9, 66–7
Last Flight Home, 216, 228–30
Laura's Choice, 216, 226–8
legacy, 134–50, 239
León, Jorge, 113–18
Les Pal·liatives, 53, 59–60
Lessons for the Living, 72, 74–5, 87
life narratives, 175
The Light Inside, 53, 59–64
liminal, 125, 164, 198–9, 211, 222
Live and Let Go: An American Death, 216, 223–5
Living while Dying, 195–7, 199–202, 210–11
Living Your Dying, 72, 80–2, 87
Looking Death in the Face, 195–6, 198–200, 203–6
Love in Our Own Time, 154, 156, 159–60, 169–70, 240
The LuLu Sessions, 216, 220–2
Luostarinen, Kiti, 163, 195–6, 198–200, 203–6

Marika's Passing, 136, 145–50
medicalisation, 31–5, 37, 40–1, 44, 47–8, 71
moment of death, 82, 154, 158, 163–5, 167–8, 171, 187, 205
Murray, Tom, 3, 154, 156, 170

Nathan – Free as a Bird, 175, 184–8
Navasky, Miri, 30, 40
Nollet, Roel, 175, 184–8

O'Connor, Karen, 30, 40
observational documentary, 154–7, 171

245

Pennybacker, Robert, 72, 80–1
The Perfect Circle, 5, 154, 159–64, 170
performativity, 115–31
Persson, Nahid, 53, 56, 58
phenomenological film studies, 12–14, 86, 175–80
Prison Terminal: The Last Days of Private Jack Hall, 136–41, 149–50

Russell, Charlie, 94, 195–7, 209–11

Seven Songs for a Long Life, 1, 4, 114–15, 123–9
social issue documentary, 6–11, 18–21, 39, 64, 91, 181, 235
Solace: Wisdom of the Dying, 72, 77–80, 82, 87
Spain, Jay, 216, 223
speech act, 43, 78, 115–16, 123, 177–8, 199
spirituality, 72–87
subjective, 2–3, 11, 19–20, 76, 78, 83–4, 86–8, 120, 144, 196–8, 201, 203, 207–12

Terry Pratchett: Choosing to Die, 94, 195–7, 199, 208–11

testimonial, 46, 63, 81–2, 87, 99–100, 102, 106, 187, 196, 218, 230
Theroux, Louis, 30, 33–5, 94
Timonen, Jenny, 72–4
Timoner, Ondi, 216, 228–9
Tosi, Claudia, 5, 154–5, 161–3, 238–40
transcendental testimony, 82–6

Valls, Marta, 53
Veda's Choice, 175, 181–3
Venrooij, Jesse van, 175, 177, 180
Villerius, Jessica, 175, 181
voice, 4, 11, 17–21, 30–1, 38, 41–6, 72, 77–8, 81, 85, 103–4, 114–15, 118, 121, 134, 156, 179, 182–5, 190, 196, 206–7, 215, 218–19, 237, 240–1

Wallenius, Peter, 136, 145–6, 163
Wilson, Tim, 163, 195–8, 206–7, 235
witnessing, 12–18, 59, 65, 73, 80–1, 83, 85, 115, 118, 127, 136–7, 140, 156, 167, 169, 171, 176, 178–9, 189, 197, 204, 206, 208–11, 240
Wong, S. Casper, 216, 220–2

Zheutlin, Cathy, 195–7, 200–2, 211